LACAN AND LITERATURE

SUNY Series in Psychoanalysis and Culture
Henry Sussman, Editor

Lacan and Literature

Purloined Pretexts

Ben Stoltzfus

State University of New York Press

Cover Illustration: *The Reading* by Pablo Picasso
2 January 1932
Oil
130 x 97.5 cm

Published by
State University of New York Press, Albany

Printed in the United States of America

For information, address State University of New York Press, State University Plaza, Albany, NY 12246

Production by E. Moore
Marketing by Fran Keneston

Library of Congress Cataloging-in-Publication Data

Stoltzfus, Ben, 1927-
Lacan and literature : purloined pretexts / Ben Stoltzfus.
p. cm.
Includes bibliographical references and index.
ISBN 0-7914-2931-8 (alk. paper). — ISBN 0-7914-2932-6 (pbk. : alk. paper)
1. Lacan, Jacques, 1901-81. 2. Psychoanalysis and literature. 3. Criticism. 4. Literature, Modern—20th century—History and criticism. I. Title.
PN98.P75S76 1996
801'.92—dc20

95-405
CIP

10 9 8 7 6 5 4 3 2 1

For My Students

One has only to listen to poetry . . . for a polyphony to be heard for it to become clear that all discourse is aligned along the several staves of a score.

—Jacques Lacan, "The agency of the letter in the unconscious or reason since Freud"

The unconscious text is already woven of pure traces, differences that bring meaning and force together, a text that is present nowhere, constituted by archives that are *always already* transcriptions.

—Jacques Derrida, "Freud or the scene of writing"

This transferring of responsibility from the text to its readers is what the lines ask us to do—it is the essence of their experience—and in my terms it is therefore what the lines *mean*.

—Stanley Fish, "Interpreting the *Variorum*"

Contents

Acknowledgments

I am grateful to Peter Preston, Keith Cushman, Scott Donaldson, Vicki Mistacco, Raymond Gay-Crosier, and George Slusser for reading portions of the manuscript and for their wise counsel.

I benefited from discussions with my colleagues John Fisher, Carlos Cortez, Mark Gottdiener, Diana Garber, Dwight Furrow, and Bernd Magnus at the Center for Ideas and Society, University of California, Riverside, during the Winter Quarter of 1991. For the past several years the exchange of ideas with my students, both graduate and undergraduate, has been invaluable.

This project has been supported by ongoing grants from the University of California and the Center for Ideas and Society.

I thank Clara Dean for her skills at the word processor and her dedication to correcting negligent spelling and typographical errors.

I also thank Mary Reyes for preparing camera-ready artwork for all the figures in the book.

Judith's encouragement has been essential and Jan's, Celia's, and Andrew's understanding has been exemplary.

Translations from French into English of Jacques Lacan's *Écrits* are from Alan Sheridan's *Écrits: A Selection.* Occasionally I provide my own. All translations from other texts are mine.

We are grateful to the following for permission to reproduce copyright material:

Cambridge University Press, 1990, for "A Sliding Discourse: The Language of *A Farewell to Arms,*" from *New Essays on* A Farewell to Arms, ed. Scott Donaldson. Éditions Gallimard, 1962, for quotations in French from *Le Malentendu, La Femme adultère,*

Caligula, *L'Étranger*, and the preface to the American school-book edition of *L'Étranger* by Albert Camus; these texts appear in the first volume of the Pléiade edition, *Théâtre, récits, nouvelles*. Éditions Gallimard, 1965, for quotations in French from *L'Homme révolté*, *Noces*, *L'Envers et l'endroit*, *L'Été*, and *Le Mythe de Sisyphe* by Albert Camus—texts that appear in the second volume of the Pléiade edition, *Essais*. Greenwood Press, 1994, for an abridged version of "Fantasy, Metafiction, and Desire," in *Robbe-Grillet and the Fantastic*, eds. Virginia Harger-Grinling and Tony Chadwick—an imprint of Greenwood Publishing Group, Inc., Westport, Connecticut. Hamish Hamilton for quotations in English from *Le Malentendu*, *La Femme adultère*, *Caligula*, *L'Étranger*, *L'Homme révolté*, and *Le Mythe de Sisyphe* by Albert Camus. *American Journal of Semiotics*, 1987, for a modified version of "A Post-Lacanian Reading of Hemingway's *Garden of Eden*." The Hemingway Foreign Rights Trust for quotations from *A Farewell to Arms* by Ernest Hemingway. Copyright © 1929, Charles Scribner's Sons. Copyright renewed 1957 by Ernest Hemingway. *The International Fiction Review*, 1992, for a modified version of "Lacan, Robbe-Grillet and Autofiction." *Modern Fiction Studies*, 1989, for a modified version of "Towards Bliss: Barthes, Lacan and Robbe-Grillet." W. W. Norton & Company, Inc., 1977, for quotations from *Écrits: A Selection* by Jacques Lacan, translated from the French by Alan Sheridan. Copyright © 1966 by Éditions du Seuil; English translation copyright © 1977 by Tavistock Publications Limited. Penguin USA, for quotations from "Future Religion," and "The Man of Tyre," from *The Complete Poems of D. H. Lawrence* by D. H. Lawrence, edited by V. de Sola Pinto and F. W. Roberts. Copyright © 1964, 1971 by Angelo Ravagli and C. M. Weekly, executors for the Estate of Frieda Lawrence Ravagli. Used by permission of Viking Penguin, a division of Penguin Books USA, Inc. and Laurence Pollinger Ltd. Random House, for quotations from *The Man Who Died* by D. H. Lawrence. Copyright © 1928 by Alfred A. Knopf, Inc. Also Random House for quotations in English from *Le Malentendu*, *La Femme adultère*, *Caligula*, *L'Étranger*, *L'Homme révolté*, and *Le Mythe de Sisyphe* by Albert Camus. Copyright © by Alfred A. Knopf, Inc. Scribner, an imprint of Simon & Schuster, Inc. for quotations from *A Farewell to Arms* by Ernest Hemingway. Copyright © 1929, Charles Scribner's Sons. Copyright renewed 1957 by Ernest Hemingway. University of Texas Press, 1989, for a modified version of "Camus's *L'Étranger*: A Lacanian Reading," from *Texas Studies in Literature and Language*, Volume 31. University of Wisconsin Press, 1988, for the reproduction of two diagrams from *Rhetorical Poetics: Theory and Practice of Figural and Symbolic Reading in Modern French Literature* by Donald Rice and Peter Schofer. Copyright © Madison: The University of Wisconsin Press. The Picasso Museum, Paris, France, for the use of *The Reading* by Pablo Picasso for the book's dust jacket.

INTRODUCTION

> *The unconscious is that chapter of my history that is marked by a blank or occupied by a falsehood: it is the censored chapter. But the truth can be rediscovered; usually it has already been written down elsewhere. Namely:*
>
> *—in monuments: this is my body. . . .*
> *—in archival documents: these are my childhood memories . . .*
> *—in semantic evolution . . .*
> *—in traditions . . . and . . . the legends which . . . bear my history;*
> *—and, lastly, in the traces that are inevitably preserved by the distortions necessitated by the linking of the adulterated chapter to the chapters surrounding it.*
>
> —*Jacques Lacan, "The function and field of speech and language in psychoanalysis"*

Jacques Lacan says that the unconscious is structured like a language.[1] Because language envelops everything we do and say we can apprehend the unconscious in dreams, jokes, and slips of the tongue. Literature as narration is language functioning at a higher level where connotation overrides denotation, where form obscures meaning, where ambiguity devalues message. Indeed, literature and the unconscious enjoy a special affinity because language is the magnetic field that joins the two, but it is a union that can function only when a reader activates the circuit between them. James Mellard argues that by focusing on language and the mechanisms of language found in tropes, "Lacan brings his analysis immediately into the domain of literary analysis."[2] Within this domain, according to Ellie Ragland-Sullivan, the literary work represents a reader's ego to itself through the language of the text—a text that exerts a "magnetic pull" on the reader "because it is an allegory of the psyche's fundamental structure."[3]

But consciousness is also structured like a language, and this means that "language is the one agency that 'contains' the author, reader, work, and world in the only ways available to the critic."[4] Language not only structures our perception of reality, it is, says Anika Lemaire, "the precondition for *the act of becoming aware of oneself as a distinct entity*."[5] Like a Klein bottle, in which the outside and the inside are reversible, we contain language, but language also contains us. In tropes there is neither an inside nor an outside and it is this reversibility that allows the unconscious, when veiled by figural language, to reveal itself. Indeed, the it (*ça*) and the ego are not entities destined to remain separate forever. According to Juliet Flower MacCannell it is the very idea of limits or boundaries that is constantly at issue in Lacan's texts. "We do not . . . have a sense that we are trapped in the prison-house of language."[6]

Although language has a material reality it also contains the reality of the unconscious.[7] Lacan's work thus provides the basis for a theory of narration within the context of an unconscious discourse that he calls the "discourse of the Other." It derives from the Symbolic presence of paternal authority—the figure of the Law or the *non/nom du père*—that is responsible, in the early stages of the child's development, for the repression of desire. Repression, in turn, enables us to understand, as Robert Con Davis phrases it, "how language in literary texts is constituted, buoyed up, permeated, and decentered by the unconscious."[8]

Lacan's analysis of narration begins with language and proceeds to rediscover the discourse of the Other that is embedded in speech and literature. The blockage of desire, along with its corollary, repression, produce a neurosis whose narrative symptoms are metaphorical. In the production of narrative, unconscious content is condensed as metaphor and displaced as metonymy. This narrative process embodies the same characteristics of Freud's dream work, and the function of the literary critic is to show how conscious discourse veils unconscious meaning, that is, how the signifiers resolve simultaneously into manifest signified (metaphor and metonymy) and latent referents (the repressed). Lacan's formula, S^1 over S^2, means that the signifier can have two signifieds. If the dream is the iconic, although masked mirror of the unconscious, fiction is its linguistic reflector.

If we accept the premise that the unconscious is structured like a language, then literature contains repressed material that engenders a never-ending dialog with the Other—a fictitious self made up of the confluence of the Imaginary and Symbolic. The Symbolic is the Law, the father (*le non/nom du père*), eventually all *doxa*. The Imaginary is that displaced self that has to come to terms with the postponement of satisfaction, the repression of desire, the nurturing of discontent, in short, the maturation and acculturation that civilized adults claim to value. In this context literature emerges as the melding of the conscious and unconscious realms of the psyche.

Between 1950 and 1970 psychoanalytic critics tended to analyze the characters in novels and plays because these personnae were seen as projections of the author's psyche. Over the years psychoanalytic criticism has shifted its emphasis from psychoanalyzing the author, as Marie Bonaparte did in 1933, with her study of Edgar Allan Poe, to privileging the text.[9] However, in moving from the author to the text, Freudian theory has never been comfortable with the textual limitations of the New Criticism of the 1930s and 1940s, and when Ernest Jones's study of *Hamlet* was published, it transgressed the confines of intrinsic or internal information to include extrinsic or external references to the Oedipus complex.[10] Fortunately, criticism today is no longer trapped within the prison of the intrinsic text.[11] This means that extrinsic knowledge is now viewed as indispensable material for its elucidation. It is possible, indeed essential, for psychoanalytic criticism to apply the same kind of distortion, condensation, and displacement to texts that Freud described in 1900 in his *Interpretation of Dreams*.[12] Although formalist criticism certainly has its place, it is much more interesting when linked with other fields and theoretical considerations be they anthropological, historical, Marxist, mythic, or psychoanalytic. According to MacCannell, Lacan's appeal to readers of literature derives from his emphasis on the cultural context of the interhuman situation.[13]

Today, the influence of the cultural dimension on literary criticism is very strong. In this climate the new *beacons* marking the land and sea of "critifiction," as Raymond Federman calls it,[14] and paraphrasing the title of Charles Beaudelaire's poem "Les phares," are Ferdinand de Saussure and Roman Jakobson in linguistics, Claude Lévi-Strauss in anthropology, Michel Foucault in cultural history, Jacques Derrida in philosophy and deconstruction, Roland Barthes and his eclectic socioliterary criticism, and Jacques Lacan in psychoanalysis. There are many other lights in this luminous array and they all enlighten the necessary violation of literary boundaries in order to include information from other disciplines. We are in fact in the midst of an interdisciplinary explosion in all fields of learning and this dissemination of knowledge is a fertile one insofar as it affects the practice of literary criticism.

Because readers bring different sensibilities and varying degrees of knowledge to their reading, the emphasis since about 1970 has shifted from the text to the reader's response to it. Marcel Duchamp once said that there is no masterpiece without an audience. Although we can argue that within the interpretive community there are masterpieces by consensus, they still need someone to activate them. Consequently psychoanalytic critics such as Norman Holland began to look at the ways a work generates wishes and fantasies in the reader's mind. Whereas the act of reading actualizes a work's fictive referents, the act of interpretation completes the process. Only then do the world of the novel and art generally and that of the reader coalesce. It is important to understand, using Roman Ingarden's term, how this *concretization* takes place.[15] Shoshana Felman, Barbara Johnson, and others have shown in different ways that although a critic may analyze a text, a text can also "read" the reader. Although we don't always know why a work will touch us so profoundly, Mellard believes that this "power of affect is the one that comes from the unconscious, whether it lies in us or in the texts that seem to bring it up or from which we bring it up."[16]

According to Peter Brooks it is *transference* that allows the reader to activate a text. A transferential model, says Brooks, "allows us to take as the object of analysis not author or reader, but *reading*, including, of course, the transferential-interpretive operations that belong to reading."[17] Meaning comes not only from the text, nor is it the exclusive fabrication of the reader, but from "the dialogic struggle and collaboration of the two."[18] This struggle activates textual possibilities during the process of reading. Holland, however, is more concerned with the reader than with the text. In an essay entitled "The 'Unconscious' of Literature" he does not analyze Robert Frost, the man, but his poem "Mending Wall," because the poem, whatever Frost's intentions may have been, may be read as an appeal to the psychology of the reader and the latent wishes or fantasies of his or her unconscious.[19]

Despite degrees of interpretive difference among all these critics, the approach they share is an insistence on the active role of the reader. I too will use the strategy of reader response in order to concretize meaning from the texts I will be analyzing. My sample is necessarily limited, and it focuses on twentieth-century writers, but it is part of a larger endeavor by readers and critics, some of whom I have already mentioned above, who have looked at the relationship between psychoanalytic criticism and writing. Piece by piece the figure in the carpet is being fleshed out. The briefest of samplings will give a sense of the work that has already been done: *Oedipus Rex, Oedipus at Colonus, Hamlet, Othello, Daniel Deronda, Tristram Shandy, Bleak House, La Rabouilleuse, La Tentation de Saint Antoine, The Scarlet Letter, Le Rouge et le noir, Frankenstein, The Heart of Darkness, Ulysses, The Turn of the Screw, Under Western Eyes, To the Lighthouse, Absalom, Absalom!, La Condition humaine,* "The Garden of Forking Paths," *The Maids, The Catcher in the Rye, Malloy, Malone Dies, The Unnameable, The Dead Father,* and, of course, Lacan's own seminar on "The Purloined Letter."[20] Fortunately for me, and perhaps for the reader, my selections from D. H. Lawrence, Ernest Hemingway, Albert Camus, Roland Barthes, and Alain Robbe-Grillet have not yet been subjected to the critical strategy of Lacanian analysis and reader-response criticism.

When Lacan stated that the unconscious is structured like a language, he opened a royal road between literature and the unconscious, one for which Freud had already cleared the way with, among other essays, his psychoanalytic reading of E. T. A. Hoffman's "Sandman." Also, although Freud's analysis of dreams drew attention to linguistic structures, he was unfamiliar with Saussure's seminal work in linguistics which was to have such a profound influence, despite their subsequent modifications, on the oeuvre of Lévi-Strauss, Lacan, Barthes, Derrida, Foucault, and many others.[21] Therefore, in bringing together literature and psychoanalysis we need to incorporate Freud's *Interpretation of Dreams*, Saussure's *Course in General Linguistics*, and Lacan's *Ecrits* as the triad from which a psychoanalytic theory of reading can be developed.

In dreams, Freud's theories of condensation and displacement match Lacan's definitions of metaphor and metonymy because both dreams and tropes are signifiers pointing to the presence of an absence. Figures of speech coalesce in the life of the subject (the author, his or her characters, and the reader) both as dreams dramatizing unconscious imagery and as somatic manifestations of rhetorical functions. Bodily acts are comparable to the so-called manifest content in dreams because, says Lacan, "the symptom *is* a metaphor whether one likes it or not, as desire *is* metonymy, however funny people may find the idea" ("le symptôme *est* une métaphore, que l'on veuille ou non se le dire, comme le désir *est* une métonymie, même si l'homme s'en gausse").[22] The symptom in the dream or in the text veils the presence of the unconscious. Because of this veiling, the latent meaning of a somatic symptom corresponds exactly to the latent meaning of a dream. Dreams and symptoms have their manifest content and both wear metaphorical disguises that mask the truth.

For Lacan, the truth is to be found in the unseen but unmistakable presence of the unconscious which, from behind the scenes, so to speak, prompts us in the roles we play in full view of the audience. Because we are all acting out composite roles, whether we know it or not, these performances are played out on the stage of language. Without language the world as we know it would not exist. Moreover, the structure of the unconscious is the invisible text that determines our role(s) and its voice(s) dictate(s) the repetitions, the pratfalls, and the tragedies of our lives.

This is the language of drama, be it life or art, and its text is subject to and is the subject of semiotic analysis. The symptom (metaphor) is a manifestation of unconscious speech (*parole*) and it contains all the idiosyncracies of an individual utterance. A hysterical pregnancy, for example, is an unconscious trope. It mimes the real thing and the figure swells but there is no fetus. It is all an act and the symptom is *parole* treating the body as language (*langue*). Since we all have bodies and we use them, sometimes individually in sports or collectively in the body politic, these bodies are comparable to English as a language. We use English or French in order to communicate with each other or to write a set of laws with which to govern a state. Violations of the law are symptoms of unrest and examples of a criminal *parole.* In sociology the collective body of society or a group is the text, in anthropology the kinship relations of the Nambikwara are Lévi-Strauss's text, and in the case of conversion hysteria a person's body is the text.

This use of the body as a metaphor for language is a ready and useful concept that also happens to reflect wide usage. In addition to the body politic we also have the social body, the body of evidence, the body of knowledge, the body of the text, and it goes without saying, our individual bodies be they tall, short, thin, or fat. All bodies are repositories of language and experience. The story of my body is the history of my life and every text I write is part of that story and a stage in its history. The history of the United States is the story of its collective body, seemingly rational at the time of the founding fathers, hysterical during the cold war and the McCarthy era. A collective body also has its symptoms that can be analyzed in rhetorical terms because the unconscious is present in the symptom, and the symptom is essentially a trope.[23]

It is the body of written texts, literature in particular, that interests us here as well as the response of readers to the disguises of figurative language. The reading of literature is a rhetorical activity and for those analyzing its unconscious weave the task is to construct a latent text from the manifest one. It is the evocative power of literature rather than its message that communicates its magic to the reader. After a fiction tells its story we need to focus on the story of telling, a procedure that foregrounds language and the enchantment of the text. The reader's accomplices in this endeavor are the tropic, symbolic, and homonymic traces that are embedded in its tissues. Because Lacan privileges metaphor and metonymy we will be looking mainly at their programmatic disguises but also, when appropriate, at synecdoche, irony, and humor. Language in literary texts, like the images in Freud's dreams, is constantly being displaced, condensed, deformed, and dramatized. Indeed, rhetorical language is a second sign system that functions in collusion with character, plot, and suspense, but is also independent of them. Moreover, the literariness of the text, in Jakobson's sense, gives us freer access to the voice of the Other which, in Lacanian terminology, is the voice of the unconscious.

Whenever we focus on the literariness of a text we are less interested in its message than in how meaning is circulating through it. In essence, the reader produces meaning and in order to do so the creative role of the audience is indispensable. Without active readers a trope is inert. It is a lifeless combinatory mass waiting for someone to animate it, to give it form, to make it sing, to reveal its latent mysteries. The frequent indeterminacy of texts suggests that the reader must step in to give plausible explanations for redundancies, gaps, and contradictions. Textual aporia may well mean that something has been repressed and that the magnetic field of this black hole needs to be explored and its energy brought into play in the name of the father, the son, and the mother—that holy trinity of the Oedipus complex.

However, as Ragland-Sullivan points out, the aim of Lacanian poetics is not to psychoanalyze a text but to "study the paralinguistic points of join between visible language and invisible effect."[24]

Nonetheless, this invisible effect has its origin in the mirror stage and in the Oedipus complex when the subject's fragmented self is unified in the specular image of its m(Other). During that moment of misrecognition (*méconnaissance*) when the subject gains access to language, he or she is in effect being constituted by language and subsists in a system of differences, in the gap between the signifier and the signified.[25] The subject, like language, is defined by difference and it is this affinity between fictional aporia and the gaps in the structure of the self that no doubt explains in part the magnetism between the reader and the text.

Another energizing source for the reader from the text is humor, slips of the tongue, and the like, which Freud has analyzed in *Jokes and Their Relation to the Unconscious*, a work that Lacan, who is renowned for the elliptical nature of his writings, has characterized as Freud's most transparent text. There is perhaps a pejorative judgment in Lacan's reference to such transparency, but the fact remains that the relationship between jokes and the unconscious is a source of mirth and truth of which Lacan approves and that he exploits vigorously in his seminars and in his writings. No stone is left unturned in Lacan's efforts to uncover the hieroglyph written "in the sand of the flesh" (*"sur le sable de la chair"*).[26]

The reader is invited to collaborate in the creation of a parallel text to the one the writer has scripted and in doing so the reader forms his or her own tropic network using the holes, traces, words, repetitions, sentences, structures, paragraphs, and figural motifs. Underlying all this is the voice of the Other caught in the folds of the text and which the reader unfolds so that the body can be heard and seen and touched and felt almost intuitively in what Barthes describes as orgasmic bliss (*jouissance*).[27] The pretext for happiness is the game of writing, the play of reading, and the sweep of similitude that gives the reader a leading role in rewriting the text. In reading a trope the reader has to figure out the semantic transposition from a sign that is present to one that is absent. The reader has to work from the macrotext of the plot to the microtext of the traces embedded in it. Somewhere between, around, over, and under these pulsive forces the points of join between visible language and invisible effect come into play. The reader works through the different levels of the written and unwritten text (Freud's *durcharbeiten*) in order to weave his or her network of associations. Tropes and traces are the flesh and blood of this figurative body and its tissues.

The warp and woof of this weave are metaphor and metonymy. Metonymy, says Lacan is "the one side (*versant*) of the effective field constituted by the signifier" ("le premier versant du champ effectif que le signifiant constitue"),[28] and the example he gives is the substitution of "thirty sails" for "thirty ships." However, in rhetoric, the substitution of a part for the whole defines synecdoche, that is, one of the signified is also a semantic feature of the other signified. A sail is part of a ship and this is its semantic feature, whereas in the example "he assaulted her vengeance in hand," the word "vengeance," in collusion with the word "assault," describes the man's intention, but the signifier obscures the weapon. Is it a knife, a stick, a rope, a sex pistol? We don't know. The word "vengeance" may be substituted for any one of these hypothetical weapons without being a semantic feature of any of them. The substitution, in this example, is a whole—one signifier for another in its entirety—and not for any of its parts.

Lacan, however, seems to make no distinction between metonymy and synecdoche, but he does distinguish between metonymy and metaphor, metaphor being the other side (*versant*) of the effective field. The example he gives for metaphor is from Victor Hugo's poem "Booz endormi" in which the metaphorical spark illumines the fact that the sheaf of wheat that "was neither miserly nor spiteful" ("n'était pas avare ni haineuse") belongs to Booz.[29] The word "sheaf" has displaced Booz in the signifying chain and now occupies the place that would normally be his. If we compare this metaphor with Freud's analysis of dreams, the sheaf becomes the manifest content and Booz is its latent meaning. Phrased differently, the sheaf is the signifier and Booz is the signified. There is an unmistakable relationship between rhetorical poetics and the dream work. In both, a substitute signifier veils the signified. Booz does not signify "sheaf" but the sheaf, inevitably and necessarily, signifies "Booz." The reader's role in all this is to work through the chain of substitutions and displacements by linking them together in order to craft significant connections between the different parts and the whole.

Metaphor and metonymy occupy an intermediary zone between the plot of the macrotext and the particles of the microtext. As tropes they inscribe their mnemonic traces on the reader's mind and it is these tracings embedded in the text and in the reader that invite rereadings so that a polyphony can be heard, "for it to become clear that all discourse is aligned along the several staves of a score" ("pour que s'y fasse entendre une polyphonie et que tout discours s'avère s'aligner sur les plusieurs portées d'une partition").[30] Lacan's musical analogy is an apt one because tropic traces coexist in the reader's mind and it is their simultaneity that allows him or her to move backward and forward along a horizontal axis. The scoring of a text resonates with connotations and contexts that Lacan says are suspended vertically,[31] but I would say also horizontally, because it is the simultaneity of these horizontal units that gives the text its musical presence and vertical reality. All this is analogous to a pianist striking chords with both hands so that the vibrations of each note will be heard in unison.

These pulsive forces inscribe their passage on the mind. Derrida calls it a *frayage*, whereas Freud's metaphor for such inscriptions is the magical writing pad. Although the pad's inscriptions may be erased they do, nonetheless, leave a mark—a trace that can be seen when the pad is examined at a certain angle and under certain lighting conditions.[32] In writing, such traces leave conscious and unconscious trails. They may be hidden or disguised or barely noticeable, but their presence can be felt and it is the reader who apprehends and organizes them into meaningful units. These units of meaning circulate within a text energizing the activity of writing and reading. They reinforce the tropes and the voice of the Other, they disrupt realism and representation, they form gaps, and in collusion with the floating signifiers, they bar the way to the signified. For example, in Derrida's *Glas* the phoneme *gl* shares the bell's resonance, reverberating throughout the text. Vincent Leitch points out that the *gl* of *glas* mimes the sound tolled by the death knell (*glas*). It both separates (*glose*) and joins (*glu*). "As *glace*, it is icing on the cake and flaw in the gem, mirror and window. Like *gleet*, the *gl* makes up bodily discharges like phlegm and mucus (*glaire*)." Overall, it is the cry of an *écriture* (*glapir*).[33] The effect of such paronomasia is to foreground the materiality of language by shifting the reader's attention away from its "transparency" to the "opacity" of the signifier. The interplay of signifiers and their traces, whether orchestrated by the author or the reader or both, stresses the text, the intertext, the context, and the subtext. The reader's role is to listen to the world of signs and to entertain their diversity because the voice of the Other is always speaking.

Traces take on meaning through their differential opposition to and in combination with other traces. Lacan's readiness to play with sounds is legendary: the word *lettre* becomes *l'être* (being), language becomes *lalangue*, linguistics evolves into a pejorative *lin-*

guisterie, and everything ends up as *litière* (litter—letter). There is also the ostrich from which Lacan develops *la politique de l'autruiche*, a word enriched by the denomination of one letter and the familiar head-in-the-sand proverb.[34]

The quarrel between Derrida and Lacan over the phallus as transcendental signifier, notwithstanding, we as readers, if we value our creative roles, will play the writing game with a joyous Nietzschean affirmation, nimbly dancing over, around, and within the interstices of the letter where the Other resides. The writer writes because he or she has to and in order to be recognized (read). The reader, in turn, derives pleasure from the text and they (we) both play with the materiality of words. In order to experience the bliss to which Barthes refers in *Le Plaisir du texte* the body of the text must be pressed into action so that desire—the desire embedded in the writing and in the reader—may be heard and felt. The good reader resonates with what is unconscious in the writer's conscious communication.

Traces and dissemination confirm the fact that no signifier ever refers only to itself. Moreover, because language is a system of signs distinguished from one another only by their mutual opposition, no element in a discourse can function as a sign without referring to another element that is absent. In formulating a theory of reading I am borrowing from Derrida and Lacan despite the fact that Derrida's dissemination claims to contradict Lacan's Law of the phallus.[35] The dispersion of meaning throughout the text, the fragmentation of the "letter" (signifier) into *semes* that inseminate the narrative with multiple meanings—a narrative whose center is everywhere and nowhere—is a dispersion that has a material reality which, when reassembled, like Osiris, can nonetheless constitute a whole. Never mind that Osiris's phallus is still missing. Isis in search, like any castrated male, can, as in D. H. Lawrence's *Escaped Cock*, recover plenitude and bliss with the "man who died." Lawrence's hero ascends to the Father with an erection that, considering his previous rejection of sexuality, rises to the occasion. In *The Sun Also Rises* we can reassemble the Oedipus complex from fragments that are scattered throughout the text. Like Isis in search of the missing phallus, Brett Ashley is also on the go, questing after substitutes for Jake's missing part. The signifier may be unstable and its dispersion inevitable but the parts can be reassembled.

My use of Lacan and Derrida is a form of *bricolage* that emphasizes the play of traces throughout a text. Traces in language exercise both conscious and unconscious functions, and their combinatory horizons are limited only by the reader's ability and willingness to set the machinery in motion. Traces in *The Sun Also Rises* may leave visible, potentially conscious marks such as *pères, Mumms, Zizi,* and *pipi*—oedipal synecdoches that mark the channels of desire—or they may be unconscious lesions reflecting structural entities that need realignment, as in "La Femme adultère," Albert Camus's story in which the cold wind of the desert and a midnight sky redolent with stars become the objective correlatives of Janine's repression and desire.

The apperception of the ego can be a quest that the scriptor and the reader undertake together. After the tolling of the bell (*glas*) we may wonder for whom the writer writes. For whom, indeed, if not for thee? Thus, the prospective reader (listener) is the Lacanian other (small *o*) and the subject (writer) who rereads hears the voice of the Other (capital *O*) who is none other than the Other and who, in a sense, has already been found because speech (writing) "always subjectively includes its own reply, that Pascal's 'tu ne me chercherais pas si tu ne m'avais trouvé' simply confirms the same truth in different words" ("à savoir que la parole inclut toujours subjectivement sa réponse, que le 'Tu ne me chercherais pas si tu ne m'avais trouvé' ne fait qu'homologuer cette vérité").[36] If playing (writing) with the body of a text is the symbolic reenactment of the *Fort!/Da!* then it too contains both the deferral and the pleasure of such dramatization.

In this game for four players the reader's unconscious responds to the writer's unconscious, that is, the voice of the Other in both players (the writer and the reader) is the inaudible yet present sound that addresses them. The ego and the id of the writer (the text) is being read by the ego and the id of the reader (the act of reading). The manifest content of the text is in the reality of its immediate discourse: plot, structure, and character. The invisible thread that links the text's latent content with the reader's desire to know is the force that binds the two in a symbiotic relationship. The text has found an audience and the reader is listening to the voice of the Other that is embedded in the text's discourse and also in him- or herself—the voice that the writer is speaking while seeking—the voice (the bell and the belle) that resonates in the reader's unconscious.

What, we may ask, is the message that this tenuous line transmits? It is always a message of desire—a desire that "is neither the appetite for satisfaction, nor the demand for love, but the difference that results from the subtraction of the first from the second, the phenomenon of their splitting (*Spaltung*)" ("le désir n'est ni l'appétit de la satisfaction, ni la demande d'amour, mais la différence qui résulte de la soustraction du premier à la seconde, le phénomène même de leur refente (*Spaltung*)").[37] For Lacan, metaphor is related to knowledge whereas metonymy derives from desire, and the truth lies at the axis where the two meet. The goal of the subject's desire is to meld once again with the mother but the Law forbids it. This "death" of the subject that submits to the greater power of the Symbolic has as its consequence the fragmentation of the self and its alienation into language and fabulation. Despite this symbolic death the desire of the organism to live and to die in its own way and in its own time persists.[38] Writing, speaking, reading, playing, and living are thus an affirmation of life as a deferral of death. As long as the deferral is in play, life and death remain radically opposed, although indissolubly linked. There is the unavoidable biological linkage of time and old age but there is also the symbolic linkage of the primal scene, the acquisition of language, and the affirmation of subjectivity and difference. The phallus, the incest taboo, the *non/nom du père* are all implicated in that primal scene that gives birth so to speak to the Other—an Other whose voice will accompany us throughout life and whose promptings are the foundation and structure of language. Each life is a forest of symbols, and to paraphrase Baudelaire once again, these living pillars speak in garbled tongues. Nature, in the poem "Correspondances," may be viewed as a temple wherein a coded language is imprinted on us and from which the mystic cant is heard.[39]

This primal song is inscribed on the body. It is in Adam's rib and in the Eve of his seduction. This loss of paradise is the mother of desire, the absence and presence of the fragmented body whose reality is elsewhere. In French, the maternal sea (*la mer matricielle*) has homonymic traces (*la mère/la mer*) that bind these two words in an indissoluble embrace. It is this irreversible linkage that the Other in Camus's oeuvre claims and manifests. The sea in his writings is a pretext, the signifier of a signifier: "I have to write as I have to swim, because my body demands it" ("Il me faut écrire comme il faut nager, parce que mon corps l'exige").[40] Camus is indeed a constant swimmer in the waters of creative endeavor and in such works as *L'Étranger*, *Noces*, and "La Mer au plus près" we can chart the metaphorical tracings and their referential relationships that exhibit common semantic features. Immersion in the sea of language—the mother tongue—is an ontological state that he himself recognized as indispensable to his well-being.

According to Derrida, the rhythm of writing mimes the rhythm of the waves and it is this cadence, this measured relationship that immerses us in its symbolic sweep. "We know that *rythmos* has come to mean both the cadence of writing and the undulation of the waves" ("*Rythmos*, on le sait, en est venu à signifier à la fois la cadence d'une écriture et l'ondulation des flots").[41] However, the sea's cadence is regulated by deep currents whose waves in time unfold along the shoreline. There, time splashes over the footprints of my (your) history, washes away the marks of passage, except for the flotsam and jetsam, perhaps a bottle with a faded message inside that can almost be deciphered and whose symbolic script needs the imagination and ingenuity of a random beachcomber to determine its provenance (the objective chance of an encounter)—a fortuitous meeting that is beautiful and worthy of the surrealists' best couplings. It will have been unpremeditated—ruled by chance—a chaste response to the unimaginable tragedy that is the loss of innocence and oneness, the primal storm that has carried her away to sea and replaced her with the Other—mother.

Because the unconscious is structured like a language, the father's rule is threatened whenever the subject plays with words, with tropes, and the combinatory power of language. This combinatory power may be conscious or unconscious. For example, Derrida's *Glas* is a voluntary gesture in which sound directs the play of meaning, whereas Freud's *Jokes and Their Relation to the Unconscious* argues in favor of the involuntary and unpremeditated display of linguistic comedy. "Through the word—already a presence made of absence—absence gives itself a name in that moment of origin whose perpetual recreation Freud's genius detected in the play of the child" ("Par le mot qui est déjà une présence faite d'absence, l'absence même vient à se nommer en un moment original dont le génie de Freud a saisi dans le jeu de l'enfant la recréation perpétuelle").[42] Little Ernst's game of *Fort!/Da!* is the paradigm for such retrieval—the embodied presence of an absence and the substitution for it of the symbolic act and its object. Because the world of words creates the world of things,[43] symbolic language replaces absence, be it breast or mother, generating contact with the body of one's mother tongue. The father prohibits the language of incestuous longing and belonging, but the subject strives to circumvent his name (*nom/non*). Humor, jokes, puns, and slips of the tongue are indeed a circumvention, and paronomasia is the currency of intervocalic mirth. However, this economic exchange is suspect because its potency and its value derive from impotence. The gaze into the mirror is a *méconnaissance*, a misrecognition, a substitution of the Imaginary (hence counterfeit) self for the real one.

In the real world a currency's value is measured against the false, but in the realm of the Symbolic the displacement, compression, condensation, and dramatization of the neologism override the prosaic. Freud's "alcoholidays" derives its linguistic sparkle from the compression of two words: alcohol and holidays, and also from the three letters "hol," which they share. The ending of one word is the beginning of another. The meaning of one word has been displaced and it coincides with our recognition that the practice of drinking during the holidays is a frequent cultural ritual. We smile knowingly at and with the complicity of the neologism.[44] In "The Rocking-Horse Winner," D. H. Lawrence's play with the words *lucker* and *lucre* also exploits the fortunes or misfortunes of pronunciation, homonymy, and spelling. Camus's repetitive usage of the word "mother" as the homonym for the word "sea" (*la mer/la mère*), while not exactly humorous, manifests a similar displacement and compression. Ernest Hemingway's interlinguistic paronomasia in *The Sun Also Rises* is yet another example. While Jake Barnes is waiting for Brett's telegram in San Sebastian, after the fiesta in Pamplona, he sees a one-armed soldier in the park who, in French, would be called a *manchot*. After Jake receives Brett's telegram asking him to go to Madrid to rescue her he says: "that meant San Sebastian all shot to hell."[45] San Sebastian was a man shot with arrows and martyred but he did not go to hell. The ironic play on "man shot" and *manchot* depends entirely on the reader's alertness and knowledge in picking up on a French word and on Roman history. This example confirms the reader's necessary role in generating meaning.

Bill Gorton's admonitions about irony and pity are important reminders that Jake's front—his missing penis and impotence—derives from the Italian joke front where the joystick in the airplane, like the tricycle that allegedly wounded Henry James, is the cause of his physical impotence. Ironically the "joke front" of the novel's protagonist is also the source of Hemingway's verbal potency. There is mirth in such "irony and pity" and stoic merriment in the recognition of and triumph over dysfunction.

The act of writing is a triumph over symbolic impotence. It is a deferral of death tied to the pleasurable effects of repetition and retrieval (*Fort!/Da!*). In *Roland Barthes*, Barthes deliberately assembles short paragraphs of unrelated subject matter that are organized quasi-alphabetically because he believes this fragmentation of the self dramatizes and illustrates the splitting of the child's identity during the mirror phase. Barthes's autofiction (*Roland Barthes*) is an artifact in which writing in the mother tongue is the symbolic equivalent of playing with the mother's body; an act of retrieval and a source of bliss. In *Mythologies*, but also in most of his writings, Barthes's subversion of *doxa* is a devaluation of the *nom/non du père*—a retrieval of potency that challenges the Law.

Alain-Robbe Grillet's metafictions are also a challenge to the tenets of classic realism. His assault on the classic realist text—a text that relied on character development, linear chronology, and plot—in favor of the dispersion of characters (Johnson, Johnston, and Johnstone may or may not be the same person in the novel *La Maison de rendez-vous*), indeterminacy, circular chronology, and the absence of plot challenges the notion of the well-constructed novel. His emphasis on generative themes, the foregrounding of the creative process at the expense of story line, and his general disregard for the conventions of realism characterize the kind of nouveau roman he writes. Despite Robbe-Grillet's deliberate unveiling of the practice of writing and of the creative process, the voice of the Other is there, embedded in the sexual imagery and the exaggerated, comic-strip violence of erotic fantasy.

The American, British, and French authors I have selected and the works I analyze range from modernism through existentialism to postmodernism. Two of D. H. Lawrence's shorter fictions, *The Escaped Cock* (the preferred title these days to *The Man Who Died*), and "The Rocking-Horse Winner," illustrate the displacements, metaphorical slippage, and humor within the unconscious. Three Hemingway novels, *The Sun Also Rises*, *A Farewell to Arms*, and *The Garden of Eden*, address the game of *Fort!/Da!*, parallel discourse, the doubling of the narratee, and paradise regained. Several works by Camus, *L'Étranger*, *Noces*, and "La Femme adultère," reveal homonymous veilings, the use of metaphor, and the voice of the Other as quest. I discuss Barthes's and Robbe-Grillet's autofictions (*Roland Barthes*, *Le Miroir qui revient*, and *Angélique ou l'enchantement*—their fictional autobiographies) as discourses of fantasy and bliss and finally, in the conclusion, using the metaphor from Hans Christian Andersen's "The Emperor's New Clothes," I unveil the body of the text as metafiction in a creative and critical replication of the Lacanian style. Throughout this study my frames of reference are Freudian, Lacanian, reader-response, and postmodern. A postmodern sensibility guides my reading of traditional texts such as *The Sun Also Rises*, where I find traces of Derrida's "dissemination," Freud's *Fort!/Da!*, and Lacan's voice of the Other. Metafiction is more difficult to analyze because it is more self-consciously post-Freudian, but the traces of dispersion, discontinuity, and play are strong marks of deferral and bliss—practices that accompany the subversion of the Law.

Ultimately, the theme that brings all of these works together is the voice of the (m)Other—the trope of loss and desire that guides the discourse of each writer. From modernism to postmodernism, from Lawrence to Robbe-Grillet, the linguistic weave in all the texts reveals almost identical patterns of deferral and displacement. Despite differences in vision and narration, the materiality of language and the reality of the unconscious provide the warp and the woof with which the reader weaves a common figural motif.

Chapter 1

D. H. Lawrence: *The Escaped Cock*[1]

For the phallus is a signifier, a signifier whose function, in the intrasubjective economy of the analysis, lifts the veil perhaps from the function it performed in the mysteries.

—Jacques Lacan, "The signification of the phallus"

In the novella *The Escaped Cock*, D. H. Lawrence's treatment of Christ after his "resurrection"—a Christ who repudiates the Law of the Father—is a narrative in which the repression of sexuality (symbolic death) and desire reenact the tenets of Lacanian theory. At the height of his newly found sexual identity, as Christ "rises" to the Father in the temple of Isis, Lawrence gives us a formulaic image of a mythical union worthy of the Oedipus complex.[2] The difference, however, in this instance, is that instead of castration, the son recovers his manhood, possesses the mother symbolically, and ascends, like the sun, illumining the ego with the "dark rays" of the id. Christ recovers from his impotence and, redeemed at last, he is part of "the great rose of Space."[3]

Freudian critiques of Lawrence (Lacan staunchly maintained that he was a devout Freudian) tend to look for the author behind the work, whereas Lacanian criticism frees the text from this umbilical cord.[4] The text thus becomes a free-floating construct in which metaphor, metonymy, synecdoche, homonymy, aporia, puns, indeed every combination possible, contribute to the artistic space that defines the work. Lacan privileges the text over the artist's life because the text already contains everything we need to know. Indeed, Lacan wrote his "Seminar on 'The Purloined Letter'" in order to demonstrate that meaning, the letter, the signifier are displaced and circulate throughout the text whether or not we refer to Edgar Allan Poe's biography. As a signifier, the letter is "the letter of the unconscious" and it is a paradigm that functions independently of the author's life.[5] Every text contains repressed material that manifests an ongoing record of the Other's presence. It is the play of language, its gaps, puns, repetitions, metaphorical slippages, and homonyms—the spaces wherein desire lurks—that reveal the discourse of the Other. Language manifests desire because desire was proscribed by the Law (*le nom/non du père*). It is during the infant's so-called mirror phase, when it misrecognizes itself as Other, that the child accedes to language. This accession to language coincides with the primal repression of desire (union with the mother and displacements of desire), which then lingers on, embedded in the subject and his or her language.[6]

For Lacan, the unconscious is structured like a language, whereas for Lawrence the unconscious is the life force, the soul, the individual self generated spontaneously at the very moment of conception when the sperm penetrates the ovum. The unconscious, says Lawrence, is the "active spontaneity which rouses in each individual organism at the moment of fusion of parent nuclei," and it "brings forth not only consciousness, but tissue and organs also."[7] The true unconscious "is the spontaneous life-motive in every organism," and it begins where life begins.[8] For Lawrence, the concept of repression is a false unconscious, whereas for Lacan, repression and accession to language form the unconscious. Lawrence believes in a phenomenological and ontological sense of presence, whereas for Lacan and for Derrida, a self constituted by language, whether consciously or unconsciously, is a fragmented, decentered, and problematic self. Because of this decentering Lacan says, playing with Descartes' *cogito*: "I think where I am not, therefore I am where I do not think" ("Je pense où je ne suis pas, donc je suis où je ne pense pas").[9]

Despite their differences, Lawrence and Lacan frequently seem to be moving in the same direction. A discourse that in Lacanian terms has to remain unconscious, when applied to Lawrence, seems to have been contrived consciously, as though Freud's "Wo Es war, soll Ich werden," which Lacan translates as "Là où fut ça, il me faut advenir," or "Là où c'était . . . c'est mon devoir que je vienne à être," were part of Lawrence's agenda and not opposed to it.[10] The English version ("Where the id was, there the ego shall be"), according to Lacan, mistranslates the German, insofar as the German does not say *das Es* (the id) nor *das Ich* (the ego). It only says *Es* and *Ich*, namely *it* and *I*. Lacan substitutes the word *it* for id, and even more radically, the letter *S* (signifier) for *Es*, because, for the subject, every symptom is a signifier. In psychoanalytic terms, the only way to close the gap between the subject and the signifier is to strive for a melding of the two: "Where the it was, I must be."[11] The *it* is not, strictly speaking, the id, nor is the *I* necessarily the ego.[12] "The Other is, therefore, the locus in which is constituted the I who speaks to him who hears, that which is said by the one being already the reply, the other deciding to hear it whether the one has or has not spoken" ("L'Autre est donc le lieu où se constitue le je qui parle avec celui qui entend, ce que l'un dit étant déjà la réponse et l'autre décidant à l'entendre si l'un a ou non parlé").[13] The metaphorical discourse of fiction is the answer I have already heard if only I have ears to hear. The Other is always speaking, but what does the Other want for me?[14] Since the speaking I is already in the Other, the passage toward consciousness for Lacan, as with Lawrence, is from *it* to *me*. What does the unconscious want to say and what does it want for me? Lawrence's *Escaped Cock* may provide some answers.

"I tried to compel them to live, so they compelled me to die."[15] These are the words of Lawrence's Christ—a man who survives his death because they took him down from the cross too soon, and, having survived, he repudiates his past by saying that "the day of his interference is done. The teacher and savior are dead in me."[16] Indeed, the man who died rejects his previous message of salvation in favor of a new earth-centered philosophy. "No man can save the earth from tillage," he says,[17] and he concludes that "virginity is a form of greed,"[18] that preaching was a mistake,[19] that care is a noose that can strangle,[20] in short, that he had run to excess because he gave more than he took, and that such excess was also a form of death.[21] The man who died rejects a theological idealism that is consonant with Lawrence's own repudiation of it. Having cast off the excesses and the compulsions of his previous existence, the man moves in another direction that, although radically different from the first—he seeks a sexual fulfillment that will allow him to "ascend to the Father"[22] differently—has its own compulsive force. Lawrence embarks his character on a mystical, mythical quest that allows him to meld the Christian crucifixion and the myth of Isis and Osiris into a parable for modern-day man.

In view of Christ's ordeal on the cross, his desire for a life of physical, as opposed to spiritual fulfillment, is perhaps not unreasonable. However, a new and different obsession asserts itself primarily, although not exclusively, within Lawrence's discourse, through the use of nouns and verbs of touch. The sound of the cock crowing "made him shiver as if electricity had touched him."[23] As a metaphor of the phallus the rooster adumbrates the novella's climax. While the priestess of Isis watches the sleeping stranger, his presence touches her with the same "flame-tip of life"[24] that surges through the "rocking vibration of the bent bird."[25] Before making love to her, the man who died wonders if he dare "come into touch? . . . into this tender touch of life"?[26] Touching her "was like touching the sun."[27] The stranger believes that if he is naked enough for this *contact* (my emphasis), he has not died in vain.[28] The priestess "*rubs* [my emphasis] the scar on his hand with oil,"[29] and then anoints and rubs all the scars with oil.[30] The man lays "his hand softly on her warm bright shoulder" and he sees "the white glow of her white-gold breasts. And he touched them, and he felt his life go molten. 'Father!' he said, 'why did you hide this from me?' And he touched her with the poignancy of wonder, and the marvelous piercing transcendence of desire. 'Lo!' he said, 'this is beyond prayer.'"[31] Then the priestess envelops him with her arms, and, after making love and referring to his scars, he says: "'They are suns! . . . They shine from your touch. They are my atonement with you.'"[32] Satisfactions of the flesh have, at last, displaced prayer and spirituality. Afterwards, all around him, the dew touches the darkness of the starry sky that is like a rose.[33] "The world is one flower of many petalled darknesses, and he is in its perfume as in a touch."[34] He sleeps in his cave "in the absolute stillness and fullness of touch,"[35] and when the dawn comes, he says: "'This is the great atonement, the being in touch. . . . the invisible Isis and the unseen sun are all in touch, and at one.'"[36]

Christ's death—his repressed sexuality and failed desire[37]—embody a need for contact with life that is ongoing and all-inclusive. He will strive for union not only with a woman, but with the whole phenomenal world—a conjunction that will heal the wound and soothe the scars of his crucifixion—a harmony that restores his body and his soul. The man who died feels the need to get in touch with himself and with the realm of living things, and the force that will make this possible is the sun. Indeed, Lawrence uses the word *sun* almost as obsessively as he does the word *touch*, but he uses both words deliberately, despite the remarkable congruity of his metaphors with Lacan's analysis of how unconscious discourse manifests itself. For example, at the end of *Apocalypse*, Lawrence writes: "Start with the sun, and the rest will slowly, slowly happen."[38] And in *Psychoanalysis and the Unconscious* he says that "it is necessary for us to know the unconscious . . . just as it is necessary for us to know the sun."[39] He equates the word *sun* with the word *soul*, since the sun is as invisible as the soul and we know the sun by "watching his motions and feeling his changing power. The same with the unconscious."[40] The hypothesis of a partially premeditated metaphorical discourse in *The Escaped Cock* is reinforced by Lawrence's conscious equation between the words *sun*, *soul*, and *unconscious* in a context of "getting in touch." A passage from the "Future Religion" confirms the process:

> The future of religion is in the mystery of touch.
> The mind is touchless, so is the will, so is the spirit.
> First come the death, then the pure aloneness, which is
>   permanent
> then the resurrection into touch.[41]

The man "dies" and is resurrected only after he gets in touch with his unconscious—contact with the inner sun ascending to the Father. This need for contact does, nonetheless, have its incestuous connotations because, initially, the priestess of Isis embraces the man in the same way a mother embraces her child. The priestess heals the man's howling wounds even as a mother soothes her crying infant's hurt. Also, the word *sun*, as a homonym for the son of the father, considering the importance that both Freud and Lacan attribute to the play of language, reinforces the incest motif. Paronomastic associations thus help to unveil the latent discourse beneath Lawrence's otherwise lucid metaphorical structures.

Lacan's discourse of the Other corresponds to the latent content of unconscious desire veiled by every manifest narrative. In order to unveil the Other, Lacan applies Freud's theories of condensation and displacement in dreams to the tropes of realistic discourse. Indeed, Lawrence's story has a dreamlike subtext in which the cock is the phallus, the sun in the sky veils the son of the father, and the man's erection is tantamount to resurrection.

As striking perhaps as the dreamlike quality of the narrative is the fact that a force greater than death prompts the man in the cave on the narrow wall of rock to awaken "from a long sleep in which he was tied up."[42] He is literally and figuratively bound and hobbled, like the cock, whose "body, soul and spirit were tied by that string."[43] For Lacan, the repression of desire means that the emotions are tied into a knot. Indeed, as Jane Gallop points out, the slang word in French for penis is *noeud*, meaning "knot."[44] Moreover, the essential problem in psychoanalysis is how to slice through the knot that binds and inhibits change. In Lawrence's novella the cock denotes rooster, but it connotes phallus and it is the life-force of the cock that overrides death: "something had returned to him, like a returned letter,"[45] because, despite the cold, the nausea, and the forlornness, the man pushes at the bandages on his face, his shoulders, and his legs. He unties himself, the linen swathing-bands fall away, and he leaves the cave, stepping "with wincing feet down the rocky slope, past the sleeping soldiers."[46] Because *The Escaped Cock* reads like a case study in psychoanalysis, the sleeping soldiers guarding the tomb behave like Freud's metaphorical censors who are asleep on the job and therefore allow the unconscious to act out its dream imagery. Indeed, the man who died is free to set forth on his mythical quest only because the guardians of the Law are derelict in their duty.

It is quite remarkable that Lawrence should use the analogy of the returned letter, the analogy that both Lacan and Derrida also use in order to explain the meanderings of the unconscious. One of Lacan's essays in *Ecrits* is entitled "The agency of the letter in the unconscious" and one of Derrida's essays in *The Post Card* is entitled "Le Facteur de la vérité," in which the word *facteur* means both factor and mailman.[47] The truth, according to Derrida, being that a letter does not always necessarily reach its destination, whereas for Lacan it does. Poe's "Purloined Letter" is the basis for the disagreement and exploration of the workings of the unconscious by both Lacan and Derrida. Despite their differences, the event in Lawrence's story that redirects the letter to its addressee is death, not real death, but the symbolic death of a man who consciously rejects the ideology for which he was crucified. He repudiates the Father's Law, that is the *doxa* for which he was tried and which he now finds so objectionable. His insight frees him from the tangle that had bound him, and, in due course, he rises to the Father, resurrected, and no longer subservient to His Law. The man who died understands that the coercive nature of the Law is a form of death in life. He accepts the meaning of his past and the symbolic death of the man who no longer exists. He is free to go forth in search of a new self based on a vibrant sexuality, "the flame-tip of life," that had for so long been repressed and which he still only vaguely apprehends.[48]

Lawrence's novella provides the answer to Lacan's question: "What does the unconscious want for me?" The answer being that it wants me to live, and to live productively, and, in living, it overrides the death instinct that Freud formulated in *Beyond the Pleasure Principle.* Thus, the compulsion to repeat, the *Fort!/Da!* episode of little Ernst, whose "game" recovers the absent mother, is, as Derrida points out in *The Post Card,* not the negation of the pleasure principle, but its extension.[49] The behavior of the man who died acts out the principle that iterative subservience to the Law is death, whereas the need to "get in touch" with life, although perhaps also compulsive, dramatizes the ongoing force of the pleasure principle. The decision of the man who died to repudiate the Law and to go forth in search of fulfillment is not, therefore, a regressive death instinct, as classical Freudians might argue, but its opposite—the affirmation of Eros over Thanatos.

The Escaped Cock can be read as a metaphor of Lacanian theory in which the Law—God—proscribes desire. Christ's "death" is a reenactment of the primal scene—a prohibition that is experienced as castration and as a death of the self. On the denotative level, Lawrence's story has the vivid immediacy of realism, but on a psychoanalytic level his "wound" connotes all the hurt of the primal repression. When Christ does finally creep down from the cell of rock in which he had been entombed, Lawrence tells us that "it meant full awakening," movement accompanied "with the caution of the bitterly wounded."[50] And he thinks of his own mission and "how he had tried to lay the compulsion of love on all men,"[51] and for which he was crucified. In *Fantasia of the Unconscious* Lawrence had already asserted that because the Ideal was evil no idea should be raised to a governing throne. "It is the death of all life to force a pure *idea* into practice."[52] It should not surprise us, therefore, that when the man who died comes in contact with the cock, he sees "not the bird alone, but the short, sharp wave of life of which the bird was the crest. . . . and the voice of its life, crowing triumph and assertion, yet strangled by a cord of circumstance."[53] It is the "cord" of the Law that hobbles—a circumstance that Lawrence weaves into the fabric of his discourse. In the end, Christ overcomes his "wound"—the Ideal that the Law had imposed on him and that was responsible for his symbolic death—retrieves the phallus, and makes love to the priestess of Isis. He is now literally and figuratively in touch with the goddess Isis, the Magna Mater. It is Isis who rewards the priestess's quest and Christ's quest, since they are both searching for the same thing—the lost phallus. Finally, the symbolic reunion of the son and the mother is possible only in the temple of Isis. The priestess dreams that the stranger is the lost Osiris,[54] and he, the son of God, connects at last with the sun/son within himself, a homonymic union that was sundered when *le nom/non du père* intervened to split the child from the mother. Before his crucifixion, Christ's ego is the will of God—the Father and superego for whom he "dies"—but having died, and having freed himself, he sets out to discover himself as subject. The self has been decentered and the *it*, namely the sun, the phallus, the life force can assert itself and ascend. It is this displacement and acceptance of a repressed sexuality that transforms this novella into a specimen-story of Lacanian theory.

For Lacan, every symptom of aberrant behavior is a metaphor. According to Lawrence, the symptoms of Christ's aberrance are virginity, excess, preaching, and the need to compel others in their beliefs. In structuring Christ's quest after he died, Lawrence orients him and the reader toward the reenactment of a scene that dramatizes the child's repressed desire for the mother. Although the priestess is not the mother, Lawrence's discourse, imagery, and metaphors weave a web of enchantment that returns the Christ-child to the maternal womb where he, the son, reestablishes contact with his dead self. Only then does he achieve fulfillment. Christ's erection and "resurrection" would not have been possible without this backward journey. Let us track the slippage of Lawrence's metaphors and pursue their traces in the text.

In part 2 of *The Escaped Cock*, Lawrence anthropomorphizes nature and objects, imbuing them with the colors and symbolism of womanhood. Isis, nature, the priestess, and space become one maternal network contributing to the resurrection of the son. The temple of Isis stands on a "tongue of land between the two bays."[55] A causeway of rock is "the neck of her temple peninsula."[56] The peninsula is also "humped"[57] and pine-covered and the light falls on it "triumphantly."[58] Lawrence's tropological weave introduces a decidedly human pattern—a point of view that transforms the four wooden pillars of the temple into stems of "the swollen lotus-bud of Egypt."[59]

The shadow of the afternoon "washes" over the pillar-bases.[60] The little world of the peninsula is "sacred."[61] The sunshine "pours," is "royal," and is "pure." A black-and-white pigeon flies over the "immaculate loneliness" of the sea "like a ghost."[62] Objects are animated, shadows "wash," sunshine "pours," and the sea is "lonely."

There is a human complicity at work that imbues nature with human attributes. A peninsula can only be sacred if a person describes it that way. This is also true of the adjective "royal," as in "royal sunshine"—another example of the way man's use of language contaminates nature and objects. How can the sea be lonely? It knows nothing of its loneliness. These pathetic fallacies are disguised forms of perception that give us little real information about nature but say a great deal about the person who is speaking figuratively. The same anthropomorphism links the pink and white temple, which is "like a flower in the little clearing,"[63] to the priestess dressed in yellow and white—the exact colors of the "narcissus sparkling gaily in the rocks."[64] Can flowers be gay? People, yes, but flowers? The gaiety of a flower can come only from one source, which is a human source. The flowers animate the temple with qualities that belong to the priestess thereby transforming the whole scene into a vast pagan evocation of the Holy Ghost over which the Egyptian goddess presides. Thus, the adjectives "royal," "immaculate," and "pure," while used to denote the landscape, connote a sacred entity that is embedded in a non Christian setting.

Formerly, the man who died was known as the son of God, the Father, but he will soon become the son of Isis, the Mother. Language establishes a metaphorical complicity with nature and motherhood. The stranger spends the first night in a cave in a little gully where a rock basin fringed with *maidenhair* (my emphasis) contains a dripping mouthful of water.[65] The man eats bread and he dips it into the water (not wine)—the new source of his life—the spring fringed with maidenhair.[66] Every paragraph contains metaphorical associations and anthropomorphized images. The priestess is a virginal lotus bud, or a narcissus, or "the deep interfolded warmth, warmth living and penetrable, the woman, the heart of the rose!"[67] The heart of the rose is "like the core of a flame,"[68] and the flame, as an earlier passage tells us, is life. In due course the world becomes "one flower of many petalled darknesses" whose perfume brings the stranger and priestess together.[69] The world and everything in it is now alive, and the man who died experiences his resurrection as a universal oneness. Lawrence's metaphorical equations state, in essence, that woman is a flower, that a rose has the life force of fire, that woman is therefore life itself, and that space is female, fertile, enveloping, maternal.[70]

The metaphorical complicity that moves inexorably toward the maternalization of nature and space is a necessary prelude to the man's ascension. He, like the priestess, is still "in Search,"[71] and he seems unable to fulfill himself without reliving the original mother/son union that was severed by the father. "Sun beyond suns had dipped her in mysterious fire, the mysterious fire of a potent woman, and to touch her was like touching the sun."[72] The man feels not only the sun's warmth, but homonymically speaking, the child within himself. His face shines with the invisible violet light of "the dark sun."[73] He is ready for the climax, but still impotent, "faced by the demand of life, and burdened still by his death."[74] The scar on the man's side "is the eye of the violet"[75] and the wound is the source of "the re-born man."[76] The wound has healed externally but not internally, and this sexual impotence cannot be overcome until the man unites symbolically with Isis. Only this union can heal the inner cry by conjuring the lost mother and retrieving the absent breast. In *Psychoanalysis and the Unconscious* Lawrence speaks of birth, pain, and the child's desire to heal the wound. The child seeks the mother's breast in order to reinstate "the old organic continuum—a recovery of the pre-natal state."[77] Indeed, "the nipples of the breast are as fountains leaping into the universe, or as little lamps irradiating the contiguous world, to the soul in quest."[78] The man's wound is like a baby's mouth seeking to recover the warmth and comfort of the lost breast. Accordingly, the priestess puts "her breast against the wound in his left side, and her arms round him, folding over the wound in his right side, and she pressed him to her, in a power of living warmth . . . And the wailing died out altogether, and there was a stillness and darkness in his soul, unbroken dark stillness, wholeness."[79] The breast and the embrace heal the wound and the wailing—the child's silent ongoing and unconscious wailing—is silenced only after this primal, maternal contact has been reaffirmed.

It is the ascent, the rising of the unconscious, the *it/ça* that is "coming up in him, in the perfect inner darkness of himself."[80] This inner darkness is the unconscious, and the voice of the Other that has been veiled for so long by the Law is unveiled in the temple of Isis. It is like the rising of a new sun. But this sun is now the son of Isis, and as the sun illumines the I, the two together see. Truly, the man who died, echoing Freud, can say, "The id and I are now one," or, as he prefers to say "'Now I am not myself. I am something new.'"[81] The new man, no longer impotent and at last in touch with the primal mother says as he feels himself ascending to the Father:

> "I am risen!"
> Magnificent, blazing indomitable in the depths of his loins, his own sun dawned, and sent its fire running along his limbs, so that his face shone unconsciously.[82]

The sexual union of the man and the priestess of Isis is, in Lacanian terms, a metaphor for moving the contents of the unconscious into the light of day. Hence the role of the sun in its denotative and connotative forms. The mystery and power of the sun generate the "flaming buds of life" and "the foaming crest of the wave"; the revivifying power of the goddess Isis in contact with the sun-god heals the stranger on the shores of Lebanon. This is the message of the unconscious that is manifest in the puns, metaphors, and slips of language that, like a letter, always has a destination (what does the unconscious want for me?), even though sometimes it may not get there. What had been silenced and repressed by ideology was the phallus. The man's erection is the resurrection and retrieval of wholeness. The child's wound has been healed, and the dead man is finally alive. Lawrence's novella relives with formulaic accuracy the events of the so-called primal scene.

The Son, the Father, and the Holy Ghost are now one, insofar as the resurrected man incorporates all three: the unconscious, his I, and the displacement of the Father by his own impending fatherhood. The man is now in constant touch with the principle of life—universal motherhood—and free at last to pursue the calling of his own identity. This inner radiance, Barthes would surely have called it *jouissance,* with its incestuous connotations, is the happiness of freedom, wholeness, fulfillment, and absence of care. The priestess is also happy because she is "full of the risen Osiris! . . ."[83] The phallus, as Lacan points out, is a signifier and its function is to lift the veil from the Other so that the id may speak, rising to the occasion one might say, and becoming the subject, a subject who can at last assume his identity in the Father.[84] *The Escaped Cock* demonstrates that Freud's "Wo Es war, soll Ich werden"[85] is not an incursion of the ego-ideal into the id, but its opposite, namely the illumination of the ego by the rising sun of the unconscious.

The new father sleeps in the cave "in the peace and delight of being in touch . . . the invisible Isis and the unseen sun are all in touch, and at one."[86] Isis, the earth-mother, watches over the man in the womblike cave with its spring and its maidenhair, and he sleeps in this protective enclosure as a child sleeps in its mother's womb. Lawrence's novella can thus be read as the discourse of a man in search of the mother, and of the son's primal contact with her. When he finds her and himself, then the son of the father and the sun that shines ascend together as one heavenly body. The sexuality of the unconscious illumines the whole.

But the son who died is now also the new father, and his eventual departure from the temple means that his child will be raised by the mother, the priestess of Isis. "The man who had died rowed slowly on, with the current, and laughed to himself: 'I have sowed the seed of my life and my resurrection.'"[87] Nature has displaced the mother, and the mother is nature, and this new oneness is the retrieval that resurrects the son. Now that he is healed and whole, he will venture forth, once again, into "the great rose of space" in which he is "like a grain of its perfume."[88] The man's desire is not to merge with a caretaker mother, although the mother is present, but to function as an individual within the maternal realm of the universe. In the final analysis, both Lawrence's message and his achievement, at least in *The Escaped Cock*, show that his mother fixation is not emotionally and artistically crippling, as some commentators allege, but ennobling. As a future father, the man who died has proved his manhood, and he is now ready to assume his place in the world as a free, independent, integrated person.

Although I find it impossible to say where the deliberate metaphorical weave ends and the discourse of the Other begins, it is reasonably clear that *The Escaped Cock* contains both conscious and unconscious material. The two function together, simultaneously, and they attest to Lawrence's profound need to incorporate the mother as an artistic, psychological, and visionary presence within a novella that, near the end of his career, marks an important synthesis of values.[89]

The novella demonstrates that Lawrence believes in the oneness of a world that has been feminized. However, this symbolic incest with Isis, the Magna Mater, and "the rose of space" also confirms the obsessional recurring patterns to which Leigh Travis objects.[90] Nonetheless, *The Escaped Cock* objectifies Lawrence's need and desire to transcend the problem of death, castration, and lost identity. In the end, the son recovers the phallus and ascends to the Father as a renewed and now whole "Osiris." He rejects the-name-of-the-father—the Law and ideology that crucified him. I am tempted to say that he will now be able to live without the Law, without the transcendental signifier to which Derrida objects so strenuously, were it not for the fact that the phallus of self-identity becomes the new Law on which he will found his system. There is a fundamental difference, however, between the two Laws, a difference the existentialists have been stressing for a long time. One is imposed from without and is unauthentic, whereas the other is self-generated and authentic. Unauthenticity stems from encratic language, that is, the use of clichés and the acceptance of ready-made values, whereas authenticity is the by-product of choices consciously made after the rejection of *doxa*. Lawrence's novella points toward a phallic authenticity and presence based on a rejection of ideology. This authenticity is accompanied by insight and bliss. Symbolic death and the primal scene have been exorcized in a reenactment and dramatization of phallic possession. The sexual psychodrama that has been staged in the temple of Isis puts the subject (ego) in touch with the it (id), thus opening the way to insight and fulfillment.

All this has been made possible by the illumination of the I by the dark sun of the unconscious. The repressed has been incorporated into consciousness and the I is where *it* was. The Law disappears with the resurrection of the phallus because the I's wholeness has now been affirmed. Union with the symbolic mother heals the pain of symbolic castration, desire has been satisfied, and the unconscious no longer functions as the repository for the-name-of-the-father. The man who died may no longer be the subject of a *méconnaissance*, the misrecognition of identity that accompanies repression. He is now himself, whole and resurrected—the new father.

Chapter 2

D. H. Lawrence: "The Rocking-Horse Winner"

Condensation, displacement and indirect representation—have become known to us as peculiarities of the dream-work. Does not this agreement suggest the conclusion that joke-work and dream-work must, at least in some essential respect, be identical.
—Sigmund Freud, "The Relation of Jokes to Dreams and to the Unconscious"

What the psychoanalytic experience discovers in the unconscious is the whole structure of language.
—Jacques Lacan, "The agency of the letter in the unconscious or reason since Freud"

In the previous chapter we saw how the mythical retrieval of the phallus and the melding of the id and the ego made it possible for the man who died to have his erection and to fulfill his resurrection. He is now whole, at last, and a future father in his own right because the symbolic ascent transcends the death of the primal repression. The new man overcomes the death-dealing compulsions of his previous existence by incorporating and acting upon the life-giving power of the phallus. In contrast with the regenerative forces of *The Escaped Cock*, "The Rocking-Horse Winner" foregrounds the tragic consequences of a repetition compulsion that kills. In order to understand what really happens to Paul, the boy rocker, we need to frame the story within Freud's *Jokes and Their Relation to the Unconscious* and Lacan's "Agency of the letter in the unconscious." They will explain the metaphorical slippages of language in relation to jokes and the metonymical desire of rocking in terms of the signifier.

"The Rocking-Horse Winner," one of a group of Lawrence's tales of the supernatural, appeared in October, 1926, in Cynthia Asquith's *The Ghost Book.*[1] It combines the mundane concerns of realistic fiction with the mystery of fantasy and fable[2] and, like all good fairy tales, it has complementary references to social, familial, and psychological levels. "On the social level, the tale reads as a satire on the equation of money, love, luck, and happiness."[3] On the familial level, the tale dramatizes the idea "that mothers shape their sons into the desirable opposite of their husbands."[4] On the psychological level, which is the one that interests us here, the story uses the rocking-horse as a symbolic extension of desire. According to W. D. Snodgrass, the sexual area is "the basic area in which begins the pattern of living which the rocking-horse symbolizes."[5] Its symbolic extensions are "the story's chief structural feature."[6] As Snodgrass, Janice Hubbard Harris, and others have observed, Paul, the preadolescent boy, frequently retreats to his room where, in secrecy, he mounts his hobbyhorse and rides himself into a trance. Snodgrass maintains that even a brief reading of Lawrence's essay, "Pornography and Obscenity," in concert with "The Rocking-Horse Winner," should convince us that Paul's ecstasy is not only religious but also sexual and onanistic. "Just as the riding of a horse is an obvious symbol for the sex act, and 'riding' was once the common sexual verb, so the rocking-horse stands for the child's imitation of the sex act, for the riding which goes nowhere."[7] Harris, like Snodgrass, believes that rocking and its results echo Lawrence's description of and objection to masturbation in "Pornography and Obscenity."[8]

In addition to Snodgrass's and Harris's equation of rocking with masturbation, W. S. Marks's essay on "The Psychology of the Uncanny" is the most ambitious Freudian essay to date on "The Rocking-Horse Winner." Marks analyzes the tale in light of Freud's *Collected Papers* and he alludes to "the kind of verbal ambiguity Freud delighted in exploring as a clue to the repressed life of his patients" but he makes no connection between *lucre*, *lucker*, and Freud's analysis of *Jokes and Their Relation to the Unconscious*, or the *Fort!/Da!* in *Beyond the Pleasure Principle.*[9] Nor has anyone analyzed rocking as a signifier without a signified. The essays of Snodgrass, Harris, and Marks point in the right direction but we need to take rocking beyond onanism into the realm of the Symbolic where the signifier can act out its proper role on the scene of language.

If Paul rides his rocking horse long enough and hard enough he can foretell the future. With uncanny insight the boy is able to predict the name of the next winning horse at the races. Paul wants to be lucky, desperately, and he succeeds, or so it would seem, because before he dies, and as a result of naming the winner, he earns 80,000 pounds. He wants to be lucky because his mother says that she and her husband, the boy's father, are "unlucky." Also, because the house whispers *"There must be more money! There must be more money!"* The words come "whispering from the springs of the still-swaying rocking horse."[10] Although no one speaks it, the whisper is everywhere.

"The house came to be haunted by the unspoken phrase," and all three children hear the whisper that springs continuously from every corner.[11] The horse, the dollhouse, and the puppy also hear the whispering as the story shifts from realism into the realm of the fantastic. However, if the story is to "get us there," the way rocking illumines Paul, the reader, like the boy, must believe in the horse's superior powers. But Paul's divination works only when he plays with his toy, furiously. Only his frenzied rocking gives him the names of the winning horses: Sansovino, Daffodil, Lively Spark, and Malabar.

The story's fantastic element derives in part from the strange collusion between the organic and the inorganic: the house has become a living, breathing, sentient entity that orchestrates a whispering campaign. "Oh-h-h; there *must* be more money. Oh, now, now-w! Now-w-w—there *must* be more money!—more than ever! More than ever!"[12] The voices in the house come from "behind the sprays of mimosa and almond-blossoms, and from under the piles of iridescent cushions" in an orgasmic "ecstasy" that frightens the boy.

Paul wants to stop the whispers and he wants to prove to his mother that he is lucky. Although the rocking frenzy "gets him there" and gives him the luck he craves, this same rocking madness also eventually kills him. The horse rocks back and forth between the plausible and the uncanny even as the boy slips in and out of his trances—trances in which God ostensibly communicates to him the name(s) of the winning horse(s). "It's as if he had it from heaven," says Bassett.[13]

One day Paul asks his mother if luck is money and she says "no," luck is "what causes you to have money."[14] Subsequently the boy rocks himself into the lucky kingdom of lucre in order to stop the house's whispering and make his mother happy. He also states that God told him that he was lucky despite his mother's assertion that God "never tells."[15] God is invoked at the end of the story when Uncle Oscar says to his sister, the boy's mother: "My God, Hester, you're eighty-odd thousand to the good, and a poor devil of a son to the bad."[16] Although casually invoked, allusions to the supernatural give an "impossible" story its plausibility. Binary oppositions, such as God and the devil or good and bad, reinforce the story's rhythms such as breathing in and out and rocking back and forth. It seems inevitable that living and dying should also be part of the pattern. Although mounting and rocking are unlikely agents of luck, they are also sexual metaphors that, when deciphered, transport, shall we say rock the reader beyond the story's realism into the realm of the unconscious where Freud's analyses of jokes and Lacan's "agency of the letter" perform their inevitable magic.

Although the boy may play with his horse and adults may play the horses, there is also a semantic "free play" at work that activates the back and forth play of signifiers. In addition to child's play and the connotation of gambling, play also functions linguistically and psychoanalytically—linguistically, with the continuous slippage of the floating signifiers, and psychoanalytically, with the similarities between Paul's compulsive rocking and little Ernst's *Fort!/Da!* game with the spool that Freud describes.[17] The horse and the spool have become substitutes for the mother because rocking back and forth and throwing the spool across the crib are games of control that stem from the boy's desire to reduce the pain of loss and enhance the pleasure of Symbolic presence. Ernst sends the mother away, symbolically, with each *Fort!* and he retrieves her with each *Da!*, a relatively innocent game compared to Paul's rocking that has highly charged erotic connotations. He may well be the "filthy lucker" that his innocent question belies.

This "joke" plays with the difference and ambiguity of two words: *lucre* and *luck*. The following conversation between Paul and his mother illustrates the slippage:

> "Is luck money, mother?" he asked, rather timidly.
>
> "No, Paul. Not quite. It's what causes you to have money."
>
> "Oh!" said Paul vaguely. "I thought when Uncle Oscar said *filthy lucker*, it meant money."
>
> "*Filthy lucre* does mean money," said the mother. "But it's lucre, not luck."[18]

The play on words derives from the boy's misrecognition of his uncle's statement concerning *filthy lucre* and his transformation of it into *filthy lucker*. In this context, *filthy lucker* seems to imply that the lucky person derives his luck from some unsavory source. In any case, it is money that connects *lucre* and *luck*. Indeed, as a result of the conversation with his mother, Paul will associate luck with money and will do all he can within his infantile power to amass it.[19]

Despite the reader's amusement, Paul and his mother show no sign of mirth because the spelling, pronunciation, and mispronunciation of the word consist "in focusing our psychical attitude upon the *sound* of the word instead of upon its *meaning*—in making the (acoustic) word-presentation itself take the place of its significance as given by its relations to thing-presentations."[20] Freud refers to children who are accustomed to treating the word as an object and who are inclined to find the same meaning in words of the same or of similar sounds. He has analyzed at some length what he calls "innocent jokes," jokes that "are likely to put the problem . . . before us in its purest form."[21] Lawrence's use of the words *lucre* and *lucker*, although seemingly harmless, is the tip of an iceberg that reveals the play of the signifier within the sea of the unconscious.

Paul, his mother, and the reader focus on sound, but sense is by no means elided because this passage, and the story itself, will ultimately depend on meaning and the contamination of meaning by this preliminary word play. Although the two are not necessarily connected, money and luck sometimes go together, despite the mother's allegation. Nonetheless, the story exploits the lucre/lucker connection. Freud says that certain usages of language are able to produce a "good" joke or a "bad" one. A good joke, such as this one, depends on double meaning or on a slightly modified word in order to get from one idea to another by means of a "short cut," in this case luck and money.[22] Freud's two examples are *Traduttore—Traditore* (translator—traitor), and *Amantes—Amentes* (lovers—lunatics). "The two disparate ideas which are here linked by an external association, are also united in a significant relation which indicates an essential kinship between them. . . . A 'translator' is not only called by a similar name to 'traitor'; he actually *is* a kind of traitor and bears the name, as it were by right."[23] The same is true of *Amantes—Amentes*. Not only do the words resemble each other, there is also an affinity between the words "love" and "lunacy," which, according to Freud, has been noted from time immemorial. Luck and lucre display a comparable association of sound and meaning.

The boy's rocking, like the above slippages of language, gets him there by the shortest route he knows: he names the winning horse, he proves that he is lucky, and he wins the money. The reader also gets there and the story works because of the senseful association of ideas. Although mother and son don't know it, the word play on lucre/lucker is a "good" joke. It would be a "bad" joke if there were only a play on sound. The boy's mispronunciation of the word sets the stage for the story's ending, when all the meaning and all the irony come into focus. Only then, when the boy is dead and his uncle calls him a "poor devil," does the full range of linguistic associative play manifest itself. Only then do words such as "God," "money," "devil," "luck," and "poor" resonate with the conversation between Paul and his mother: the times she tells him that his father has no luck, that they are "the poor members of the family," and the boy's statement that he is lucky and that God told him so.[24]

The greater the economy in words, says Freud, the more effective the joke. In word play, from the listener's point of view, less is more because economy and pleasure are related, whereas in the story, for the characters, economy (little money) and displeasure are related to the economic disproportion that the boy will try to master. Because the family is poor, the mother must economize in order to make ends meet and keep up appearances. Paul's lucky money should have pleased her, but ironically more is never enough. It's as though Lawrence had used Freud's "Mechanism of Pleasure and the Psychogenesis of Jokes" deliberately in order to structure his story around the economy of pleasure that determines what is and is not a good joke: "*This yield of pleasure corresponds to the economy of psychical expenditure that is saved,*" says Freud.[25] Verbal jokes are a source of pleasure because they exploit double meanings in the ambiguities of words. Although pleasure begins with the two related meanings in the lucre/lucker sequence, pleasure and unpleasure run throughout the story. The boy thinks that money will please his mother. Indeed, being lucky is for him a source of pleasure because his *jouissance* (bliss) derives from his ability to name the winner. Paul's mother may believe that God "never tells,"[26] but her son, somehow, "hears" the winner's name. The bliss of *j'ouïs* (*jouis*), meaning to hear and to enjoy, is "getting there," that is, naming the horse.[27] The sexual connotations of rocking also inevitably enhance the *jouissance*. As for the reader, the "technical methods of joking . . . [such as] condensation, displacement, indirect representation and so on—thus possess the power of evoking a feeling of pleasure in the hearer."[28]

The technique of jokes is thus due to a special process that has "left behind in the wording of the joke a second trace—the formation of a substitute."[29] This process has a striking similarity to the processes of condensation in dreams that also lead to abbreviations and substitutive formations.[30] But since the dream work, as we know, is the language of the unconscious, the similarities between condensation in dreams and condensation in wit point toward the discourse of the Other, that is, toward material that is repressed. The concrete (conscious) discourse of Lawrence's story veils the discourse of the Other that begins to poke through with the initial witticism. Condensation produces economy and it is this tendency to economize that produces the joke: instead of putting together a few new words, "it has to take the trouble to search out the word which covers the two thoughts."[31] Accordingly, the story's logic structures the following syllogism: a poor family must economize. If Paul's family had money his mother would not have to economize. But they have no money because they are not lucky. Paul becomes the "lucker" who will rescue the family and his mother. But there is more in the word "lucker" than a mispronunciation of "lucre." Besides, what is a "lucker"? The word does not exist in the dictionary, but its association with luck (both acoustically and in its spelling) establishes its affinity with money. A purposeful association of ideas is established in Paul's mind and in the reader's.

However, because Paul and his mother do not laugh at the lucre/lucker witticism and derive no pleasure from it, a third person is needed to highlight the play of the signifiers. The reader's role (as the third person) is to pick up on the verbal play and give it the comic resonance it deserves. The story then becomes a formulaic account of unconscious activity, and the joke alerts us to the condensations and displacements that are unveiled by Paul's compulsive rocking. Lucky denotes winning at the racetrack but it connotes winning the mother's love, hence the S^1/S^2 algorithm in which S^1 denotes and S^2 connotes. This is indeed a weighty affair, and its success will be measured in British pounds.

Although the family has no *filthy lucre* it may have a *filthy lucker* on its hands. The humorous and derogatory sense of the first term spills over onto the second one, which has no meaning except in the boy's associative fancy. The boy creates a neologism and then goes about proving that lucre and luck are related. Nonetheless, the word *filthy* sticks to *lucker*, the new word, as the reader tries to make sense out of nonsense. The boy's association authorizes the reader's association and free play. In due course the *f* of *filthy* slides over to replace the *l* of *lucker* in order to produce the word *fucker*. We have a new noun and a new verb *to fuck* (instead of *luck*), words that the reader might dismiss were it not for the baggage of the Oedipal triangle, repression, desire, and the dissemination of verbal (psychic) traces. The term *little fucker* becomes more insistent and is consonant with the boy's compulsive rocking and frenzied playing with his toy. "Words are a plastic material with which one can do all kinds of things," says Freud.[32] Indeed, it is the structure of Lawrence's story, in the context of *desire*, that shapes *filthy lucre* into *little fucker*, the latter being an anagram of the first with a slight shift in pronunciation.

The verb "to fuck" derives from the Latin word *futuere*, the old French *foutre*, and the Greek word *ficken*. The Greek word means to strike, but in popular speech it means to copulate with. The word "fuck" thus combines the vocalism of *futuere* and the consonantism of *ficken*.[33] No wonder Paul is interested in his Greek and Latin studies.

It is the humor in the shift from *lucre* to *lucker* that also authorizes the use of the letter *f* from the word *filthy*. The words *filthy lucker* and *filthy lucre* are used contiguously and we might ask what kind of sense *f* and *lucker* produce, if not *fucker*, since fucking is precisely the content of the story that is repressed but which is, nonetheless, manifest in the symptom "little rocker." The shift from and associations with *lucker* and *lucre* invite other transpositions based on phonetic and phonemic similarities: rocker = focker = fucker, all of which seem to generate the boy's brain-fever and the reader's illumination through the dissemination of paronomastic traces.

Derrida's and Lacan's emphasis on the inherent instability of the signifier and the resultant dissemination of meaning in structuring a reader's response encourages the kind of semantic free play that underlies all jokes.[34] If we subscribe to the generative possibilities of linguistic dissemination and the subversion of the father that writing represents (the boy rocks in order to compensate for the fact that his father is not lucky), then the letters in *filthy lucre* may be rearranged to produce the anagram *Lucifer*.[35] In this context, worldly pleasures are Lucifer's temptations, even as the reader is tempted to associate the word filthy with the activities of the "little fucker" who wants more lucre. The reader's riches and pleasures are in the story's joke and in its irony. Indeed, the uncle's allusion to his sister's "poor devil of a son to the bad"[36] is consonant with these shifts and transpositions insofar as we are dealing with a text that mimes the unconscious—that realm where the free play of the signifier encourages these otherwise implausible and perhaps outrageous slippages of sound and meaning.

We must not forget that jokes and dreams survive only on displacement, condensation, and irony. Surely the ending of the story is ironic in that, despite the son's unusual powers, he is now a poor and dead devil, whereas his mother is 80,000 pounds to the good. But what good are all the riches in the world if she loses her son? With regard to luck, she was right to say that God never tells, because God is love, not lucre, and the one thing that Hester was incapable of doing was loving her children.[37] Because money is what she wanted more than anything, her wish has been fulfilled. The uncle's "My God" resonates with appropriate irony as we grasp the significance of Hester's relationship with her son and the fact that she has unconsciously sold him to Lucifer for lucre—the money that is the object of her greed and the source of Christ's temptation in the desert. The word *whisper* has a homonymic resemblance to the mother's name *Hester*, which appears only once, at the end of the story, where it echoes the house's whispers of the opening pages. Hester's whispers are what the boy constantly hears and acts on. The house is Hester, both symbolically and psychoanalytically, and the "ecstatic" whispers are charged with a sexuality to which the boy responds.[38] He needs his mother's love but she cannot love him because she loves money. If Paul could only give her enough, since his mother wants someone who is lucky, then she might be able to love him. He could then recapture the happiness that now eludes him—the green paradise of the preoedipal phase when he and his mother were as one and not yet separated by the Law.

Moreover, Lucifer comes from the Latin word meaning "lightbearer." The word "light" is also related to "luster" because in Latin, *lūcēre* means "to shine"; and "light-bringing" comes from the word *lūx*, which is light. Even without the anagram, the word *lūcifer* in Latin leads to *Lūcifer* in both Latin and English. *Lūx* also evolves into *luna* (the moon), and *fānāticus*, that is, living in the moon, hence lunatic, trances, mad, and epileptic. These illuminating associations from the Latin *lūx* all apply to Paul in one way or another. The anagram only serves to confirm the demonic source of the money, rather than its God-given origin. If Paul is lucky, his lucre comes not from God but from the devil. We, like Paul, need to study our Greek and Latin in order to understand the connection.

Whenever Paul rocks his horse his eyes are described as "blue fire" or "blazing" or "having a canny cold fire" in them or "blazing with a sort of madness." Only in his coma do they look like blue stones. To name the winner Paul must indeed be illumined. In fact, there is an unusual congruence of light and rocking during the climactic moment when he names Malabar—the winning horse at the Derby. Paul is in his "dark" room plunging to and fro on his horse at one o'clock in the morning. His mother has returned from a party in town and goes upstairs.

> She switched on the light, and saw her son, in his green pajamas, madly surging on the rocking-horse. The blaze of light suddenly lit him up, as he urged the wooden horse, and lit her up, as she stood, blonde, in her dress of pale green and crystal, in the doorway.
>
> "Paul!" she cried. "Whatever are you doing?"
>
> "It's Malabar!" he screamed in a powerful, strange voice. "It's Malabar!"
>
> His eyes blazed at her for one strange and senseless second, as he ceased urging his wooden horse. Then he fell with a crash to the ground.[39]

The mother switches on "the light" and the "blaze" illumines her and the boy. She cries "Paul," he screams "Malabar," and his eyes also "blaze." What is the meaning of Malabar?[40]

Mal, from Latin and Old French, signifies *bad* and is usually a prefix, as in the word *malfunction.* In French, the word *mal* means "evil," as in *le mal*; *Le Malin,* in French, is the devil. This is indeed a "bad (evil) joke" that resonates ironically with the "good joke" in the text and Freud's analysis of verbal play. The disseminated meaning of *mal* echoes the "poor devil to the bad," thus connoting the evil of possessions (lucre), since the mother's obsession with money is a form of possession (by the devil) as is the boy's compulsion to be lucky: "Oh, absolutely! Mother, did I ever tell you? I *am* lucky!"[41] These are the last words Paul speaks before he dies. His eyes are now like two blue stones, his mother's heart has turned to stone, and his father's voice is stony. Happiness, if that is what luck and money might have brought them, has eluded them. Lucre is all they have. Is it a coincidence that the boy rocking in the dark names Malabar when the light shines on him? Is it a coincidence that Lucifer, the light-bearer, fell from grace and that the boy falls from his horse? After his fall and before he dies, Paul is sick for three days with brain-fever. It is sometimes said that high fever is the result of demonic possession and that spirit control is exercised from without. The spirit is said to have entered the person in order to foretell the future or to proclaim the will of a god. Paul does foretell the future, when he can "get there," but his trancelike rocking and the lucre/lucker connection seem more demonic than Godlike. However, if Lucifer's light shines on the 80,000 pounds, it does not necessarily illumine the unconscious play of the signifier. To do that we must shed linguistic and semiotic rays on those invisible and repressed parts of the story where the devil may or may not be present.

It may be useful to focus on Lacan's "Agency of the letter in the unconscious or reason since Freud," because, as a metaphor of the unconscious "The Rocking-Horse Winner" highlights the play of the signifier and the role of the symptom that veils desire.[42] Indeed, the veiled sexual activity of rocking has a triple function: getting there, naming the winner, and winning the money which, in effect is winning the mummy. Whereas the father is unlucky, the son, by winning, proves to himself and to his mother that he is lucky. The homonymic slippage between the words *money* and *mummy* is consonant with the mother's compulsive need for money and the house's repeated whispering.

"Words," says Lacan, "are trapped in all the corporeal images that captivate the subject." They "undergo symbolic lesions" and they "accomplish imaginary acts of which the patient is the subject" ("Les mots sont pris dans toutes les images corporelles qui captivent le sujet. . . . les mots peuvent eux-mêmes subir les lésions symboliques, accomplir les actes imaginaires dont le patient est le sujet"). Lacan cites Freud's example of *The Wolf Man* and the word *Wespe* (wasp) whose *W* is castrated in order to become the subject's initials, S.P.[43] Words in the Lacanian system are less stable than they are in the Saussurian (and even less so in the Derridian), so that the traces, erasures, and slippages that affect signifiers are the "symbolic lesions" that help the subject to "accomplish imaginary acts." For example, Paul mounts his horse in the house of the mother. The difference between "horse" and *house* is in the letters *r* and *u*. If the house is the mother's displaced signifier (because the house, like the mother, wants money) and rocking is the symptom of desire, then mounting the horse and rocking it in the mother's house, or in the mother's name, in order to get there, that is, acquire money (mummy) is tantamount to mounting the mother. To be lucky is to get mummy (money) and that is what all the rocking is about. Rocking is a variant of the *Fort!/Da!*, a game in which Paul is indeed the "lucky fucker." Rocking the horse is fucking the mother (filthy lucre/little fucker), and climax is the horse's winning name inscribed in the boy's head—the name that wins the money but maybe not the mummy, since she can never have enough. Money is power and power is potency and money pleases the mother. Her lack is that she wants money, a classical Freudian case of penis envy that inscribes itself on the boy's psyche. He wants the phallus because he is not yet a man and the mother wants the phallus because she is a woman, yet the *non/nom du père* and biology deprive them both of what they want.

The inscribed lack materializes the bond between mother and son. Death and desire are bound together, inextricably, as the boy rocks himself to death listening to the mother's lullaby. The maternal house (voice) whispers "more money," and the boy who cannot sleep because he doesn't have the answer, rocks endlessly in the darkness of his room in order to get there. In the final episode, when his mother switches on the light, the name Malabar inscribes itself on the boy's inflamed mind and he falls into a coma. Malabar wins, but winning his *Ma* is the *grand mal* that kills him—be it sin or the penalty for violating the Law.[44] Visually, the boy's green pajamas and the mother's green dress are the symbolic link between the two. The word "arrested" also links mother and son because Laurence describes the "arrested prance of the horse" and Hester standing outside her son's room with "arrested muscles."[45] The word "arrested" and the color green connect the mother, the son, and the horse in one unmistakable triad that features arrested development.

The rocking process bridges the time gap between childhood and adulthood, between fantasy and reality. A biological time warp is impossible, yet getting there is what Paul achieves symbolically. This is perhaps the meaning of the brain-fever that kills him. On the realistic level Paul's ability to predict the winner is impossible, but on the symbolic level his rocking materializes (wins) the letter of the unconscious. The "little fucker" gets his filthy lucre.

Lacan's "agency of the letter" designates the structure of language insofar as the subject is implicated in it. The *Mal* (evil) within the name Malabar comes from the substitution of language for the thing. Desire implicates the subject, but it is language that names him. The gap between the signifier and the signified is not only a function of the aporia of language, but also a function of substitution. It operates metonymically. Playing with the toy horse—the compulsive rocking that names the winner in order to win the money (mummy)—names a "real" horse in the adult world where money is potency—a world in which money and potency are important because Paul's parents are the poor members of the family, that is, they have been castrated of their wealth. Winning mummy in the boy's world is a form of metonymic potency, but once again it underscores the gap between the signifier and the signified, between the unconscious and the conscious worlds. "Rocking" is a sign that denotes serious play whose purpose is to name, but it connotes "mounting the mother" in an equally serious although unnamed game of retrieval. The letter of the unconscious thus designates the very structure of language, literally, from which the subject (the boy) borrows the material support of his conscious and unconscious discourse. The brain-fever that afflicts him before he dies may be construed as the impossibility of crossing the Saussurian bar (S/s), as in Mal/a/bar, or of ever reconciling the difference between the signifier and the signified. The difference is forever deferred in the play of the sign, in the compulsive rocking that names a symptom that is also forever displaced. The letter of the unconscious is the "material support that concrete discourse borrows from language" ("Nous désignons par lettre ce support matériel que le discours concret emprunte au langage"),[46] concrete discourse being the act of rocking, the activity itself that names. The letter of the unconscious is the material support that sustains the rocking/mounting, that is, the Imaginary and the Real. The "real" letter, as in Edgar Allan Poe's story "The Purloined Letter," is hidden, but in a place so evident that no one sees it. Indeed the letter has a certain materiality and it occupies a space but this "relation to place" is always an "out of place" (*un manque à sa place*),[47] that is, a displacement, and the symptom (compulsive rocking) is the material sign of the displacement. The problem to be solved and the letter to be found is in recognizing the symptom and the significance of its displacement. The letter of the unconscious is not where we think it is, although it is always in plain view and, as with Oedipus, when he finally "sees" who Jocasta really is—his mother—he blinds himself in order to atone for the fact that his eyes had failed to see what had for so long been staring him in the face.

We are back to Oedipus, which is what the letter of the unconscious is all about—the message inscribed in the subject's unconscious, the voice of the Other that manifests itself in symptoms—the displacements and condensations of a Symbolic language. The subject is installed by the Other on the rocking horse of desire where the symptom is played out in the game of loss and retrieval, impotence and potency, where the loser (Paul dies) wins the Derby (money/mummy). This is yet another example of the anteriority of language in relation to the individual, of an inscription that accompanies the misrecognition (*méconnaissance*) of self during the "mirror phase," evidence of the inevitable aporia between the Imaginary and the Real. Language is the symptom and lesion of this primal inscription where desire rocks back and forth in the energized game of foretelling. This foreplay is a matter of life and death in which the message ostensibly comes from God—the absent transcendental signifier who "never tells." Nonetheless, desire confirms the presence of the Law and the name-of-the-father is Malabar. The evil (*mal*) of crossing the Saussurian "bar" is in naming the unnameable—the impossibility of the sign and the failure of its unity. Although Lawrence had no knowledge of Saussure's *Course in General Linguistics*, Malabar is such a fortuitous and convenient word that it would be sinful, even demonic, not to exploit its potential and symbolic link between presence and absence as well as the story's formulaic accuracy in defining the agency of the letter in the unconscious.

All evil (*mal*), says Lacan, stems from the conception of language in relation to the thing.[48] According to Jean-Luc Nancy and Philippe Lacoue-Labarthe, Lacan destroys the sign "in order to consolidate the science of the letter" in the unconscious.[49] The sign of rocking the horse is under erasure because it no longer signifies rocking. The rocking itself has been displaced in order to signify something else. The S/s algorithm is a sign (under erasure). It is not destroyed, but then again it is not functioning as it should. The signifier, signified, and signification are still there, but the system has been perverted. It is being asked to perform differently. Malabar accents the "evil" (*mal*) of the Saussurian "bar" because accenting the bar highlights the division in the sign. The burden of signification is displaced from the signified, that is, the denoted, to the signifier because what is connoted is what is "absent," and it is absent only because it is in the unconscious and inaccessible to the subject. In the place of the signified (rocking) another function (fucking the mother) is introduced that erases it and, in terms of unconscious desire, replaces it. Rocking the horse goes nowhere, except symbolically, because of its signified denotation, but "getting there" has its function because the repetition of the *Fort!/Da!* foregrounds the role of the signifier. The signifier, not the signified, makes connotation possible, and that is why the lucker/lucre joke is so significant. The play of the signifier is "confirmed in its threefold determination: materiality/localization/symbolization."[50] The connotation (fucking the mother) displaces the denotation (rocking), but what was immaterial, unlocalized, and nonsymbolic suddenly assumes all three functions in a new and positive role of signification. We are dealing with the difference between the denoted and the connoted, but the reality of the symptom—the meaning that it displaces—is as real (perhaps more real) than the meaningless and impossible task of rocking a toy horse into a winning position.

The function of rocking is to overcome the Law (the incest taboo)—a Law that is temporarily under erasure, or at least as long as the rocking continues. The Law, among other things, emphasizes the difference between adults and children, but the rocking suspends the difference symbolically so that the boy can get there, name the winner, and, in naming the biggest winner of all (Malabar) the story inscribes the signifier over the signified. The "bar" is the slash (S/s) and the so-called evil (*mal*) is in elevating the role of the signifier and in downgrading the signified. The triumph of the signifier is already present in the title of the story in which the letter of the Law manifests itself as difference: lucker/lucre, money/mummy, filthy lucre/little fucker. The dissemination of letters and phonemes, the "litter" of the "letter" to which Lacan alludes,[51] encourages the free play of the signifier which is not unmotivated because the slippage of meaning, as in the *Fort!/Da!*, is sustained by desire.

The concrete discourse may be little Ernst's game of tossing and retrieving the spool or Paul's equally compulsive rocking, but the symbolic discourse is in the signifier that displaces the spool or the rocking-horse in order to replace them with the mother. The boy, however, remains symbolically separated from signification by the rocking-horse and/or Malabar, so that the meaning of his act eludes him. Whether rocker or bar, the sign of difference is inscribed by the algorithm S/s that displaces the signified. The boy's green pajamas and the mother's green dress illuminated by the light connote symbolic union. The color green is an entry into the signified. It is the "go ahead" signal and it "gets us there." The signifier crosses the bar and it rocks the horse in order to produce meaning. This is a signifying operation based on structural conditions that Lacan calls *articulation*: "the structure of the signifier is, as is commonly said of language, to be articulated" ("la structure du signifiant est, comme on le dit communément du langage, qu'il soit articulé)."[52]

The signifier's dual function of denoting and connoting is also linked to what Lacan calls *signifiance*, which is the operation of the signifier when it has "passed over to the level of the signified," when it comes "to be charged with signification" ("Qu'il est passé à l'étage du signifié . . . autant à se charger de signification").[53] If *signifiance* is not, strictly speaking, the same as signification, it is, nonetheless, what makes signification possible. Signification is thus constituted as the presence of the signifier "in the subject"—hence the "agency" of the letter—a letter that articulates the entry of the signifier into the signified. The subject's concrete discourse (rocking the horse) signifies "*something quite other* than what it says" ("*tout autre chose* que ce qu'elle dit").[54] *Signifiance* will therefore function as a regulated generalization of connotation, thereby displacing the denoted meaning of rocking which is, nonetheless, essential if the subject is "to know the truth." The boy must rock furiously in order to "get there," in order to name the winner. He can, if he knows the truth (and he says he does) "make it heard in spite of all the *between-the-lines* censures" ("la faire entendre malgré toutes les censures *entre les lignes*").[55] The truth is *Malabar*: the name that connotes the agency of the letter in the unconscious as well as getting the money/mummy.

The subject has access to the denoted truth (rocking and Malabar) but the Lacanian subject is incapable of "knowing the truth" of connotation. As Nancy and Lacoue-Labarthe point out, "It is precisely this subject deprived of knowledge who can be the subject of a connotation which is *purely and simply detached or demarcated from denotation*."[56] In one sense "truth" is the same as speech, since it "is founded by the fact that it speaks" ("puisque la vérité se fonde de ce qu'elle parle")[57] and *Malabar* as an utterance is sufficient unto itself. The boy, however, has no access to the metalanguage, that is, the *signifiance* that Malabar connotes.

For Saussure the reciprocity of the signifier-signified relationship was essential: each *signifier* referred to its particular *signified* in an arbitrary coupling based on linguistic convention. For Lacan, however, the line between the S/s relationship is a *bar* indicating that the signifier does not have access to the signified. The signifier slides in a sea of signifiers in search of its signified, but encountering only other signifiers in a continuous systemic indeterminacy. As François Raffoul and David Pettigrew point out, "signifiers can only *slide along* the bar in an indefinite deferral of meaning."[58] According to Freud there is an unconscious purpose that "drags the preconscious thought down into the unconscious and there gives it a new shape."[59] This is where the sliding indeterminacy of the signifier occurs: "For, as we have learnt from the dream-work, the connecting paths which start out from *words* are in the unconscious treated in the same way as connections between *things*."[60]

Lacan's originality is to have combined linguistics and psychoanalysis into the "science of the letter,"[61] and in doing so he has reinterpreted metaphor and metonymy—the two main axes of language—in their relation to desire. Metonymy becomes the trope of desire while metaphor is the operation of substitution of one signifier for another. Paul's desire (metonymy) rides the horse toward luck and lucre (metaphor), the signifiers that keep sliding along the bar where lucker/fucker, money/mummy, house/horse rock each other back and forth in their ongoing and frenzied indeterminacy. Paul's desire is the lack (luck/lucre, money/mummy) that articulates the signifiers. This is the *truth* of his condition. Rocking the horse is the metaphor of this lack. Lacan articulates the truth of desire in the very letter that "materializes the agency of death" ("matérialise l'instance de la mort").[62] The signifier, the letter of the Law that kills Paul, is Malabar, the name of the winning horse for which he bought his "lucky" ticket. Ironically, St. Paul, his namesake says: "The letter killeth, but the spirit giveth life" ("La lettre tue, dit-on, quand l'esprit vivifie").[63] A further irony is that Lacan's quotation from St. Paul should apply to Lawrence's story with such uncanny precision.[64]

In the final analysis, we have a pleasure principle in the service of the death instinct: desire to please the mother on the conscious level and the desire to ride the mummy on the unconscious one. However, the brain-fever is the frenzied symptom of a compulsion that kills. The agency of the letter and the materiality of words, the signifiers, play themselves out in the life and death of the boy. Having named Malabar, the horse Paul *knows* will win the race, the boy falls into a coma and dies three days later. He has, literally, been consumed by the truth—his desire to know, that is, to get there—but the truth remains censored because the *signifiance* of naming Malabar (the signifier) does not give Paul access to the signified—the truth from which desire springs and which remains repressed. The truth is inscribed in the signifier and lucre/lucker is the joke, the letter's agent, that sets the rocking horse in motion. The brain-fever is the symptom of the letter—the letter that kills—that "innocent joke" that whispers "Oh, now, now-w! Now-w-w—there *must* be more money!"[65] The homonymic slippage to "more mummy, more mummy, now!" is the veiled truth for which the boy gives his life.

Freud's truth, which is also Lacan's truth, is that the only "good" father is a "dead father."[66] Naming Malabar is the boy's biggest win, a win motivated by his desire to displace the father. But the Law cannot be displaced. Rocking can name the truth but it cannot understand or overcome it.[67] The coma and the brain-fever are the sign of its inaccessibility. The censor triumphs, the son is dead, the father and Uncle Oscar remain, and Hester is 80,000 pounds to the good.

Chapter 3

Ernest Hemingway: *The Sun Also Rises* Writing the Pleasure Principle in a Postmodern Context

These are the games of occultation which Freud, in a flash of genius, revealed to us so that we might recognize in them that the moment in which desire becomes human is also that in which the child is born into language.

We can now grasp in this the fact that in this moment the subject is not simply mastering his privation by assuming it, but that here he is raising his desire to a second power. For his action destroys the object that it causes to appear and disappear in the anticipating provocation *of its absence and its presence. . . .* "Fort! Da!"

—*Jacques Lacan, "The function and field of speech and language in psychoanalysis"*

In the preceding chapter we explored the ramifications of compulsive rocking in the behavior of a boy who rides his hobbyhorse as a substitute for riding his mother. We move next to *The Sun Also Rises*, Ernest Hemingway's first novel which, like "The Rocking-Horse Winner," was published in 1926. Like Paul, Hemingway's protagonists are also riders, but their vehicles of choice are taxis, carriages, and trains. Although different in kind, the compulsive behavior of the "lost generation," particularly Jake Barnes's and Brett Ashley's displacements, reenacts Freud's *Fort!/Da!* game of loss and retrieval. In order to understand the role that language plays in the game of occultation, the reader needs to respond to the novel in the context of a plot that is necessarily postmodern.

For many commentators Jake is an active hero, whereas for others he is a passive recorder of events, chronicling the decadent lives of "the lost generation" that contrast with Spanish *afición*.[1] For some Jake is a trustworthy narrator whereas for others he is untrustworthy. For some he is an existential hero whereas for others he is a Catholic believer on a pilgrim's mission. For some the novel's conclusion is a dead end whereas for others it is upbeat. For some Brett is a nymphomaniac whereas for others she is merely promiscuous. For some she is spoiled and self-centered whereas for others she is a caring, liberated woman. Some believe that Jake dominates Brett whereas others see him as submissive to her whims. Some believe that the novel is circular and that Jake's and Brett's relationship goes nowhere whereas others argue that Jake changes after his disgrace in Pamplona and his "cleansing" experience in San Sebastian. Some argue that Jake's love for Brett is as romantic as Robert Cohn's whereas others believe that Jake, the narrator of the novel, has the grace and control of Pedro Romero, the bullfighter. Some view Jake's infirmity in tragic terms, others stress the dialogues of "irony and pity" as manifestations of comedy. Some believe that Cohn deserves the ostracism he receives whereas others see it as a reflection of anti-Semitism. Some view Hemingway's celebrated dialogues as an expression of artistic realism, others as the quintessence of stylistic compression and omission.

Despite the plethora of contradictory views, what everybody does agree on is that Jake is impotent, an impotence that leaves his desire intact because he still has balls, but who, despite desire, cannot fulfill himself sexually. Although the novel itself is vague about the exact nature of Jake's injury, in his interview with George Plimpton, Hemingway insisted that Jake "was capable of all normal feelings as a *man* but incapable of consummating them,"[2] that the "wound was physical and not psychological and that he was not emasculated."[3]

If the novel's meaning is so problematic, perhaps, in Susan Sontag's words, we need to go "against interpretation"[4] and look at something else, at words, homonymy, and traces of words as generators of sense and at language as the figure (character) of (in) the text. Perhaps the real hero or heroine, in the postmodern sense, is language and writing and not the characters. Hemingway's craft of omission and the need for audience complicity certainly point in this direction. If *the* overriding metaphor in *The Sun Also Rises*[5] is impotence (Jake's wound and the reader's desire to know based on the blindness of the reader's temporary castration) then we need to look at the meaning of impotence and writing in psychoanalytic terms. Because postcards, telegrams, letters, newspaper dispatches, and fiction, in addition to riding (sounds like writing) in taxis and trains, may be symptoms of deferral, desire, and of the repressed, we need to ask what these symptoms symbolize. If writing and riding are similar and, because of their homonymy, textually related then, in the context of Freud's *Beyond the Pleasure Principle,* the novel's love games and train trips, and the characters' goings and comings assume special (spatial) significance. Messages are being dispatched and destinations are reached but they say more than any realistic reading of the text can reveal.[6]

Perhaps we need to look beyond the Cartesian level of signification—a textual matrix whose meaning derives from the paradigmatic chain of "difference"—toward Lacan's "discourse of the Other" and Derrida's "dissemination."[7] Instead of focusing on linear discourse, we need to see what a simultaneous discourse can reveal, a simultaneity that results from the privileged overview of rereading when special moments and significant things come into focus to form a spatial oneness that may, at first, go unnoticed. It will be similar to a vertical discourse, that is, the combined verbal chords of Lacan's musical analogy. Lacan's discourse of the Other is as much a part of any text as Derrida's traces are, but we need to track the metaphorical and metonymical structures in addition to the phonemic and syllabic repetitions and verbal associations that trigger responses in the reader's mind. Michael Reynolds has begun to unravel the meaning of these repetitions that resonate in "our mental matrix," but the metafictional implications of such dissemination need closer scrutiny.[8] It is certainly true, as Reynolds points out, that "unconsciously the reader picks up these repetitions" and it is important to understand the cumulative value of words such as "hell," "nice," and "value," or actions such as "bathing" and "paying the bill."[9] In this connection, John Atherton says that it is the narrator's "total recall," and I would add the reader's recall as well, that "restores to words their capacity to play *between* situations."[10] Lacan calls it a "resonance in the communicating networks of discourse" ("résonance dans des réseaux communicants de discours").[11] Indeed, Nina Schwartz, John Atherton, Robert B. Jones, Elizabeth D. Vaughn, and others believe that *The Sun Also Rises,* despite its realism, exhibits postmodern characteristics.[12]

In realist writing the reader sometimes mistakenly believes that the words in the text are people, objects, and events in the real world. A Hemingway story, for example, may provide enough descriptive detail to convey the illusion that X, Y, and Z are flesh and blood characters in an historical setting. Clearly, his descriptions of Paris streets, the Basque landscape, and the Pamplona fiesta evoke a vivid and accurate sense of place. In postmodern texts, however, meaning derives not from such realism but mainly from a network of interconnecting signs. This network emphasizes words, images, and connotations that function independently of the codes for people, chronology, and causality. The play of different voices occurs as a spatial unfolding of language that speaks independently of any one character. In essence, the reader produces meaning from an elaborate web of associations that contribute to the thickening of the plot. Joseph Frank refers to it as a pattern of internal references that can be apprehended as a unity.[13] Although he has the language of poetry in mind, the principle applies also to fiction whenever the structural complexities of the text foreground what Jakobson calls its "literariness." Frederic Joseph Svoboda points out that Hemingway himself wanted to write a prose that would "work on his readers with the subtlety normally associated with such a genre as poetry."[14]

Murray Krieger reminds us that words have a dual power, that in addition to newspaper language (Jake, like Hemingway, is a newspaper man who is writing a novel), words can work with and against each other. A poem, in contrast to newspaper language, remakes language as a web, a tissue of interrelationships that foreground the weaving process. The reader must therefore be attentive to the force that words generate among each other because "they function both as intelligible, transparent carriers of meaning, . . . and, simultaneously, as dense, sensible entities on their own."[15] These verbal manipulations—a form of language play—perform another function while obstructing our conventional use of newspaper language. When words are transparent we focus on the story, when they are opaque we fix on the verbal surfaces in order to apprehend them as separate entities instead of pointers to objects, people, or events in the "real" world. Whenever this happens fictional discourse swerves away from the story toward a system of internal relationships whose parts are sustained by "mutual justification instead of by reference to outside realities."[16] However, if we are looking for meaning or reference, these networks may also help to unveil the unconscious (with its reference to death, desire, and impotence), or they may be seen as mimetic signs of impersonal, random, and entropic events—the cosmic "Game" that Kostas Axelos refers to.[17]

A theoretical text (such as this one) has to mediate between the rigors of philosophical or psychoanalytic discourse and the practical work of criticism. Having said this and in addition to the obvious patterns of *The Sun Also Rises's* plot and its characters, there are floating signifiers denoting and connoting sex, money, value, hell, and death, among others, disseminated throughout the text. For example, there is a passage that involves Jake, Brett, Count Mippipopolous, and a Greek artist named Zizi. The word "*zizi*" in French is a boy's penis. The "pippi" sound in Mippipopolous has juvenile scatological traces when its two phonemes are read backward. The count's allusion to "big doings" in London, and Brett's cryptic statement, "Enormous," are comical, in part, because the connotation contrasts the size of a boy's "*zizi*" with an adult's.[18] This is also the context of Jake's "accident," which occurred on the Italian "joke front" and is supposed to be "funny,"[19] but which, in reality, despite the wit and the irony, makes him one of the wounded, like all the other expatriates who suffer in one way or another, either physically or emotionally. The word "joke" resembles the word "Jake" when we substitute the vowel *o* for the vowel *a*. The impotence inscribed on Jake's body at the Italian "joke front" has become a "hell of a joke." The conversation in chapter seven between the count, Brett, and Jake foregrounds the connection: joking is used as a verb nine times and is linked directly to Jake with statements such as "you don't joke him" and "I wouldn't joke him."[20] "Jake" and "joke" are interchangeable, and the floating signifiers and vocalic traces belong to the text's resonating network. The joke and the irony derive from the fact that Jake's "*zizi*" is neither small nor big, but absent. The "joke front" is also a pun on Jake's front—the front part of his anatomy—his missing penis, a penis that is neither seen nor described in the mirror scene, as Jake prepares for bed one evening in his Paris apartment. This part of *The Sun Also Rises* reads as though Hemingway was consciously incorporating Freud's theories concerning "jokes and their relation to the unconscious."

Phallic absence, which fits in so well with the theory of castration, regulates the structure of the novel. In one sense Jake's creativity overrides his impotence (he is writing the novel we are reading), but in another, this impotence, both directly and indirectly, affects everyone in the cast, from Brett to Cohn to Romero. Brett's promiscuity is, in large measure, a reaction to Jake's inability to make love, but Jake's relationship with Brett and her relationship with him are a dramatization of the *Fort!/Da!* game that little Ernst plays in *Beyond the Pleasure Principle.*[21] Little Ernst's game of tossing the spool across the crib (*Fort* = gone) and retrieving it (*Da* = here), which Freud interprets as the game of retrieval of the absent mother, is like Jake's game with Brett. Jake is Ernst (in more ways than one) and Brett is the mother-spool. She may go away temporarily, but she always comes back or he goes to her, as though they had each other on a string. Her infidelities may be painful but they are tolerated, and the nature of their relationship—a connection with strings attached (postcards, wires, and telegrams)—is that she does return. As with Ernst's spool, which is tossed across the crib, Brett's destination is inevitably someone's bed.

Within the context of the symbolic bed and the absent "*zizi*" there is an undercurrent of the primal scene and of the repressed, and it derives in part from the cumulative effect of words such as *Saint Pères*, royalty, father, boy, "little friend Zizi," hard, mummy, *Mumms*, *Veuve Cliquot* (referring to the widow Clicquot whose widowhood on the bottle's label identifies the champagne—Hemingway misspells *Clicquot* and *Mumm*), love, desire, money, and values.[22] Together, these words create a network of interconnecting signs—a spatial (special) unfolding that connotes the primal scene (Laius, Jocasta, Oedipus) while contributing to the work's literariness.

Money, in contrast with impotence (no penis), has power and potency, and it buys things, sex, and pleasure. Money, like impotence, is one of the pervasive themes of the novel. Indeed, the frame of reference shifts quickly from the boy's "*zizi*" to the adult world of "big doings" where the actors play out their "stuffed" lives on the stage of monetary exchange. Count Mippipopolous knows the "values," he has lots of money, and he gladly pays for all his pleasures. In a material economy everything has value and this value supplements Freud's psychic economy of impotence and the need for love. In time (time, like the sun that rises, is another word that resonates throughout the text), the less experienced actors pay for everything they do and get and, sometimes, as Brett and Jake do, comment respectively on that fact: "Don't we pay for all the things we do, though?"[23] and "the bill always came."[24] Jake not only counts his money, adding it up in his checkbook, he also pays the bills that inevitably come due. There is both realism and resonance in the bills that are due, but in order to produce meaning (the writerly and resonant level) the reader moves from realism (the readerly level) to linguistic interplay—an essential element of metafiction and of post-modern critical strategy.

This shift is a relatively recent phenomenon in Hemingway criticism. Not so long ago (1950), critics such as W. M. Frohock, in "Violence and Discipline," said that "it might be impossible for anyone opening the book now to find anything much, other than irrelevant digression, in the pages about the self-made Greek Count."[25] Within the last decade, however, critics such as James Hinkle have been emphasizing the fact that "playing with multiple meanings inherent in words is a pervasive feature of Hemingway's writing."[26] Atherton points out that comic operations on language open up the signifier to a form of free play, that Bill Gorton's repetition of words such as "wonderful," "never be daunted," and "utilize" lose their denotation through ludic insistence.[27] Verbal play, like irony, also contributes to the novel's disguises. It conceals the devastating effects of Jake's wound with wit and humor, it hides the empty lives of the expatriates with merriment, and it masks the *Fort!/Da!* game of repetition-compulsion with postcards, telegrams, and trips to San Sebastian.

Jake's impotence is, in fact, responsible for everything that happens, and it is his war wound, his symbolic impotence, that both generates and regulates the machinery of the novel. Jake is the narrator of events and it is his discourse that keeps things moving. What also keeps things moving is the expatriate's pursuit of pleasure.

They bring their moveable feast from Paris to Pamplona where the fiesta, literally, explodes in their faces. Brett (Circe) reduces men to swine, Jake becomes a pimp, a churlish Cohn fights with Jake, Mike, and Romero, and, except for Cohn, they all get drunk. They behave in ways that are decidedly not "nice," and Brett, who cannot resist what she wants, leaves for Madrid with Romero. The expatriates' behavior in Paris was perhaps dissolute, but in Pamplona, by Montoya's standards, it is degraded. At first Montoya forgives Jake for his friends because he is *aficionado*, but after the pimping episode he is no better than they are. Jake, like the steers, is both physically and morally deballed. He is doubly impotent. He cannot stop his friends' slide into disgrace or his own. But why would Jake dishonor himself by sending Brett off with Romero? Are not love and honor supposed to be more important to a man than life itself? Cohn fights in order to protect his idea of a chivalric code, and Romero's code, whenever the occasion demands it, is to face death in the bull ring. Has Jake no sense of honor? Is he not aware of the values? Why, since he knows Spain so well and loves the *corrida* so much, should he defile his honor and alienate Montoya?

The answer is perhaps not self-evident. Jake's behavior, like that of the other expatriates, is subject to the pleasure principle. His love for Brett overrides the reality principle. If he now seems indifferent to Spanish honor it is because his impotence and love for Brett have changed the rules of the game. Or have they? This will not have been the first time Brett has gone off with another man. There was Cohn before Romero, and before Cohn there were others. It's as though Jake and Brett, together, were playing the *Fort!/Da!* ritual—the game of going away and coming back. Jake fixes Brett up with a man, she goes away with him, but her departure, in essence, assures her return. "That was it," says Jake.

> Send a girl off with one man. Introduce her to another to go off with him. Now go and bring her back. And sign the wire with love. That was it all right.[28]

The desire that Jake experiences (perverse as it may seem) thus assimilates the reality principle. The symbolic pleasure of the game is the new reality principle and he subordinates everything to it. Indeed, Jake's relationship with Brett illustrates Derrida's contention that the pleasure principle is stronger than the death drive, or rather, if repetition compulsion is a symptom of the death instinct, then the pleasure principle remains dominant—dominant because it incorporates the reality principle.[29] Instead of returning to Paris after the fiesta, like the others, Jake goes to Biarritz and then on to San Sebastian. Why? In part because he knows Brett has gone off without money, but also because we are witnessing the climax of the *Fort!/Da!* game that the two have been playing all along.

The pleasure principle, like Ernst's string and spool, reels the characters in, connecting them with letters, wires, postcards, newspaper dispatches, and words. If writing is a deferral that reenacts the primal loss, be it breast or mother, then this retrieval inscribes pain and pleasure as the new reality principle. Hemingway adumbrates the process with his Paris sidewalk description of jumping frogs and boxer toys being manipulated by strings.[30] And when Brett, who is so infatuated with Romero that she can't stand it any more, says that she's "a goner,"[31] the reader knows that she is voicing the *Fort!* and that she will soon be back, *Da!* Strings, wires, and writing are the metaphoric ties for this compulsive and repetitive behavior activated by the pleasure principle.

Sending Brett away represents Jake's unconscious strategy to retain control over their relationship. In the *Fort!/Da!* game little Ernst sends his mother away symbolically in order to experience the pleasure of bringing her back—the *Da!* of retrieval. Loss and retrieval are a form of control that Brett also plays whenever she sends Jake away. Thus Jake's ritual of repetition-compulsion—the substitute men with whom he sends her away—is his effort to maintain mastery over the situation.

The city of San Sebastian, like Ernst's crib, regulates and binds the goings and comings of both Jake and Brett. Topologically, San Sebastian is a nodal point between Paris and Pamplona, a point toward which all the characters gravitate. For several years Jake has passed through the city on his way to the bull fights. Brett and Cohn have an affair in San Sebastian and Brett sends Jake a postcard of the Concha. Although the postcard is a scene of the beach area, the word *concha,* in Spanish, is the signifier for both shell and cunt. She and Mike Campbell, her fiancé, stop off there on their way to Pamplona. Instead of going fishing with Jake and Gorton, Cohn returns to San Sebastian in order to be with Brett. After the fiesta, Jake stays in San Sebastian waiting for a message from Brett. When her two telegrams arrive asking him to come to Madrid because she's in trouble, he says: "Well, that meant San Sebastian all shot to hell."[32]

Sebastian, as a historical figure and favorite youth of the Emperor Diocletian, was martyred because he had embraced Christianity. Diocletian ordered that he be shot with arrows, but he survived and, in time, after his sanctification, became a frequent subject for religious paintings. For example, in Andrea Mantegna's work (about 1455–60) 15 arrows pierce Sebastian's head, body, and legs. He is depicted standing, naked (except for a loincloth), enduring his misfortune. His wounds are visible and his suffering is tangible. It is appropriate, therefore, that San Sebastian, the city, act as a magnet for the novel's expatriates. Like him, they too were martyred, this time by World War I, and their suffering epitomizes a loss with which they are trying to cope.

In a postwar context of arrow wounds (Mippipopolous), oedipal scars, suffering, and impotence, Jake's comment about San Sebastian being "all shot to hell" has an irony that connotes not only

Sebastian's martyrdom, but one that also echoes the ninety times or so that Hemingway uses the word "hell" and the thirty-five times he uses the words "damn" and "damnation." A *man shot* resonates paronomastically with the one-armed soldier Jake sees in the park in San Sebastian. In French, a man with one arm is a *manchot* (man shot), another wounded specimen of the war. Jake knows French, as Hemingway did, so the verbal play and slippage of meaning from Sebastian to shot, to one arm is easy to follow. Jake speaks and understands French and he reads French newspapers, even the letters to the editor.

In due course Brett's telegram arrives. Jake dispatches his own telegram of reassurance and catches the Sud Express for Madrid. The telegram (wire) is like the string on Ernst's spool. It is the symbolic link between presence and absence. Also, when Brett's telegram arrives, Jake, fittingly, is in San Sebastian, the city named after the wounded martyr. It is also the city of the *concha*. In essence Brett's telegram says "come and get me," and Jake's says "I'm coming, the wire connects us." The telegrams are an act of retrieval using the connecting wire of words and language. The wire, by synecdoche, links the telegram (a short version of a longer message) with writing, with the writing of *The Sun Also Rises*. Hemingway's novel is another act of retrieval and deferral, because language, as Barthes so aptly phrases it, gives the writer an incestuous relationship with his mother tongue.[33] If writing is a compulsion, and most writers admit that it is, then this constant return to language is part of the ritual.

The telegram is written, but we hear each of the two characters speaking. Their utterances of commitment to each other may be spoken (at a distance) but they record the inscription of the *Fort!/Da!* that binds (wires) one to the other. The telegram illustrates the *différance* but like writing (when wiring) it is also a deferral of death—a deferral that manifests itself because we see that the pleasure principle has triumphed over the reality principle. This is what Derrida seems to mean when he says that the repetition compulsion can converge with the pleasure principle in order to from an intimate partnership.[34]

What is repeated in Jake's and Brett's departures is not some secret fantasy of Hemingway's, but the symbolic displacement of a signifier, in this case a person, through the insistence of the signifying chain. Each person's departure and return is not one of sameness but of difference, a differential interrelationship in which what returns is an other.[35] Brett goes to San Sebastian with Cohn and returns to Jake in Paris, whereas after she goes to Madrid with Romero, Jake goes to San Sebastian and then follows her to Madrid. The structural significance of the repetition compulsion is determined by this difference and the sequential reenactment of it.

Two other intimate partnerships are worth noting: the relationship between Jake and Brett, of course, but also the dissemination of words and their traces throughout the text—the patterns that structure its spatial form. It is the partnership of kindred traces whose genealogy generates a family of surplus resemblances that gives the reader essential supplemental information with which to organize the shifting marks of the signifiers. By transgressing the canon of realism and foregrounding dissemination and the unconscious, the reader achieves levels of insight that would otherwise go unnoticed. These strategies apply with renewed pertinence to the final scene of the novel whose symbolic wiring with everything that has preceded it makes the ending so unusual.

The ending of *The Sun Also Rises* has generated as many contradictory interpretations as the novel itself. In general critics are divided between those who think that it is upbeat and those who think it is not, between those who say that Jake and Brett have a future together and those who say they do not. At the risk of repeating an ending that is already too familiar, the last lines read as follows:

> "Oh, Jake," Brett said, "we could have had such a damned good time together."
>
> Ahead was a mounted policeman in khaki directing traffic. He raised his baton. The car slowed suddenly pressing Brett against me.
>
> "Yes," I said. "Isn't it pretty to think so?"
>
> The End

Jake has just retrieved Brett from the Hotel Montana, they have taken a taxi to the Palace Hotel for drinks (martinis), have arranged for berths on the Sud Express back to Paris, and have lunched at Botin's where Jake drinks more than three bottles of *rioja alta*. After lunch they take a taxi ride around Madrid. The above exchange occurs as the taxi turns onto the Gran Via and Jake puts his arm around Brett.

If we focus on the words "mounted" and "taxi," Jake's conversation with Gorton concerning stuffed animals and the taxidermist who *mounts* them comes to mind. Although elements of *The Sun Also Rises* function primarily on the level of Lacan's unstable signifier, words such as "hell," "taxi," "taxidermist," "stuffed dogs," and "dead" leave mnemonic traces whose meaning emerges only by following the marks left by their passage. A taxi may have one destination at a time but the intersecting tracks of words and phonemes create the resonating network. The word "hell," for example, may appear on a page anywhere from one to five times.[36] The words "damn" and "damned" are less frequent, although on page 143, "damn" appears five times. Sometimes the words "damn" and "hell" appear on the same page where they are used casually, descriptively, in anger, as insults, and as expletives. Together, they build a network of associations, a topology that defines the psychological landscape of the lost generation.

In addition to the words "hell," and "damn," the word "taxi" has its own deferred and disseminated meanings. Whether in Paris or Madrid, taxis are the expatriates' vehicles of choice. It is in the comical and yet ironic context of destination, values, and hell that the pyrotechnics of Gorton's verbal play manifests itself. The traces and the slippages of meaning within different passages generate clusters of meaning that reverberate throughout the novel. "Here's a taxidermist's," says Gorton. "Want to buy anything? Nice stuffed dog? . . . Simple exchange of values. You give them money. They give you a stuffed dog."[37] The "exchange of values" revives the conversation with Count Mippipopolous concerning money and values and the unconscious economy eliciting the need for love. Moreover, words such as "taxidermist," and "stuffed race-horses" connote a semblance of an outer life that is devoid of inner substance, particularly when we learn and remember (in view of his drunken behavior in Pamplona) that Campbell, Brett's fiancé, is "in the stud-book and everything," meaning one of the blue-bloods.[38] If, in the context of Gorton's humor, Mike is a stud for stuffed race-horses, then the connection between the wounded, the walking dead, and their taxis produces a species that we might call a "taxi-derm." The walking dead are all also so "nice," and they know their values, particularly money. The word "taxidermist" appears on pages 72 and 75 and by the end of page 75, in a context of dead and stuffed animals, it has been coupled with the word "taxi" four times. Thus, whenever one or more characters gets into a taxi, the mnemonic effects of the word "taxidermist" accompany their displacements. Together, the words "taxi," "taxidermist," and "hell" spin a web of connotations to which the reader responds and from which he or she produces meaning. We are not surprised to learn from Gorton that the "road to hell [is] paved with unbought stuffed dogs."[39]

The novel's ending contains the embedded traces of feelings, conversation, and meanings that transcend the immediacy of descriptive realism. It is the layered simultaneities that make the spatial form of the novel so complex. The apparent surplus of dissemination is not just something left over, but material that is essential to a full reading of the text.

What makes the ending so rich (best value for your money) is the symbolic act of the policeman's raised baton which, judging from the suddenly slowing taxi means "stop." In any case, he is the one directing traffic. The policeman's gesture, both literally and figuratively, is the Law, the civil law to be sure, but also Lacan's Law of the phallus and all the psychoanalytical meanings ascribed to it: the name-of-the-father (*le nom/non du père*), the incest taboo, repression, castration, and death. The raised baton (the phallus) is also the prohibition (do not proceed) inscribed by the father onto the child when the Law separates the infant and its mother. This prohibition is responsible for the feelings of death and castration experienced by the child. It is a symbolic event—one that never really happened—but, according to Lacan, it is the origin of language because the mark of this inscription and its *frayage* leave such a profound impression on the mind.[40] The *Fort!/Da!* game is a symbolic reenactment of impotence and desire and it is this symbolic level that the policeman's baton addresses.

The words of the book's ending denote an event that takes place at a street intersection in Madrid, but they connote the dual inscription of Hemingway's intentional and unintentional tracings. Insofar as word play facilitates the unveiling of unconscious discourse we should look at some of the connotations of the word "not" contained in the sign of the raised baton. It signifies "do not proceed!"—the same interdiction that Oedipus experiences when Laius (the father) blocks his way. But the word "not" is also a homonym for "knot." Such homonymic play is an important element in Lacan's strategy because for him, "the unconscious castration complex has the function of a knot."[41] From the point of view of the Law, says Lacan, "castration should be the punishment for incest."[42] The raised baton provides the missing element—the pallus—to the game Jake and Brett have been playing. It puts into perspective and gives symbolic castration (Jake's impotence) its necessary meaning. Without Jake's wound this novel would not have been written. Its symbolic language exists in the form of a knot (not)—a knot to be untangled and a prohibition to be understood. The letters, postcards, telegrams, and the writing of the novel are its symbolic untangling. The reader's role is to unravel and connect all the lines.

On another level, however, the raised baton is not a prohibition but a warning. If Jake and Brett are hell-bent in a taxi that is driving over a well-intentioned pavement of unbought stuffed animals (Gorton's admonition), then they have indeed reached a dead-end—the "stop" of the policeman's raised baton. Brett's "damned good time" is full of irony and Jake's "pretty to think so" is appropriately doubtful. Moreover, the words "The End" are inscribed at the end of the novel, thus reinforcing the dead end of an impotent relationship that has reached the "end of the line."[43]

Finally, the raised baton and the slowing taxi have two simultaneous and contradictory meanings. The text's realism and the symbolic connotations of the baton signal, in Derrida's and Maurice Blanchot's system an *arrêt de mort*,[44] which can mean both a death sentence and the suspension of death.[45] It comes from the French word *arrêter*, meaning to stop and, like Derrida's use of the word *pharmakon* in *La Dissémination*, it has two meanings.[46] In the same sense that *pharmakon* was both remedy and poison, the raised baton signifies both life and death. It is within the power of the Law to administer both and the ending of the novel serves either possibility.

The baton is the Law that defines "the end of the line" and the beginning of the game because death and desire are both inscribed in the policeman's gesture. The reader's unconscious resonates with the text's unconscious, but the ending reads the reader as often as the reader reads it, hence the frequency of contradictory exegeses. Together, Brett and Jake play the game of *Fort!/Da!*, just as little Ernst did, and as Freud did in writing *Beyond the Pleasure Principle*.[47] The reader's unconscious responds to the symptom of compulsion repetition. The Symbolic in the text activates the Symbolic in the reader and they resonate together as the baton, like the clapper of a bell, tolls the letter of the unconscious on both sides of the divide.

In conclusion, San Sebastian is the *point de capiton*, the nodal point that gathers together the different strands of the novel. The memory of San Sebastian (the man) is a metaphor for the wounded generation that has survived the shooting of World War I, but only as traumatized survivors of the conflict. San Sebastian, the city, is the symbolic crib from which and through which Jake and Brett, little Ernst's Siamese twins, reenact their game of loss and retrieval. It is worth keeping in mind that Hemingway, according to Reynolds, "knew his Freudian theory."[48] Moreover, *Beyond the Pleasure Principle* was published in Vienna in 1920. The first English translation appeared in 1922, and the Boni and Liveright edition appeared in 1924. In 1925 Boni and Liveright published *In Our Time*, and in 1926 Scribner published *The Sun Also Rises*. There is thus every reason to believe that Hemingway, when writing *The Sun Also Rises*, had read *Beyond the Pleasure Principle*. Not only do the characters, verbal traces, and linguistic connotations dramatize the pleasure principle and its beyond, it is as though Hemingway had taken to heart Freud's speculative admonition to his grandson (little Ernst) that he play with trains and not with spools. Indeed, Hemingway's taxis, his trains to San Sebastian, and the Sud Express to Madrid ("the end of the line") are part of the game that Freud wished his grandson would play.

However, in the final analysis, whether Hemingway had read Freud or not is irrelevant because, as Barthes maintains, "the author is dead."[49] Also, reader-response theoreticians quite correctly privilege the reader at the expense of the author and his or her intention, and, insofar as every text manifests desire, it is inevitable that all writing, in one form or another, stage the pleasure principle as a reenactment of Freud's *Fort!/Da!* episode. Writing manifests desire and deferral, simultaneously. If modernism stages deferral as difference, then postmodernism embeds the traces of desire within this *différance*. Writing, riding in taxis and trains, wires, telegrams, postcards, fishing lines, railroad lines, the end of the line, the lines of the novel are all strings that bind absence to presence, loss to retrieval—ties that link desire with life and the postponement of death.

San Sebastian thus functions as the symbolic knot of Jake's missing organ, his *zizi*, and his "impotence" organizes the writing game, the novel, the wires, the string of words, and the *son* (Jake) who cannot have an erection except and insofar as the *sun* also rises. This ascent traces the arrows' trajectories linking pippi, zizi, big doings, enormous, money, and the economy of value with the scars of repressed feelings whose unspoken content ("cuntent") and inscribed messages weave the unconscious into the manifest texture of Hemingway's first major work. The reader, in responding to these trajectories, regenerates the pleasure principle in a postmodern context.

Chapter 4

Ernest Hemingway: *A Farewell to Arms* Pronominal Shifts and Metaphorical Slippage

The realization of perfect love is a fruit not of nature but of grace—that is to say, the fruit of an intersubjective agreement imposing its harmony on the divided nature that supports it.

—Jacques Lacan, "The function and field of speech and language in psychoanalysis"

Who, then, is this other to whom I am more attached than to myself, since, at the heart of my assent to my own identity it is still he who agitates me?

—Jacques Lacan, "The agency of the letter in the unconscious or reason since Freud"

Three years after *The Sun Also Rises* appeared, Scribner published Hemingway's *A Farewell to Arms* (1929), a novel about two star-crossed lovers whose perfect love is destroyed by war, circumstance, and the incompetence of doctors. The pronominal shifts and metaphorical slippage of Frederic Henry's narration reveal the presence of an Other within the interstices of language. *A Farewell to Arms* is the story of a young man who narrates certain events. Frederic writes about the war, his love for Catherine Barkley, and her death, in order to sort through the devastating nature of his experience.

Although Frederic is ostensibly telling his own story, the narrative contains two simultaneous voices, Frederic's and

Hemingway's. Together, they give us the simultaneity of a sliding discourse—a simultaneity that allows Hemingway to superimpose two time schemes: one corresponding to the events as they first occurred, and the other to hindsight.

Although the novel is written in the first person, on five different occasions Frederic shifts from the first-person pronoun "I" to the second-person "you." In these passages he is not addressing another character, as we might expect, nor is he using "you" in the general sense of "one." Is this a narrative lapse on Hemingway's part, or is the opacity deliberate? Furthermore, in addition to the "I/you" shifts, there are also at least four passages in which Hemingway uses the pronoun "we" in a context that does little to clarify to whom, besides Frederic, the "we" refers.

These pronominal shifts are embedded in a discursive weave that contributes to the opacity. It is not until Chapter 5 that the narrator is identified, an American in the Italian army, and not until Chapter 12 that his first name is mentioned in Italian: Federico. The narrator's full name, Frederic Henry, does not appear until Chapter 13. Meanwhile, he has been wounded at the front and is convalescing in a Milan hospital. Why, we wonder, has Hemingway deferred naming his narrator, and why has Frederic, repressed his own name? Part of Hemingway's strategy is to force the reader to ask who is telling the story, but also, as Gerry Brenner points out, Frederic "is unsure of who he is."[1] Even after his identity is established, the pronominal shifts continue to destabilize it. Names imply differences, and indeed there is a difference between the innocent lieutenant of Book One and the *educated* Frederic Henry of Book Five. The narrative does not only defer identity. It multiplies the differences among Hemingway, Frederic, and Frederic's two selves.

On the biographical level, Frederic's narrative can be construed as Hemingway's displaced version of his love for Agnes von Kurowsky, the American nurse with whom he fell in love in the Milan hospital after he was wounded on the Italian front during World War I. According to her, Hemingway left Europe thinking that she would soon join him in the United States and that they would be married.[2] Carlos Baker, quoting Marcelline, Hemingway's sister, says that after Hemingway's return home from Italy, his brooding about Agnes reminded her of someone "put in a box with the cover nailed down."[3] When Hemingway finally received Agnes's "Dear Ernest" letter, he "ran a temperature and was obliged to go to bed."[4] Clearly, he felt her loss acutely, and, although unlike Frederic, he does not sit down immediately to write their story, he does, in time, do exactly that. Also, unlike Frederic, Hemingway had had time to assimilate the experience in order to write about it with a detachment that enabled him to structure it not only as the telling of a story but as the story of telling. *A Farewell to Arms* is a novel about writing. It is not simply Frederic trying to muddle through an experience that has left him devastated; Hemingway's narrative foregrounds the writer as artificer. The rain motif, for example, which many commentators have analyzed, and whose role as an objective correlative adumbrates the tragedy of Catherine's death, is one of many devices that belies innocent storytelling.

Innocent or not, some readers believe that Frederic is selfish, irresponsible, and infantile, whereas others argue that he is caring and even committed to his relationship with Catherine. Some argue that Frederic is running from his obligations, whereas others believe in his deep involvement. Robert W. Lewis, Jr., for example, argues that Frederic escapes to "the simplicity, isolation, and irresponsibility of an idyllic life with his beloved," but that "in the depths of his mind Henry is really glad that Catherine dies."[5] Ray B. West, Jr., also believes that Frederic tries "to escape from the obligations which life imposes."[6] Scott Donaldson emphasizes Frederic's immature attitude, his selfishness in love, and the heresy of Catherine's words when she says "you're my religion."[7] Faith Pullin maintains that Catherine "is crippled by self-hatred and by the sexual nausea that pervades the novel as a whole."[8] West, on the other hand, sees Catherine's love for Frederic as fundamentally moral, as does Jackson J. Benson, who defends the depth of Frederic's and Catherine's commitments to each other and the caring nature of their love.[9]

Robert Penn Warren suggests that these divergent views fit into a larger context. He says that *A Farewell to Arms* is a love story that establishes a connection between secular love and divine love. He defines Frederic as "the sleepless man, the man haunted by nada," the man who evolves from sensory love as appetite and discovery to another kind of love in which one does things for others: "The priest's role is to indicate . . . the true meaning of love, the 'wish to do things for.'" After he leaves, Frederic "muses on the high, clean country of the Abruzzi, the priest's home that has already been endowed with the symbolic significance of the religious view of the world."[10] This is the same "home" to which Benson refers. Thus Benson and Warren argue that the purpose of the novel is to make Frederic's and Catherine's secular love equal in value to the priest's divine love. This is the equivalence that emerges from Catherine's statement to Frederic ("You're my religion.") and the priest's statement concerning love, service, and sacrifice. Arguably, Frederic and Catherine in Switzerland establish this oneness of love—a oneness that Reynolds describes as "the spirit of the flesh."[11]

Despite these divergent views, there may be a way to reconcile and even transcend the contradictions—contradictions that are based on the belief that Frederic and Catherine are real people. If we think of them as flesh-and-blood characters, in accordance with the canon of classic realism, then we judge them accordingly. Edmund Wilson, among others, laments the fact that Hemingway "has not shown any very solid sense of character or . . . any real interest in it."[12] Indeed, Frederic and Catherine are not real; they are fictions, mere metaphors within Hemingway's discursive web. Because, according to Lacan,[13] metaphors veil the presence of the unconscious, critics should perhaps not judge these characters' moral failings or virtues, but, instead should analyze Hemingway's linguistic and artistic patterns that subsume them.

Whether Frederic and Catherine are or are not shallow characters, and whether they can or cannot love properly, may be less important than the narrative Hemingway structures around them, because his pattern of pronominal shifts, deferral, and metaphorical slippage casts special light on the changes that are taking place within Frederic. The language of love and death, of desire and loss, of the conscious and the unconscious reveals, if we borrow Freud's dream terminology, both latent meaning and manifest content.[14] Metaphors, slips, and gaps in the text—the text's manifest level—veil its hidden meaning. Therefore, the metaphorical resonance of the title embedded in the text requires readerly participation if meaning is to be heard. But the shifts, although not hard to detect, are not always easy to explain. Nonetheless, it is this essay's purpose, within a Lacanian and a reader-response context, to try to make sense of the pronominal shifts, metaphorical slippage, and structural gaps. A Lacanian reading always focuses on discourse, and because in this case the discourse is Hemingway's, any analysis of Frederic and Catherine must necessarily pull aside the veils they cast on the author who weaves them.

Not all commentators approve of such a critical strategy. Indeed, despite the fact that the first full-length Freudian study of Hemingway's works appeared seven years after *Hemingway's First War*, Reynolds believes that the vein of psychoanalytic exegesis has been overworked.[15] He urges a return to the use of old critical tools, and, in using them himself, he provides valuable and useful historical and biographical information concerning Hemingway's role at the Italian front in 1918 and on his writing of *A Farewell to Arms* in 1928. Reynolds also provides important details to support his contention that Hemingway researched portions of the novel in order to give it geographical, meteorological, historical, and military accuracy.[16] He points out that Hemingway never allowed reality to interfere with his fiction, that whenever art and biography were at odds, Hemingway "would change the remembered experience to fit the needs of his writing."[17]

The point that Reynolds makes, nonetheless, is that the author's need to write fiction is psychological, as evidenced by the fact that Hemingway changed reality to suit his needs. For example, although both Frederic Henry and Hemingway were blown up at the front, Hemingway was wounded while distributing chocolate at a forward listening post along the Piave river, whereas Frederic was eating macaroni and cheese in the trenches. Although Agnes von Kurowsky and Catherine Barkley were both nurses at the Milan hospital, Agnes had short brown hair, whereas Catherine had long blonde hair. Furthermore, Catherine is a composite character of Agnes, the nurse, Hadley Richardson, Hemingway's first wife, and Pauline Pfeiffer, his second. Hemingway spent an idyllic winter in Montreux with Hadley, and he suffered through Pauline's eighteen-hour labor, followed by caesarian delivery of a healthy child. Pauline did not die, as Catherine does, nor did the baby.[18] Hemingway's novel corroborates certain facts and contradicts others. In this connection Reynolds's book provides essential information for source hunters, and it says a great deal about Hemingway's working methods. However, a return to the use of old critical tools[19] may say less about the internal meaning of *A Farewell to Arms* than strategies grounded in linguistics, psychoanalysis, and reader-response criticism.

Reynolds is correct to stress the fact that it is dangerous to read Hemingway's fiction as biography.[20] However, there are two kinds of biography: one kind tracks the places, events, and relationships of a person's external life, whereas the other records the internal passage. In the second kind, art is the autobiography of the mind and the emotions because it traces a psychic voyage. Thus, Lacanian readings of works of fiction, such as *A Farewell to Arms*, do not concern themselves with the accuracy of historical detail but with language, because language contains metaphorical displacements that correspond to the psyche's affective states. Tropes dramatize the artist's inner world—and its meaning—as opposed to the external, visible world through which the artist moves.

With reference to *A Farewell to Arms* there are, therefore, psychologically speaking, three fundamental questions: What is the meaning of Hemingway's and Frederic's wound, what is the meaning of Hemingway's and Frederic's loss, and what is the meaning of defeat? Some background information will set the stage for our inquiry. Before Hemingway began writing *A Farewell to Arms,* he and Hadley returned to Fossalta, Italy, in search of the spot where he was wounded by the exploding shell in 1918. Although Hemingway was unable to find the exact location, Reynolds sees this return as Hemingway's ritualistic "attempt to make sense out of the trauma of his wounding."[21] The wounding at the front is the first of three key events in the novel. The second one concerns the massive retreat and defeat of the Italian army at Caporetto. This is the setting for Frederic's arrest and desertion. Why, therefore, although Hemingway was wounded on July 8, 1918, did he choose to set the novel during the two-year period between 1915 and 1917? Reynolds believes that Hemingway must have chosen not to use the Italian victory at Vittorio Veneto in 1918, because "he wanted to place Frederic in the midst of a beaten and partially paralyzed army, not a victorious one."[22] For the Italians, "Caporetto stood for the entire war experience, and that experience was defeat."[23] Although Reynolds gives a cogent historical reason, for Lacan, a sense of defeat always accompanies the infant's state of mind after the so-called *mirror phase.* The father's Law that separates the child from the mother is interiorized as defeat, castration, and death. Whether historical or psychological, defeat is the bedrock of human experience, and loss is the sine qua non of the human condition. All people carry within them, not only the invisible stigmata of the primal repression but also the gnawing awareness of contingency, death, and finitude. Reynolds senses this when he says that "*A Farewell to Arms* is a massive defeat; there could be no sentimental hope left at the end."[24] The end, the third key element in the novel, is, of course, Catherine's death. Her death and the death of the baby dramatize, symbolically, the defeat of the ego after the father's *prohibition.* Defeat resonates throughout the novel both for historical and psychological reasons.

It is perhaps not insignificant that in his youth Hemingway was attracted to older women. On July 21, 1918, when he turned nineteen, Agnes was twenty-six. Later, when he married Hadley, she was seven years his senior.[25] An interesting pattern asserts itself in Hemingway's early years, although, as he grew older, the reverse would be true: he would be attracted to younger women. There is also the parallelism between an older Agnes who nurses him back to health in the Milan hospital and the role of the mother nursing the child. The novel mirrors this relationship. Indeed, when Catherine dies, and only Frederic remains, we have, replayed, the dramatic sense of the primal triad in which Catherine, the mother, is for all intents and purposes lost, and the baby (i.e., the self) dies, both events replicating a child's inner sense of loss and death when the Law intervenes. Only Frederic's wounded ego remains, a silent witness, in the rain, to the massive defeat that has occurred.

If death is a metaphor for separation (absence) as *A Farewell to Arms* most emphatically proposes, then the loss of Agnes, or Catherine, or the mother, in Lacanian terms, echoes the hurt of the child's primal loss when the phallus (the Law) represses desire and precipitates the child's accession to language. The consequences of this separation, which are also repressed, are that death and desire form the basis for the discourse of the Other. The discourse of the Other surfaces whenever there is metaphoric or metonymic interplay. Frederic's desertion from the Italian army corresponds to a rejection of the Law and the paternalistic order for which it stands. This order is violent and irrational and it will subsequently be equated with death. Indeed, one of the novel's themes is that death, in its symbolic forms, must be resisted, even though, ultimately, Frederic recognizes it as a force over which man has no dominion. In the final analysis, Frederic's and Catherine's behaviors are symptoms of a metaphoric displacement. The name-of-the-father, which separates the infant from the mother, is interpreted as a form of death—a death that is repressed but that nonetheless is an accompanying and unconscious piece of psychic baggage. Death and desire are the two components of the Law.

The novel begins with Frederic and Catherine in the Red Cross on a front they have chosen but which is not of their making. She is there to forget and perhaps to serve, and he for no better reason than that he is in Italy and speaks the language. Frederic, as Benson points out, acts like a naive tourist visiting the front.[26] As for Catherine, she behaves the way she does because her fiancé has been killed in the war. She is a person already brutalized by forces that will eventually also kill her. Frederic, in contrast, despite the fact that initially he behaves like a fraternity boy bent on seduction, undergoes a gradual change that will put him in the spot Catherine was in when they first met. He too will have been brutalized. Although, at the beginning, Catherine may have been a "little crazy,"[27] she does truly fall in love with Frederic, and, eventually, he with her.

Whatever their private motives for being at the front, their presence *appears* useful and morally responsible. Ironically, this altruism goes unrewarded and is even punished by fate, ignorance, and incompetence. In due course Frederic says farewell to the bungling strategists who are directing the war, and he bids farewell to Catherine, who dies in the delivery room in the hands of incompetent doctors. The novel's title reveals that the linguistic detonator for the succession of tragic events is the word "farewell." Indeed, the trauma of loss explains both Catherine's behavior and Frederic's behavior, because death deprives each of them of the person loved.

At first, Catherine's behavior, due to her "crazy" outbursts, seems puzzling: she slaps Frederic for kissing her, then relents, and in no time is calling him "darling," as though he had become the instant and living substitute for her dead fiancé. Although she is not as calculating as Frederic, she, too, plays the game of love, alternately attracting and repulsing him, even as he fantasizes that she will pretend he is the boy who was killed in the Somme. Catherine understands Frederic's motives and she even sees through his artifice, telling him not to lie. She also has insight into her own behavior and she comments objectively about her first irrational lapses. One evening, having almost forgotten his date with her, Frederic experiences a lonely and hollow feeling because she is ill and not available. Suddenly, her unavailability heightens his love interest. The nature of their sporadic encounters gives her a fugitive and unpredictable role. There are obstacles and a distance which, Marcel Proust says are guaranteed to whip a suitor's love into a frenzy.[28] However, it is Frederic's brush with death, more than "the vicissitudes of the heart," that accelerates his nascent love for Catherine. This brush with death mirrors the death embodied in the primal repression. When the Austrian shell explodes

> there was a flash as when a blast-furnace door is swung open, and a roar that started white and went red and on and on in a rushing of wind. I tried to breathe but my breath would not come and I felt myself rush bodily out of myself and out and out and out and all the time bodily in the wind. I went out swiftly, all of myself, and I knew I was dead and that it had all

> been a mistake to think you just died. Then I floated, and instead of going on I felt myself slide back. I breathed and I was back.[29]

Frederic has, literally, come back from the dead. His concussion is real and is not without its affective consequences—consequences that are both conscious and unconscious. Whereas the father's prohibition, which is a form of death, deprives the child of the mother, thus frustrating desire, Catherine's appearance in the Milan hospital is like a gift from heaven. When Frederic sees her, everything turns over inside of him and he says: "When I saw her I was in love with her."[30] Why should Frederic's brush with death change the game of love into actual love when his initial goal was to seduce Catherine? How can we explain such an abrupt change? In view of the child motif embedded in the text, a Lacanian reading may provide some answers.

For Lacan all discourse is always dual because of the repression of desire at the time of the primal scene when the Law cleaves the infant/mother relationship. During the mirror phase, before the separation and irrevocable exile of the self, the mother/infant unit is experienced as a oneness—a longing for the primal oneness that is subsequently incorporated into desire. This sense of exile manifests itself in terms of a paradise lost and as a form of death (castration). The combination of loss and repressed desire (for the mother) coexists throughout life influencing all behavior and all decisions. This loss is also perceived as an absence. Frederic's need to write his story, in the light of the *Fort!/Da!*, is a form of repetition triggered by the similarities between his recent experiences and the forces of the primal scene.

Desire for the mother, due to the incest taboo, is repressed, but coming back from the dead seems to have intensified Frederic's desire, and it now focuses on Catherine. She "looked fresh and young and very beautiful. I thought I had never seen any one so beautiful."[31] The "little stick" of the dead fiancé never was and certainly now is no match for Frederic's convalescing ardor, and so, he and Catherine consummate their love—their pretense of a marriage—thus unconsciously perpetuating the illicit and unconscious taboo of desire. In nursing his wounds, Catherine fulfills a maternal role and, although it is a hospital, their nocturnal trysts give the place a semblance of a hotel and the allure of a love that is forbidden.

Although hospitals and nurses, generally, in their treatment and language (as when using the pronoun "we") tend to cast patients in the role of the incompetent, or talk to them as children, Frederic's nascent identity, in addition to this hospital syndrome, emerges in a context that is suggestive of childhood. Rinaldi, the doctor at the front, repeatedly calls him "baby." When Frederic asks when the Milan hospital doctor will arrive, Miss Gage, one of the nurses, answers: "Hush. Be a good boy and he'll come."[32] When the doctor finally arrives, he too says, "be a good boy." The child motif carries over to Catherine who says, "I'm good. I do what you want."[33] These verbal exchanges equate goodness with obedience, and obedience is, generally, what adults expect from a child, or what an officer expects from his enlisted men. However, there is nothing in Frederic's demeanor and behavior, except for his wound and the fact that he is in bed, to suggest that he is a child, or that he acts like one. He is young, but he is, nonetheless, a lieutenant; he answers firmly, he holds his own against overbearing nurses, he pays the porter to bring him cognac, he insists on seeing another doctor when the three incompetent ones advise a six-month delay for the operation on his knee so that the synovial fluid can form, he makes love to Catherine, and he convalesces. Although he is cast in the role of a child, he does not behave like one: he is not obedient, and he opposes the paternalistic order that treats him as an unthinking minor. Nonetheless, death, the concussion, and the child motif, from the reader's point of view, reinforce the return of the repressed, the helplessness of childhood, and desire, since desire for the lost mother (the one who nurses) is continuously displaced and renewed.

At some point in Frederic's convalescence, Catherine conceives. Although it is not clear which contraceptives she might have been using (Frederic apparently used none), she says that her pregnancy has occurred in spite of her preventive measures. These protestations are perhaps suspect, but Frederic is too much in love to care or to notice. Although Catherine's conception violates the moral code of the day, they decide not to marry, fearing they will be separated. But this illusion of togetherness is aborted after his wounds have healed, because Frederic is sent back to the front in order to support the paternalistic order from which his wounds have given him a reprieve. His return is not without irony, however, since the unit has continued to function well in spite of his absence. Moreover, the law he serves and in whose name the war is being fought, almost kills him a second time when he is arrested by the battle police. On the unconscious level, because the ultimate threat is death, these events will be interpreted as the law's renewed attempt at castration. The sexual implications of linking death and desire point toward Frederic's growing love for Catherine, as well as his determination to endure. Although he endures and survives, he has difficulty adjusting to the events that are gradually overwhelming him.

The passages containing the pronominal shifts reflect Frederic's dilemma and disorientation. I agree with Brenner who states that "the novel hangs together best when heard on the heels of Catherine's death."[34] In retrospect, the "we" of the opening paragraph makes special sense if we reread it after finishing the novel. "In the late summer of that year *we* [my emphasis] lived in a house in a village that looked across the river and the plain to the mountains." The similarity in tone and description of this first paragraph with the opening paragraphs of Books Three and Five (particularly the latter) is striking: "That fall the snow came very late. We lived in a brown wooden house in the pine trees on the side of the mountain."[35] Leaving aside the fact that the rain and the snow (the metaphors of fear and death) come from the mountains, it is indisputable that the "we" in the brown wooden house on the side of the mountain are Frederic and Catherine.

Who then is the "we" of Book One? It can't be Catherine, because she and Frederic have not met. Does it include the other male members of the Red Cross unit? Bernard Oldsey says that the "we" signifies "we the noncombatants, the onlookers not as yet engaged in action,"[36] and that reading makes sense. However, when rereading the novel, and keeping all the pronominal shifts in mind, a more complex view emerges. Could the stylistic similarities in the opening paragraphs of Books One and Five mean that the "we" of Book One refers to an absent Catherine? If so, it reflects an imperious need to write about her and their Swiss idyll when they were as one and lived only for each other. Catherine says: "Oh, darling, I want you so much I want to be you too." To which Frederic answers: "You are. . . . We're the same one."[37] If Frederic begins writing his story immediately after Catherine's death, as I believe he does, then their oneness during the last months of her pregnancy explains his use of "we" in the book's opening paragraph. Frederic needs to understand why she has died and what has happened to him, and in writing the story of their love (she is still too much with him; he cannot dissociate himself from her) Hemingway invites the reader's participation in deciphering Frederic's motives and feelings.

For example, after deserting and after rejoining Catherine at the Grand-Hôtel & des Isles Baromées in Stresa, Frederic says that he feels guilty like a truant schoolboy. Also, "I feel like a criminal. I've deserted from the army."[38] Feelings of guilt surface, attesting a certain vacillation, despite his earlier anger that "was washed away in the river along with any obligation. . . . it was not my show any more."[39] In civilian clothes he feels like a masquerader. "I had been in uniform a long time and I missed the feeling of being held by *your* clothes"[40] [my emphasis]. This use of the possessive pronoun "your" (one of the five passages referred to earlier) alludes to his military self, as opposed to his civilian self. Because Frederic is in dialog with Henry, the clothes are the outward sign of an inner duality. His name, made up of two first names, Frederic and Henry, connotes this difference. Circumstances (the retreat of the Italian army, his brush with death) force him to desert and to reject the paternalistic order in favor of love, Catherine, and his future child. Frederic is obliged to choose new, radically different responsibilities—confusing responsibilities that are difficult to harmonize with the fraternal order of men with whom he has been fighting.

The degree to which he himself had espoused the authoritarian system is illustrated by the fact that he shoots a soldier who would desert the truck that is stuck in the mud. Nonetheless, although Frederic is a man who believes in the system, the paternalistic order treats him like a child, punishing him for making decisions that affirm his manhood. These circumstances and these events explain, in part, Frederic's dilemma, his fragmented self, and his need to tell his story. Catherine's death affirms the dominion of a chaotic authority that is allied with fate. It is "they" who punish Catherine and Frederic for having loved each other. Before dying she says, echoing an earlier passage: "I'm all broken. They've broken me."[41] And Frederic says, "They killed you in the end. . . . Stay around and they would kill you."[42] Within a Puritanical context (Hemingway's family background in Oak Park, Illinois), Catherine's death and their stillborn child can be construed as punishment for an illicit love, because they are not married and have engaged in an elaborate act of pretense in which a hotel room becomes their home and their love affair is called a marriage. Indeed, Frederic and Catherine behave like children playing at love, and when that love is threatened, they blame the world for the afflictions visited on them. Their tragic affair ends in death and separation, and *A Farewell to Arms* is the narrative of the circumstances surrounding the lovers and the feelings engendered by their relationship.

The dialog between Frederic's civilian and military selves (the "we") refers to a discourse that is trying to sort through the conflicting ideologies of opposing identities. The pronoun "we" carries with it at least three voices (four when we add the Lacanian discourse of the Other): one is realistic, two are imaginary, and one is displaced. The realistic "we" is plausible, chronological, and conventional. It refers to Frederic and his associates at the front. It is the two imaginary "we" voices (Catherine's and Frederic's two selves) that disrupt the narrative conventions of time and plausibility, because they require that readers keep in mind previous readings of the novel. If the "we" refers to Frederic and the death of Catherine, then her haunting presence dictates Hemingway's narrative strategy. If Frederic writes because he has to reconcile his civilian and military selves, then this additional duality is also incorporated into the "you" passages that follow. This splitting of Frederic's identity fits into a Lacanian analysis.

In writing the story of his love for and loss of Catherine, Frederic is also recovering the wholeness and the unity of the premirror phase—an unconscious phase—but one which, nonetheless is now replicated through Catherine's death and the triumph of the Law ("they")—the phallus. *A Farewell to Arms* thus conforms to certain classical phases of Lacanian theory. Frederic truly experiences an ordeal by (Austrian) fire (power) that initiates him into manhood. He is wounded, he falls in love, he recovers, and he returns to the front. Significantly, the shell that almost kills him also deprives him of his pistol (symptom of castration and loss of the phallus). Nonetheless, the "broken baby boy," with Catherine's help recovers his manhood, even as he convalesces, and before returning to the front he buys a secondhand pistol to replace the one that was lost. The metaphorical value of the pistol is obvious. Its phallic charge is comparable to the little stick—the toy riding crop—that her fiancé's mother sent Catherine after he was killed.

"Now *we're* fully armed," says Frederic,[43] in a context in which "I'm fully armed" would have fulfilled the requirements of narrative realism. Why the "we"? Is it rhetorical? Or is it, as I tend to think, the reflection of a renewed identity and purpose stressing the fact that his civilian and military selves are still one, that they have not yet been sundered, that he still believes in the paternalistic cause that prompted him to enlist in the Red Cross and serve in the Italian army. He does not realize that the enduring enemy is not the Austrians and the Germans, but the Law—a Law that is peremptory, ignorant, and incompetent. Frederic's wound, his rite of passage, was a passport to the war-torn country of the Law—the paternalistic system of bourgeois values. Unwittingly, Frederic begins his farewell in the massive retreat during which "the whole country was moving, as well as the army."[44] This is when Frederic is arrested by the battle police and, in spite of his protestations, is condemned to be shot as a German infiltrator. He has more to fear from the battle police, who are shooting "deserters," than from the Austrians and Germans. His earlier statement that "now we're fully armed" has an ironic echo as he is literally and symbolically disarmed while reaching for his pistol. In the ensuing struggle, the battle police pull his arm up "so that it twisted in the socket."[45]

Frederic says nothing about losing his pistol a second time, and the reader has to infer that he does, because there is no other reason for the battle police to pull his arm up and twist it. So it turns out: after pulling himself out of the river, he reveals that "they had taken my pistol at the road."[46] This first omission, considering the pistol's phallic connotations, is not insignificant. On a conscious level the omission reflects Hemingway's iceberg theory of writing. On an unconscious level Frederic's repression of it corresponds to the repression and loss of memory of the primal scene when the father's prohibition (the Law—in this case the battle police) is perceived as a form of death. Frederic is forced to bid farewell to his arm, that is, his weapon, that is, his military self—his superego. It is this loss that forms part of the "I/you" dialog. The painful impact of each loss has its psychic reverberations that will be felt metaphorically up to the very end, when Frederic has to bid farewell to Catherine's arms, as he was once forced by the Law to bid farewell to his mother's arms.

The title, as every college student knows, and as Oldsey points out, "says good-bye to military arms and to love's embrace."[47] However, *A Farewell to Arms* was not Hemingway's working title, since, according to Oldsey he rejected thirty-three projected titles before choosing the one derived from George Peele's poem. The novel incorporates three motifs —war, love, and the education of the protagonist—as overlapping categories within the rejected titles. Contrary to the idealization of love and honor in Peele's "A Farewell to Arms," Oldsey notes that Hemingway's title gives ironic emphasis to the fact that "there is very little glory or honor on the field of battle, and that human love dies in the flesh."[48] Clearly, *A Farewell to Arms* as a title reflects a deliberate and conscious choice on

Hemingway's part—a choice that reflects the novel's themes. However, there are unconscious dimensions within the title that reflect the Law (encratic language and the military) and repressed desire (Frederic's displaced love for Catherine).

The pistol scene is a pivotal passage in which the word "arm," as in the title, has two signifieds. The dual reference, to pistol and to a part of the anatomy, illustrates Lacan's theory of the repressed. It is at junctures such as this one—metaphorical junctures—that the unconscious reveals itself through verbal play. Because the unconscious is structured like a language, Lacan insists that we can see it at work, or, at the very least, experience its presence through the play (articulation) of language. Metaphors are symptoms, and in this symptomatic language we (the readers) can decipher the intentions of desire. Frederic is *disarmed* (his pistol and his arm), and he is dealt a symbolic blow that, in time, will also kill the woman he loves. The battle police, whose peremptory attitudes and self-arrogated justice are sources of instant judgment and execution, adumbrate the powers of ignorance that are responsible for Catherine's death (the two doctors at the Lausanne hospital). "The questioners [the battle police] had that beautiful detachment and devotion to stern justice of men dealing in death without being in any danger of it."[49] They speak in clichés, using phrases such as "the sacred soil of the fatherland" and "the fruits of victory."[50] They are the quintessential embodiment of the Law, be it real or symbolic, and their thinking is encratic. Firing squads constituted by ignorance are no different than the doctors' death-dealing ministrations of incompetence. Catherine's death forces Frederic to do without the consoling warmth of her embrace. His farewell to arms reinforces the metaphoric significance of the title—a title that contains the two poles articulating the novel's structure: love and death. "It was like saying good-by [sic] to a statue."[51] Catherine cannot respond, and a statue does not embrace.

The lesson that Frederic learns is that the world kills: "It kills the very good and the very gentle and the very brave impartially."[52] What he has to sort through, however, are the differences among the battle police, the doctors, biology, and fate, "they" into which these categories fall, and the world that incorporates all of them. If the world kills indiscriminately, then the absurd consequences of this existential premise are significant. What is also significant is that from infancy on we repress the fact that one of the components of the Law is death—a death whose implications Freud explores in *Beyond the Pleasure Principle.*

In addition to *Beyond the Pleasure Principle,* Freud's treatise on the interpretation of dreams enabled Lacan to show that the operations of the unconscious are themselves linguistic processes. Like the iconic nature of dreams, language and narration have a manifest and a latent content. In dreams, condensation and displacement disguise the content of the unconscious in the same way that metaphor and metonymy veil the pulsive forces of the author's or the narrator's desire, whenever language is being used. All discourse contains repressed material that structures a never-ending dialog with the Other—a two-tiered identity made up of the Imaginary and the Symbolic. The Symbolic is the Law (the father, the army, the battle police). The Imaginary is the displaced self that has to come to terms with the postponement of satisfaction, the repression of desire, the nurturing of discontent—in short, the maturation and acculturation that mark the passage from adolescence to adulthood. Although Frederic's transition from one to the other has been accelerated by the war, he copes competently and even heroically with adversity and change. Still, the pronominal shifts in the narrative reveal cracks in the facade of endurance.

Frederic is always portrayed as bigger than life: he knows his wines, his foods, his women, and his American family, which he rejects. He expounds knowledgeably on guns, birds, fish, brandy, and people. He falls in love. He is not unread. The ninety-four-year-old Count Greffi seeks out his company, and they philosophize about life and death. Frederic is also the confidant and friend of doctors, porters, nurses, enlisted men, hotel clerks, and even strangers. He survives in an icy river, and when he emerges he spends hours in wet clothes (he wrings them out, but they are still wet) in temperatures that would have knocked an ordinary mortal out with hypothermia. He rows thirty-five miles across a lake from Italy to Switzerland in one night in stormy weather. He endures and he survives—a tribute to his stamina and his resourcefulness. Perhaps because of the exaggeration, we recognize the attributes of Hemingway's code-hero, and we admire him for his extraordinary attributes. He is one of the initiated.

However, the crack in the facade can be revealed only through language, and it is Frederic's account of his exploits that unveils other selves beneath the one we see. The shifting nouns and metaphors are the gaps and clues that open up the narrative. Metaphors, like condensation in dreams, are paradigmatic. They go from a sign that is present to others that are absent. Reading a trope thus involves a series of operations that occur simultaneously whenever there is an overlapping of meaning. Figure 4.1 may be useful in detailing the process:

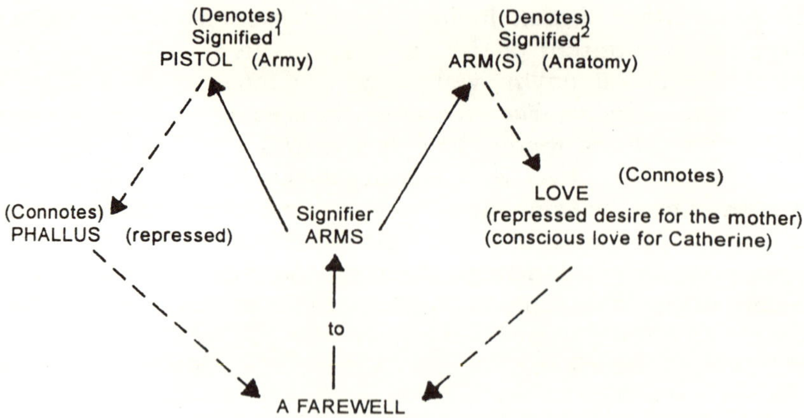

FIGURE 4.1

The solid arrows point to the telling of the story, whereas the broken arrows mark the gaps in the story of telling. The signifier ARMS has two signifieds (S^1 and S^2), each of which connotes a latent and repressed referent. Although the sign (signifier + signified) remains distinct from the repressed referent, the referent, in its contextual and extratextual functions, dramatizes the presence of the repressed. The reader constructs meaning by tracing such metaphorical relationships. Thus, the title, *A Farewell to Arms*, although not a premeditated working title, acts as an unconscious generative cell from which the novel emerges, and, like the work itself, the title has both manifest and latent meanings. The manifest meaning is the telling of the story, and the latent meaning corresponds to the story of telling. Frederic needs to tell his story in order to come to terms with loss. Catherine's death is a conscious loss, but it is superimposed on the repressed loss of the primal scene. The novel, in fact, derives its evocative power from this perfect congruence of manifest content and latent meaning, both of which elicit oedipal feelings in every reader.

In addition to its metaphoric displacement, the word "farewell" has homonyms that slide into the novel's themes. The world treats Frederic and Catherine harshly. She dies, and he loses the woman he loves. The world, according to Frederic, is not fair, because it breaks the strong and kills the innocent. The world is not *fair,* and neither protagonist *fares* well. They are both trapped, but the trap is as much existential *angst,* stemming from the certitude of death, as it is the biology of love. Only critics with severe Puritan tendencies could focus on the sexual aspect of the biological trap to the virtual exclusion of its metaphysical resonance.

John Killinger, among others, cogently develops the idea of "the absurd" in Hemingway's works.[53] Philosophers of the absurd, such as Jean-Paul Sartre and Albert Camus, believe that men exist in a contingent world devoid of a priori meaning.[54] The biological trap, in existential terms, posits that all men are mortal and that immortality is an illusion. In Camus's play *Caligula,* the protagonist states it bluntly: "Men die and they are not happy."[55] The death of Caligula's sister, Drusilla, is the beginning of Caligula's madness—a madness that reminds us of Catherine's craziness. Indeed, the death of a person we love (actual or symbolic) cannot be dismissed as readily as many commentators have dismissed Frederic's love for Catherine.

Furthermore, Camus asserts that men strive for immortality in a world that denies such longing. In this context, the absurd is defined as the discrepancy between desire and reality. The notion of the absurd leads to the conclusion that all is not well in a world in which men want happiness only to find that happiness is denied to them. It is not only bunglers, incompetents, and ignorant zealots—the battle police who arrest Frederic and the doctors who perform Catherine's caesarian—who are responsible for premature or accidental death; it is when death is perceived as a biological trap that it affects man's view of the human condition. At such times life is perceived as tragedy. Frederic and Hemingway can then state ironically that the cholera has killed only 7,000. War and cholera are not dissimilar: they both kill. Thus, men are exposed to the vicissitudes of battle, disease, chance, the biological trap, ignorance, and incompetence. All is not well in this world, and God is not in Hemingway's heaven.

Because the world in *A Farewell to Arms* is sick, the hospital is a metaphor structuring the novel's symmetry. Moreover, as William Wasserstrom puts it, "An affair that begins in a hospital bed in Milan is foredoomed to end in a hospital bed in Lausanne."[56] There is an inversion that takes place from the Red Cross flag to the Swiss flag which, as Brenner points out, is consistent and appropriate.[57] The slippage from "farewell" to "well" to "sick" to "hospital" to "wound" occurs naturally and consistently. Frederic's "wound" is tripartite: he is wounded at the front, he is aware of the biological trap as existential *angst,* and he writes in order to recover the object of his loss, whether mother or Catherine. On the unconscious level, Frederic's wound is Hemingway's wound, and both men write in order to recover an absence. The wound–psychic-scar idea is also a theme that Philip Young pursues in the "Adventures of Nick Adams."[58] The metaphoric and homonymic slippages and connotations of the words "farewell" and "arms" lift the veil of the unconscious, thereby giving us glimpses of the wound—the primal repression—from which the novel emerges.

The novel's generative cell, the oneness of the mother/infant unit (Frederic's and Catherine's idyll in the Alps), is recaptured provisionally in Switzerland. But because Catherine is as much Hemingway as Frederic is, they both manifest their author's *desire.* Catherine's quest for oneness with Frederic should not be dismissed, because her need is a facet of Hemingway's desire, namely the repressed nostalgia for oneness that is part of every sexual union. A Lacanian analysis suggests that Catherine's death and the death of the baby enable Hemingway to relive the symbolic death of desire. He, the artist, like the child in Freud's *Fort!/Da!* game, repeats and relives the masquerade of retrieving the loss of the mother. The artist plays with reality, must in fact play with it, in order to soothe the demands of the unconscious.

Although the game metaphor, as Benson points out, is "a method for ethical dramatization,"[59] it also mirrors the absurd and the unconscious. Although not foregrounded in his work as in that of such postmodern writers as John Barth, Robert Coover, and Alain Robbe-Grillet,[60] Hemingway's verbal play is nonetheless present. The freedom to play with language and to invent dramatic roles for his characters emphasizes Hemingway's metaphysical and ethical strategy. Lewis points out that *A Farewell to Arms* foregrounds many situations of masquerading and playacting. Frederic is an American in Italian uniform. He compares love to a game of chess and cards. Catherine pretends Frederic is her dead fiancé. The war itself is ridiculous and a bit theatrical. Patriots, singers, and doctors are not what they appear to be. Frederic hides empty cognac bottles even as he and Catherine conceal their lovemaking. They go to a fixed horse race. It is rumored that Germans are wearing Italian uniforms. After deserting, Frederic disguises himself first as an enlisted man, then as a civilian. In Switzerland Frederic and Catherine say they are cousins, and then they say they are married. In the delivery room Frederic wears a doctor's mask.[61] Life is theater, life imitates art, and not everything is what it appears to be. From a Lacanian point of view, art is a disguise that enables the writer to relive the truth of an experience that never took place but that, nonetheless, affects the subject with an intensity that is felt to be real. Although Frederic and Catherine are fictitious characters, together they function as Hemingway's metaphor for loss and desire.

For Lacan, the quintessential paradigm of the narration is Sophocles' *Oedipus at Colonus*, where Oedipus says: "It is now that I am nothing, that I am made to be a man?"[62] Indeed, he has nothing left to tell but his desire, and it is Oedipus' telling and retelling of his drama that prompts Lacan to say that "it is natural that everything would fall on Oedipus, since Oedipus embodies the central knot of speech."[63] It is Oedipus' tacit recognition and Lacan's conscious exposition of the indissoluble linkage among repression, death, and language that leads to symbolic formulation. "To symbolize," says Felman, "is to incorporate death in language, *in order to survive.*"[64] Hemingway's novels are the manifestation of his will to survive, and Frederic's story is the symptom of his will to carry on.

Why, we may ask—because the use of "you" and "we" as an alternate discourse is such an effective device—did Hemingway not use it more frequently in order to dramatize conflicting sensibilities? Is it because he used it only at critical psychological moments—moments that articulate the text by giving it metaphorical weight? Or do these shifts correspond to some thought process going on within Frederic? There are important passages in which there are no pronominal shifts. There is none when the shell explodes, almost killing Frederic, nor when he is on the verge of being shot by the battle police. Although these passages are central, they are moments of physical action and survival—moments that precede or preclude thought. The pronominal shifts occur only when Frederic is thinking, observing, fantasizing, or remembering. It is thought, coupled with a pronominal shift, that gives special weight to otherwise prosaic passages. Buying the pistol prompts the observation that "now we're fully armed,"[65] thus foregrounding it as an important purchase that might otherwise go unnoticed.

The first use of the pronominal "you" occurs when Frederic fantasizes he is in a Milan hotel with Catherine:

> I would put the key in the door and open it and go in and then take down the telephone and ask them to send a bottle of capri bianco in a silver bucket full of ice and you would hear the ice against the pail coming down the corridor and the boy would knock and I would say leave it outside the door please. Because we would not wear any clothes because it was so hot and the windows open and the swallows flying over the roofs of the houses and when it was dark afterward and you went to the window very small bats hunting over the houses and close down over the trees and we would drink the capri and the door locked and it hot and only a sheet and the whole night and would both love each other all night in the hot night in Milan. That was how it ought to be.[66]

A straightforward, uncomplicated passage would have had Frederic write, "I would hear the ice against the pail," not "you would hear the ice against the pail." The "you" could be construed alternately as an appeal to the reader's auditory involvement, to the generalized "one hears," to his military self (because he is now writing as a civilian), and to Catherine, because he says, "we would not wear any clothes." The "you" incorporates all of these possibilities and gives the passage a density that it would otherwise not have. The passage becomes more complex when Hemingway shifts from the conditional tense, "I would," to the past tense: "you went to the window," from which *he* sees the bats hunting over the houses. This is evidence that Frederic is writing after the fact, since the past tense shows that he remembers how it was, when in fact the passage is supposed to be a fantasy of desire. Such ambiguity gives the discourse a simultaneity that combines the past and the present into an ongoing oneness that melds the different voices. The clearest evidence to corroborate the fact that Frederic is remembering while he writes concerns the loss of the Saint Anthony that Catherine had given him. In this passage he refers to the wounding that has not yet taken place: "After I was wounded I never found him. Some one probably got it at one of the dressing stations."[67]

Another pronominal shift occurs in the first three paragraphs of Chapter 32. Frederic has escaped from the battle police, he has emerged from the river, and he has hopped a train to Milan:

> Lying on the floor of the flat-car with the guns beside me under the canvas I was wet, cold and very hungry. . . . I could remem-

> ber Catherine but I knew I would get crazy if I thought about her . . . lonesome inside and alone with wet clothing and hard floor for a wife.
>
> You did not love the floor of a flat-car nor guns with canvas jackets and the smell of vaselined metal or a canvas that rain leaked through, although it is very fine under a canvas and pleasant with guns; but you loved some one else whom now you knew was not even to be pretended there; you seeing now very clearly and coldly—not so coldly as clearly and emptily. You saw emptily, lying on your stomach, having been present when one army moved back and another came forward. You had lost your cars and your men as a floorwalker loses the stock of his department in a fire. There was, however, no insurance. You were out of it now. You had no more obligation. If they shot floorwalkers after a fire in the department store because they spoke with an accent they had always had, then certainly the floorwalkers would not be expected to return when the store opened again for business.[68]

Several identities emerge from these pronominal shifts: (1) Frederic, the writer, who remembers the event as he writes about it, thereby conjuring the feelings and thoughts of a past self; (2) a civilian self writing about a military self which has "no more obligations" because floorwalkers who might be shot are not expected to return to the store when the fire is not of their making; and (3) a loving self, because his love for Catherine reinforces his civilian identity and its different responsibilities. The sentence "You did not love the floor of a flat-car,"[69] combining the "you" and the past tense, argues strongly for a narrative after the fact, for a civilian Frederic somewhere, writing the story of his experiences. It reinforces the hypothesis that the "we" of the opening paragraph of Book One is also these two selves living together in the house in the village "that looked across the river and the plain to the mountains." However, as he watches the men passing on the road, with their cartridges bulging forward under their capes, he says that they "marched as though they were six months gone with child." The comparison, in its incongruity, is grotesque. It can only be prompted by Frederic's remembrance of Catherine's recent pregnancy thus supporting the hypothesis that the "we," in the beginning, includes Catherine.

Perhaps the most dramatic use of Frederic's "I/you" dialog occurs at the end, when Catherine is in labor and Frederic is afraid she might die:

> This was the price you paid for sleeping together. This was the end of the trap. This was what people got for loving each other. . . . So now they got her in the end. You never got away with anything. Get away hell! It would have been the same if we had been married fifty times. And what if she should die? She won't die. People don't die in childbirth nowadays. That was what all husbands thought. Yes, but what if she should die? . . . She can't, I tell you. Don't be a fool. It's just a bad time. . . . But what if she should die? She won't. She's all right. But what if she should die? She can't die. But what if she should die? Hey, what about that? What if she should die?[70]

This is the dialog of two antithetical selves: one is responsive to the moral code of the day and feels guilty for not marrying Catherine. The other self considers such a code irrelevant to what is happening and rejects the idea that they are being punished for violating it. One self tries to minimize the gravity of the situation even as the other one cannot forget the danger. The fear-of-death-self ends the dialog as the doctor comes into the room. In this passage Hemingway makes effective use of monologue by splitting it in two, thus heightening the suspense while dramatizing Frederic's dialogic selves.

Having explored these aspects of Frederic's different identities, it is safe to say, I think, that they belong to Hemingway's conscious manipulation of narrative strategy, as opposed to any unconscious symptom they may be revealing. The Lacanian discourse of the Other is not involved in the deliberate pronominal shifts from "I" to "we," or from "I" to "you." There is nonetheless, although displaced, a hint of a mirror phase, mother/infant unit, when Catherine, who has no official religion, says that love is her religion: "There isn't any me. I'm you."[71] Although this is her desire speaking, not Frederic's, as characters, they are both extrusions of Hemingway's psyche. Together they manifest his unconscious desire, a desire that, unless transcended, as it is in *The Garden of Eden*, where another Catherine appears, will, because of the nature of the primal wound, always be tragic. As metaphors of the primal unit and of loss and severance, Frederic and Catherine, in their striving for oneness and happiness, unconsciously recreate the bond that is prohibited by the Law, and whose punishment is symbolic death.

The novel rewrites the primal scene because the compulsion to repeat is the symptom of symbolic displacement. Frederic is the symbolic child who experiences death and loss. The letter of the unconscious—writing—is the symptom and the return of the repressed. Chronologically, the novel writes itself backward, since we (Hemingway) return to the metaphors of primal loss: the death of the baby is the death of oneness, and the death of Catherine is the loss of the mother. The Law (they) intervenes to cleave their oneness. The end of the novel is thus the symbolic displacement of the primal event. *Difference* is that indelible primal inscription that accompanies the unconscious meanderings of the mind. It is a difference born of separation, the difference of an identity that strives to recapture the oneness of the past by inscribing it in the present. It is the chronological simultaneity of discourse and it is motivated by desire: desire to recapture the past, to endure, and to inscribe the difference through deferral.

The discourse of the self, which is always a discourse of desire, seeks to retrieve the lost object. For Frederic, on the conscious level, it is Catherine, whereas, on the unconscious one, as it is for all of us, it is the mother. Our language is our mother tongue, and in using language, as Barthes points out, we unwittingly recover the loss of the mother.[72] Frederic writes his story in order to tell us about it, because that is all that he has left. Hemingway has thus given us two simultaneous discourses: the conscious one that Frederic provides and the unconscious one—the discourse of the Other—that accompanies it, and which Hemingway's narrative strategies veil and unveil.

Chapter 5

Ernest Hemingway: *The Garden of Eden*

What we teach the subject to recognize as his unconscious is his history . . . Thus, every fixation at a so-called instinctual stage is above all a historical scar.

—Jacques Lacan, "The function and field of speech and language in psychoanalysis"

Uncle Oscar's name in "The Rocking-Horse Winner" is a sleeper. While Paul rides his horse, his mother, Hester, rides in O's car and, by now, we know what riding is all about, particularly in Lawrence and Hemingway. Words and objects belie their meaning in the games of occultation that the id plays with the ego. Thus O's car may also be O/scar, namely the scar of the unconscious that the subject needs to recognize as his or her history. Hemingway's *Garden of Eden*, like Lawrence's *Escaped Cock*, narrates the possibility of transcending the scar by assuming the consequences of its meaning, and it implies the possibility of a rebirth (David and Marita are the new Bournes) into a pre-Adamic state of fulfillment and bliss. But I am getting ahead of myself. We need to look first of all at the controversy generated by Scribner's publication of Hemingway's *Garden of Eden* (1986)—a controversy fueled on the one hand by those who believe, as does Barbara Probst Solomon, that the "disfigurements and omissions" of and from the original manuscript are "a travesty,"[1] and, on the other hand, by critics who maintain that what was explicit in the holograph is psychologically implicit in the published version of the novel, despite the alterations, cuts, and condensations.

Solomon is distressed by inconsistencies and discontinuities that thwart the expectations of a reader accustomed to realism and verisimilitude. She laments the omission of those portions of the manuscript that reveal Hemingway's reflections on art and literature—reflections on Marcel Proust, Auguste Rodin, and Hieronymous Bosch—reflections that, she says, explain and illuminate Hemingway's interest in the creative process and in the difficulties of writing: "The real *Garden of Eden* is a sort of summa of Hemingway's aesthetics." She believes that Tom Jenks, Scribner's editor, "has committed a literary crime" because the 247 pages of the published version violate the integrity of the original manuscript in the Kennedy Library in Boston: a draft of 400 pages; another draft of 1,200 pages of Hemingway's typescript and holograph; plus another 300 pages added later.[2]

In contrast to Solomon and others, I believe that from a Lacanian point of view, the published version, despite its brevity, retains an intrinsic fidelity to the original, thereby, in once sense, confirming Scribner's "Publisher's Note": despite "a very small number of minor interpolations for clarity and consistency, nothing has been added. In every significant respect the work is all the author's."[3] I see the themes of sterility, fertility, and motherhood being expressed overtly in the original manuscript and covertly in the published version. In both versions these themes have a denotative level, emphasizing the ability or inability of the different couples to have a child, and on the connotative level, the relationship between biological fertility and artistic creativity. David Bourne and the reader are being asked to choose between Catherine and Marita, between symbolic castration (writing sterility) and the mother of a child (continued artistic output). Catherine's flight toward sexual inversion and lesbian love are opposed to Marita's supportive attitude toward David's work and her interest in motherhood.

Solomon has focused primarily on the manuscript's multiple characters, extended time span, and realistic details, which she finds lacking in the published version, whereas I am interested in the works' latent meaning which, I contend, is essentially the same in both. A Lacanian reading of *The Garden of Eden* supports the contention that what was explicit in the holograph is implicit in Scribner's version of it.

Jenks's editorial cuts have foregrounded Hemingway's Freudian connection, and it is this connection—a seemingly conscious one on Hemingway's part—that invites a Lacanian, or, more appropriately, post-Lacanian reading of the novel. The Freudian imagery, although embedded in the text, is unmistakable, and it seems to me highly unlikely that Hemingway did not know what he was doing. The iceberg theory of writing and the theory of the unconscious dovetail so nicely that they seem made to order for each other. Although it is improbable that Hemingway had read Lacan, *The Garden of Eden* reveals, nonetheless, a weave of metaphors, metonymy, the Oedipus complex, and mirrors, all of which give the novel a Lacanian flavor that is uncanny in its formulary accuracy. This should not surprise us because Lacan's writings on discourse are based on Freudian theory. However, Hemingway's apparently conscious use of Freud's theories belies a Lacanian reading of the novel, because, for Lacan, all metaphors, gaps in the text, and slips of the tongue—the interstices of language—must remain unconscious. To have structured a novel in which the unconscious dimension (the seven-eighths of the iceberg below the surface), although hidden, is deliberate, is, in a Freudian age, to move one step beyond into a post-Lacanian era. It is the formulary nature of the Freudian imagery embedded in the text that enables us to transcend the Law, castration, and the deferral of desire into the symbolic and happy ending of *The Garden of Eden* that Solomon finds so disquieting.

A quick summary of the published version will help us determine the novel's *manifest* content. Superficially, it is about a young man making love to two women in a hotel at La Napoule, on the French Riviera, at a time (before World War II) when summer was still the off season. Whenever David Bourne is not writing, the trio (the other two persons being his wife, Catherine, and a girlfriend named Marita) is swimming, drinking, eating, and basking in the sunshine. The setting and the relationships define a "Garden of Eden" of the senses, perhaps also the fulfillment of the male dream consisting of a loved wife, a loved mistress, and satisfying work in quiet, unhurried surroundings by the sea, where French cuisine, good wines, dry martinis, plenty of money, and good service guarantee a "moveable feast" of daily satisfactions.

However, there is a worm in the crimson bed of this ménage à trois. Catherine strives forcefully to assert a repressed and emerging masculinity: she gets a boy's haircut, she makes love in the dominant position while professing that she is the male and that David, her husband, is the woman. She persuades him to bleach his hair, so that it will be like hers, so that they will resemble each other completely, like "brothers." Although David is disturbed by Catherine's transformation, he acquiesces to her desires in order to please her. He loves her, but his manner is that of a child submitting to the will of a parent. Catherine has a very strong will.

Capitalizing on her newly found freedom and sexuality, Catherine, like a man, takes on a mistress, Marita, a dark, mysterious, and sensuous woman whom she shares with David. But Catherine's need to dominate and control her husband's life asserts itself beyond the bed sheets, first in seemingly insignificant temper tantrums and quarrels, then gradually in ways that strive to effeminize and castrate him. In her attempt to reverse their male-female roles, she tries to manage his writing, she burns the clippings of the reviews of his two novels, she also burns the notebooks in which he has written his short stories, and she leaves for Paris in order to make the "necessary" arrangements for *his* book with the photographer, saying all the while that she knows "what is best for him." Unable to prevent his wife's departure, David remains on the Riviera with Marita who has become his loving and supportive mistress. She has displaced Catherine. The novel began with David and Catherine alone, together, on their honeymoon at Le Grau du Roi, and it ends with David and Marita alone, together, anticipating a future honeymoon, but not, we may be sure, at Le Grau du Roi. Except for the interlude and machinations of a "crazy" wife (it is David and Marita who use this adjective to describe Catherine's "illness"), the bliss of the "Garden of Eden" is renewed and reinforced in ways that confirm a Lacanian reading of the repressed material whose latent meaning surfaces as metonymical structure and metaphorical discourse.

Lurking behind the semi-idyllic nature of *The Garden of Eden*'s manifest content is a disguised oedipal triangle embodying the latent characteristics that both Freud and Lacan refer to. Beneath the visible aspects of setting and characterization, like the bulk of Hemingway's "iceberg" under the surface of the sea, is the realm of the repressed. If we accept Lacan's theory of the repressed and look beneath the surface of Hemingway's discursive weave we discover castration, death, desire, and the Other.

David Bourne, the male character in this work, is a writer in the early stages of his career. He has published two novels, received good reviews, and is now working on a collection of short stories set in Africa. The stories are composed of semi-autobiographical episodes in which he explores his boyhood relationship with his father. Gradually, one of the stories displaces the story of the ménage à trois, thereby foregrounding the narrative and the discursive process. The text within the text is a specular device that calls attention to language and to writing. The dream within the text is another abyssal effect that calls attention to the signifying chain.

Hemingway foregrounds one of David's dreams about an eight-year-old boy on safari in Africa. David the writer, like David the boy, is tracking the spoor of a bull elephant which "smelled strong but old and sour."[4] In due course the Africa story and the Riviera story blend and overlap. David, the son, is enchanted by the old elephant which he tracks alone by moonlight with his faithful dog Kibo. The boy identifies with the ancient animal whose tusks are the diameter of his thighs. "The elephant was his hero now as his father had been for a long time."[5] The father shoots the elephant for his ivory and the boy, sickened by the death of the majestic patriarch, blames himself for "betraying" the animal who was his "brother." Before the elephant dies "his eye was alive and looked at David. He had very long eyelashes and his eye was the most alive thing David had ever seen."[6] In Lacanian theory, the "gaze" is always important and it performs the role of the mirror. From this encounter the boy takes away with him the knowledge of his mortal self. A death that was once repressed has now become conscious. "The tusks were stained with the dried blood and he scraped some of it off with his thumbnail like a dried piece of sealing wax and put it in the pocket of his shirt. That was all he took from the elephant except the beginning of the knowledge of loneliness."[7] Clearly, the elephant as a signifier is a metaphor for something other than itself. Its latent referents are sexuality and death.

Juma, the native tracker, cuts off the elephant's hairless tail, brandishes it, and exchanges a "locker-room" joke with David's father. The sexual overtones are unmistakable as Juma waves the surrogate phallus over the carcass of the animal. This is the story, along with others, that Catherine burns. She cannot stand "the dirt and the flies and the cruelty and the bestiality [and] . . . the massacre in the crater and the heartlessness of [the] . . . father."[8] Although Catherine reads and destroys all the stories, none of the others appears in Hemingway's text. There is a gap in it that veils the actual episodes of cruelty and heartlessness. This hole in the narrative is the silence of the repressed. At this point, the story is as much Catherine's as David's, since she is the one who is so profoundly shaken by it. What, we may ask, does the "massacre in the crater" allude to, if not the primal repression?

For Lacan, the act of writing posits the enticement of textuality, thereby acknowledging, unconsciously, the child's "wound" and alienation. To produce a text, whatever its conscious modes and operations, is also to relive the process by which an affective charge—a cathexis—is released from its generating poles. The writer, and eventually the reader, directs this charge, imbuing it with the Reality that both produces and attracts it. Fiction (fantasy) thus has the power to link the conscious and unconscious systems. The writer's need to repeat, rather than simply remember repressed material, illustrates the need to reproduce and work through painful events from the past as if they were present. David, the writer, repeats the death of the elephant as experienced by David the boy. The writer transcends the painful material, but Catherine cannot. What she seems to find intolerable in David's stories is her own symbolic castration (woman without a penis). Her need to generate a lack (the penis) motivates her behavior and her outrage. Her womanhood is her incompleteness, the symbolic hole that defines her. David's stories are the return of the repressed—the father's threat of castration coupled with the observation that she, like her mother, lacks a penis. The phallus thus becomes the locus of the question of sexual difference, the very difference that Catherine is trying to abolish.

Writing, like psychoanalysis, repeats the discontent of what never took place during that "time-event" referred to as the primal scene. The so-called fantasy of desire, incest, castration, death, and repression reenact not what took place, but what did not. Nonetheless, it is this scene that is replayed and reenacted on the stage of discourse as the metaphorical actors put on their veils and perform (repeat) their masked ritual.

The father, like the bull elephant, is the author of the Law. But the boy identifies with the elephant and rejects the father. The killing reenacts, simultaneously, castration and the death wish. However, David Bourne, the writer, identifies with the father and the father's need to kill, even as he comments on the boy's immaturity. Paternity has a social function through which the father lays down the law of sexual difference, of the prohibition of incest, and of language. Writing (language) becomes a substitute for the phallus, and it is David's assertion of maleness and difference that outrages Catherine. For her, the burning of the stories fulfills a double function: it erases difference while repressing the primal scene. Hemingway's novel thus illustrates the truth of the veiled/unveiled castration and of the transcendental identity of the phallus as the lack that makes the system work. It is Catherine's lack that causes her to react so violently to the African stories. Ironically, she has always wanted to go to Africa, but what she finds there, transported by David's fiction, is the phallus, not quite what she had expected. "Someone has to show you that the stories are just your way of escaping your duty."[9] Since David's duty is to his writing, Catherine's attempt to impose her law is again a desperate attempt to erase difference by asserting dominance. Although her neurosis is the symptom of repression, Hemingway's narrative reveals traces of the elephant's (symbolic) presence everywhere. The elephant's tusks and bulk prompt him to write of "the white curve of Cannes with the dark mountains behind it."[10] Catherine's "ivory white hair was like a scar across her forehead."[11] Places and characters carry within them the emotional "scar" of the elephant.

Catherine's scarred psyche prompts her to sever her emotional ties to David, allowing Marita, who began as Catherine's mistress, to become David's lover, and thus, eventually, to displace her. Although she is ostensibly David's new love, Hemingway casts her as the metaphor of the mother. Whereas Catherine is domineering and abrasive, Marita is agreeable, supportive of David's work, and at first, the mediatrix between the two. While David dreams and writes stories about himself as a young boy, Catherine and Marita play the accompanying roles of father and mother. In this case, however, we have a reversal of the normal oedipal resolution of the father's prohibition against the son. Marita and David, cast in the roles of mother and son, displace Catherine the father. By trying to change David's sex (castration) and his career (*le nom/non du père*) Catherine has, inadvertently, assumed the father's role. Desire is resolved in a new and different "Garden of Eden" in which the mother (Marita) is possessed, the father (Catherine) is banished, and incest triumphs.

Having discussed Hemingway's portrayal of Catherine as a neurotic woman and would-be father, we turn next to his metaphorical treatment of Marita as the symbolic mother. There is a revealing passage in which textual metonymy equates Marita with the sea. David and Marita are swimming in the Mediterranean, when he says in French: "*Elle est bonne, la mer, . . . Toi aussi.*" ("The water is good, . . . And you too").[12] In French, the spelling and pronunciation of *la mer* (the sea) connote *la mère* (the mother). Marita's brown breasts "were lapped gently by the movement the light breeze gave the sea. . . . then David kissed the tip of her left breast and then the other breast. 'They taste like the sea,' he said."[13] The word's homonymy in French is unmistakable, as is the sea-mother connotation. Also, Marita in Spanish means "little sea" as well as "little Mary." The context and word play of this passage connote the mother-infant relationship.

Following this episode, Hemingway repeats the patronym "Bourne" three times, thereby emphasizing this word's homonym "born." Not only is the newly born couple washed anew in the sea—the sea which is the origin (mother) of all life—but this episode is also the epiphany for a series of relationships connoting the familial structure. David and Marita may be adults, on the manifest level of discourse, and she may be the adoring and supportive woman that Catherine never was, but on the latent level, the narrative foregrounds ideas of birth, dependence, and desire.

We should not lose sight of the fact that such figural motifs or tropes represent a semantic transposition from a present sign (*la mer*) to an absent sign (*la mère*), one that is based on the perception of a relationship between one or more semantic features of the signified. In this case, we have an acoustic similarity between the two words that is motivated by a referential resemblance. David kisses Marita's breasts and they taste like the sea, that is, the mother. Within the discourse of the Other, the referent of a literary sign is both present and absent (the *Fort!/Da!* game). In Figure 5.1, recognition of the allusion to the absent referent requires substituting for the Saussurian bar a quasitriangular definition of the sign:

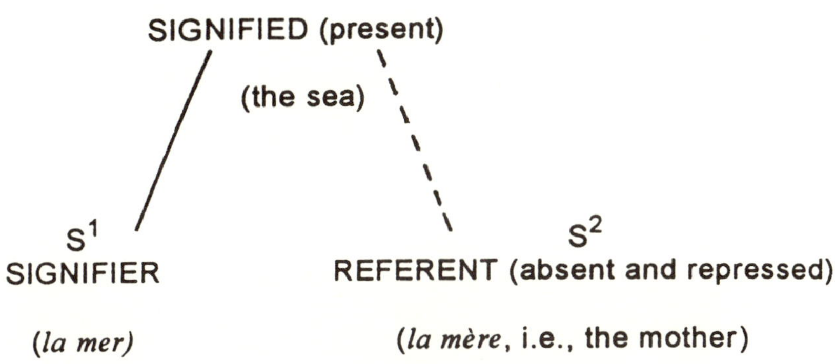

FIGURE 5.1

In this diagram, although the sign (signifier + signified) remains distinct from the referent, the referent, in its contextual and extratextual functions, dramatizes the presence of the repressed. The reader thus constructs meaning by establishing figural and symbolic traces based on metaphorical and metonymical relationships. Condensation (metaphor) is paradigmatic, going from a sign present to others that are absent, but displacement (metonymy) functions in the same way. On the acoustic level *la mer* is a metaphor for *la mère*, but on the repressed level (desire) *la mère* replaces *la mer*. The word *la mer* functions both as metaphor (condensation) and as displacement (metonymy). The word *la mer* (the sea) is the manifest actant for the latent meaning. The sea (S^1) veils the meaning of the mother (S^2).

Reading a trope involves a series of operations that tend to occur simultaneously whenever lexical or acoustic signs suggest an overlapping of meaning. Thus, in the two circles below (Figure 5.2), we have S^1 (*la mer*) overlapping with S^2 (*la mère*), with *I* as the intermediary, either on the lexical-acoustic level or on the functional level: the sea is the origin (mother) of all life, as the mother (*la mère*) is the origin of human life. In reading metaphors we cannot overlook the importance of cultural and extratextual information. For someone who knows only the dictionary definitions of *la mer* and *la mère*, the trope would be difficult to understand, especially in terms of the transfer of latent and homonymic associations referring us to desire, discourse, and repression.[14]

In this context, Hemingway's triple use of the patronym Bourne (homonym for the word "born") reinforces the latent associative referent to birth and motherhood. At this juncture the transfer of latent

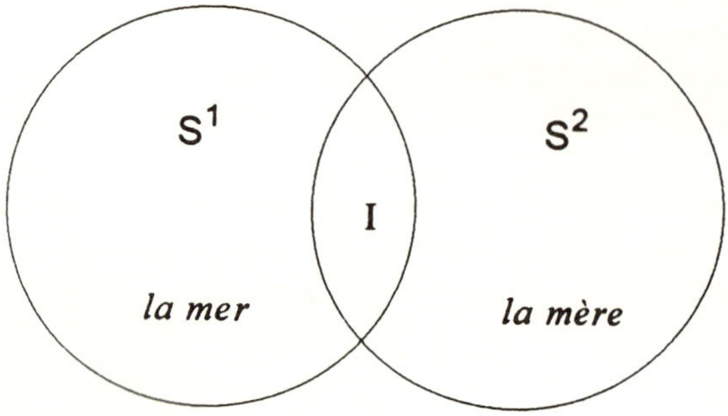

FIGURE 5.2

meaning to Marita is complete because the text tells us that she is as good as the sea (*la mer*). She is as good as the sea and she is the sea. Because her name, Marita, means little sea and little Mary, and both terms connote motherhood, Figure 5.3 diagrams the displacement and condensation of her name:

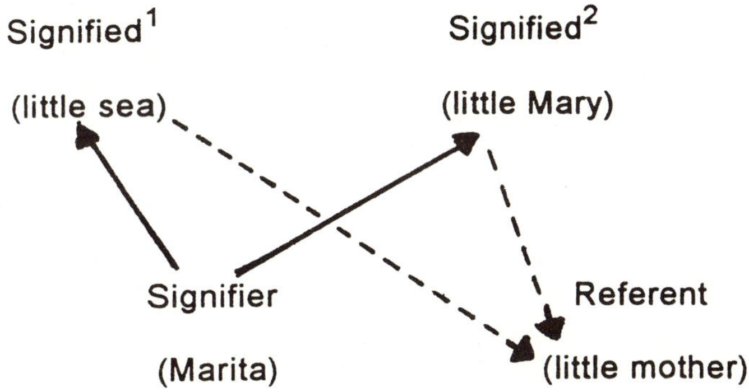

FIGURE 5.3

The signifier (Marita) has two signifieds (S^1 and S^2) and one latent referent (little mother). Both the French and the Spanish terms confirm the veiling process and the latent transposition of meaning.

The roles of the proprietors of the hotel where David, Catherine, and Marita are staying reinforce the familial traces embedded in the text. Monsieur and Madame Aurol employ a boy who is treated as a son. The words "young waiter" connote the oedipal son who must wait for his turn in order to fulfill himself as an adult (once again we have the S^1 signified and the S^2 referent). Hemingway also plays with the homonym "sun" and "son" thereby multiplying the traces throughout the text. Despite Lacan's insistence that the oedipal drama is unconscious (because it has been repressed), it seems to me that Hemingway consciously manipulates his actors and the symbolic play of events. He even inserts frequent and strategic mirrors (thereby replicating Lacan's "mirror phase" in which the child represses desire and accedes to language)—mirrors in which the characters see themselves but fail to recognize their Imaginary reflections: "He [David] looked in the mirror and it was someone else he saw."[15] There are mirrors everywhere. After Catherine's first lesbian affair, the mirror in the bedroom reflects her sense of alienation. She spends a long time in front of it, motionless, expressionless, and reactionless, as though the reflection of herself were that of another, whereas David and Marita are like the original and indissoluble mother and child: they are happy when they see themselves in the mirror together. And when Marita sees herself alone in the mirror she smiles. The mirror in the bar at the hotel, which the trio buys and installs, continuously reflects their changing moods and strategic realignments.

The use of mirrors is at least as frequent as the text's allusions to Le Grau du Roi, the small fishing village in the Camargue, where the novel begins. Le Grau du Roi (meaning the channel or harbor of the king) connects by road with Aigues Mortes (dead waters), the medieval town where Catherine had her first boyish haircut. References to Le Grau du Roi, like the mirrors, are so obsessive that they confirm the subject's need to repeat, rather than simply remember the repressed material. The compulsive repetition of Le Grau du Roi (in French, *Oedipus the King* is *Oedipe le roi*) acts like a signal, a code word for the oedipal triangle. Beyond that, what operates in the text through repetition is the death instinct, the drive toward the end, be it the end of life or the end of the story. Perhaps Aigues Mortes is Hemingway's equivalent for *Oedipus at Colonus* where the aged and exiled king comes to terms with his own death, where he assumes death as a dimension of the human condition.

Hemingway's discourse is the manifestation of his survival and it is also David's African stories about the elephant that manifest his survival. "He had not known just how greatly he had been divided and separated because once he started to work he wrote from an inner core which could not be split nor even marked nor scratched."[16] If writers write because they have to, in order to survive, then a discourse that dramatizes the exteriorization of desire goes to the very heart of language. It is a discourse within which the author reassembles the fragments of the self, and projects them onto the mirror of fiction, where we, in turn, recognize the author's metaphorical image of himself as the image of the Other. Although fiction is a mirror that distorts, it is, nonetheless, a mirror of the self.

This discourse of the self, which is always a discourse of desire, seeks to retrieve the lost object, be it breast or mother. Because language manifests the presence of the mother tongue, writing recovers an absence. The ending of *The Garden of Eden* can thus be read as a paradise regained and the fulfillment of a lack. As Marita displaces Catherine, David (the subject) recovers the mother and recreates the feeling of a lost plenitude. The elephant is killed, but David's death has been delayed because writing, and the repetition of writing, is a form of postponement. Insofar as Marita is the mythical mother whose loving presence answers all of the subject's primal needs, the incest taboo has been violated symbolically. Although Marita's origins remain obscure, and no doubt deliberately so, her femininity embodies what Freud and Hélène Cixous explicitly formulate as the dark (therefore mysterious) continent; her skin, unlike David's and Catherine's deeply tanned bodies, is naturally dark, and her features are perhaps Javanese.

The novel ends with David and Marita as the newly born couple. "We are the Bournes," they say. Hemingway has written the story of a Garden of Eden in which there is sex without guilt and in which work (writing) takes place effortlessly and perfectly. Although, at first, David feared that he would not be able to rewrite the stories that Catherine had destroyed, he is now able to recapture them in every detail:

> He found he knew much more about his father than when he had first written this story . . . not a sentence was missing. By two o'clock he had recovered, corrected and improved what it had taken him five days to write originally. He wrote on a while longer now and there was no sign that any of it would ever cease returning to him intact.[17]

Fiction is a dwelling, an enclosure, and it would seem that in writing *The Garden of Eden* as an oedipal narrative, Hemingway wished to live within that structure in a conscious rather than unconscious way. A post–Lacanian reading of Hemingway's novel thus not only confirms the explicit thrust of the original manuscript, it also suggests a radical devaluation of Oedipus, a shedding of the unconscious straitjacket of the primal repression and the discourse of the Other. By using the oedipal triangle and Freudian language in ways not originally intended, Hemingway, in effect, deconstructs desire, thereby affirming the presence of a new "garden" within which happiness is possible. Catherine fails to castrate David and, despite the burning of the stories, he now writes flawlessly from an inner core. Catherine has been displaced, the Father is "dead," and David now possesses the mother (Marita) in a pre–Adamic state of fulfillment and bliss. The death of the elephant had already raised the discourse of desire to a higher power because it had seen its own death within the oedipal narrative. In effect Hemingway's novel bans the father, gets rid of Oedipus, and affirms desire. The story and the novel end here because there is no longer any reason for postponement or for discourse as a form of repetition. "The garden of eden" is at hand, sterility (castration) is a thing of the past, and love (fertility) has triumphed.

Chapter 6

Albert Camus's Homonymous Veilings: "La Mer/Mère au plus près"

To those who have not studied the nature of language in any depth, the experience of number association will show immediately what must be grasped here, namely, the combinatory power that orders its ambiguities, and they will recognize in this the very mainspring of the unconscious.

—Jacques Lacan, "The function and field of speech and language in psychoanalysis"

We turn next to the post–World War II context of Camus's oeuvre. His work has been discussed most often in relation to the absurd and to commitment—the two poles of existentialist thinking. Psychoanalytic studies are infrequent and reader-response models tend to get lost in the morass of biographical criticism. Indeed, whenever we think of Camus and his writings, rebellion and exile are two words that come to mind frequently. The word "passion"—the third in the triadic structure that constitutes the absurd—is evoked less frequently, yet, paradoxically, passion is an essential element of the other two. Without passion there would be nothing to rebel against or for, and without a sense of exile and alienation, passion would lose its driving force. "Thus I draw from the absurd three consequences, which are my revolt, my freedom, and my passion. By a sudden act of consciousness I transform into a rule of life what was an invitation to death—and I reject suicide" ("Je tire ainsi de l'absurde trois conséquences qui sont ma révolte, ma liberté et ma passion. Par le seul jeu de la conscience, je transforme en règle de vie ce qui était invitation à la mort—et je refuse le suicide").[1]

Camus's rage to live, despite the corrosive logic of the absurd, prompts him, in his early works, such as *Le Mythe de Sisyphe*, to refuse suicide and death for an alliance with life. The rejection of death, hope, and immortality in favor of the body and the immediacy of earthly pleasures is the leitmotif of *Noces*—that lyrical essay to nature and to man's immersion in nature.[2] It is the song of man's union with the world, of his honeymoon on earth, and of his bliss in contact with the sea, the sky, and the sun: "I know that I shall never come close enough to the world. I must be naked, then dive into the sea, still scented with the perfumes of the earth, and wash the latter in the former, consummating on my flesh the embrace for which sun and sea, mouth to mouth, have for so long been sighing . . . we all display the happy weariness of a day of nuptials with the world" ("Je sais que jamais je ne m'approcherai assez du monde. Il me faut être nu et puis plonger dans la mer, encore tout parfumé des essences de la terre, laver celles-ci dans celle-là, et nouer sur ma peau l'étreinte pour laquelle soupirent lèvres à lèvres depuis si longtemps la terre et la mer . . . nous étalons tous l'heureuse lassitude d'un jour de noces avec le monde").[3]

Death, however, is the backdrop to these natural settings, and it is highlighted whenever one of his works stresses an overriding sense of the absurd: suicide is the major theme of *Le Mythe de Sisyphe*; dramatizing death and its allegorical variants is the work of *La Peste*; and Caligula's relentless logic is designed to prove that men die and that they are not happy.[4] "The exquisite corpse" that Caligula and the patricians compose together and whose topic is death, is a poem to nature and to the veiled presence of finitude manifest in intense and ephemeral moments of heightened consciousness. "A quest for happiness that purifies, / A sky where the sun is streaming, / Unusual and savage celebrations, my delirium devoid of hope! . . ." ("Chasse au bonheur qui fait les êtres purs, / Ciel où le soleil ruisselle, / Fêtes uniques et sauvages, mon délire sans espoir! . . .").[5] Camus's works foreground an awareness of life and death. One theme assumes the dominant mode and then the other, alternately. It seems natural, therefore, that the narrator of *Noces* should set out "toward love and desire" ("à la rencontre de l'amour et du désir")[6] and it seems equally natural that a pessimistic Jean-Baptiste Clamence should seek exile in the Amsterdam of *La Chute* surrounded by the circular canals of Hell. "There is no love of living without despair of living" ("Il n'y a pas d'amour de vivre sans désespoir de vivre").[7]

"The Running Sea" ("La Mer au plus près"), in *L'Été*—a poetic, even Rimbaldian evocation of a twentieth-century "drunken boat" (*bateau ivre*)—is, nonetheless, also a 1953 tribute to the affective and ongoing presence of the sea: "Rivers flow by, the sea flows and remains. This is how we must love, faithful and fleeting. I wed the sea" ("La rivière et le fleuve passent, la mer passe et demeure. C'est ainsi qu'il faudrait aimer, fidèle et fugitif. J'épouse la mer").[8] Here and elsewhere, Camus's metaphorical exaltations barely veil a pre-oedipal longing for the mother.[9] The pleasures he derives from proximity to the sea—*la mer* is a homonym for *la mère*, the mother—or embracing nature, although couched in the plenitude of presence, connote the nostalgia of absence, hence the coupling of love and death, joy and anguish, fulfillment and frustration that are manifest in the alternating images of need and desire, failure and satisfaction.[10] "There is only one love in this world. Embracing a woman's body is also to enfold this strange joy that descends from sky to sea" ("Il n'y a qu'un seul amour dans ce monde. Etreindre un corps de femme, c'est aussi retenir contre soi cette joie étrange qui descend du ciel vers la mer").[11]

The voice of Lacan's Other, in concert with the voice of the artist, structures this alternating dialectic of desire and exile, life and death. Nature, the sea, and mother earth have become substitutes for "the lost breast," and they are symptoms of retrieval, that is, writing—the signifying chain of art that repeats the *Fort!/Da!* game. Indeed, man's "nuptials" with the world are Camus's greatest source of happiness and joy: "I bit into the already golden fruit of the world, overwhelmed by the feeling of its strong sweet juice flowing along my lips. No, it was neither I nor the world that mattered, only the harmony and silence which, from one to the other, gave birth to love" ("Je mordais dans le fruit déjà doré du monde, bouleversé de sentir son jus sucré et fort couler le long de mes lèvres. Non, ce n'était pas moi qui comptais, ni le monde, mais seulement l'accord et le silence qui de lui à moi faisait naître l'amour").[12] Camus's love affair with the world has the sumptuous and sensuous trappings of erotic bliss and the repetitive force of his appeal to life that opposes death through art is, no doubt, the very theme that also appeals to so many of his readers. Resignation and impotence are not his message. On the contrary, the message is revolt against death, a passion for life, and freedom of choice. Consciousness of the absurd—the discrepancy between desire and fulfillment—might have generated resignation and despair, but instead of alienation, Camus transcends the primal wound with life-affirming exuberance. The strength of desire and the need for happiness override death and despair. Rebellion is a rejection of denial, impotence, and exile despite man's mortality and the premises of the absurd.

Camus's Other voice—not the existential logic of struggle and commitment—tells him that man's duty to himself is to return to the source of his being, to nature as a primal Eden and to the mother as the source—the "source" in *L'Étranger* toward which a sun-dazed Meursault is walking that fateful afternoon on the beach at 2:00 P.M. in order to slake his thirst. In fact, desire and the quest for happiness lead many Camusian characters toward the earth and the sea as privileged places—as the primal source. Mersault, the protagonist of *La Mort heureuse*, an earlier although different version of the Meursault in *L'Étranger*, engages in a ritual oedipal slaying, kills the rich, old invalid, Zagreus, for his money, and "buys" happiness for himself and three women in a house by the sea. There, Mersault dies happy in the knowledge that the assassination of Zagreus was an act of rebellion against the castrating forces of poverty and denial.

> Mersault noted that not once since Vienna had he thought of Zagreus as the man he had killed with his own hands. He acknowledged this faculty of forgetfulness that belongs only to children, geniuses, and the innocent. Innocent and overwhelmed with joy, he understood at last that he was destined for happiness.
>
> Mersault s'aperçut que pas une seule fois depuis Vienne il n'avait songé à Zagreus comme à l'homme qu'il avait tué de ses mains. Il reconnu en lui cette faculté d'oubli qui n'appartient qu'à l'enfant, au génie et à l'innocent. Innocent, bouleversé par la joie, il comprit enfin qu'il était fait pour le bonheur.[13]

Mersault, the name, contains the elements of oedipal desire: *mer*, the homonym for mother—*la mère*—and *sault*, the homonym for *sot*, that is, a man besotted by desire for the sea, a man who will kill and rob the symbolic father in order to buy happiness in the big "maternal" house, because the ultimate mother for Mersault and the narrator of *Noces* and *L'Été* is mother earth and the joys she can provide. "He was thirsty, hungry for love, for bliss, and the kisses thereof. The gods that were burning him cast him into the sea" ("Il avait soif, faim d'aimer, de jouir et d'embrasser. Les dieux qui le brûlaient le jetèrent dans la mer").[14] In addition to *la mer*, the word *sault* is also a leap (*sauter*) into the homonymic sea of the mother (*mer/mère*), a symbolic return to the union once severed by the name-of-the-father—*le nom/non du père*. Mersault experiences poverty as an obstacle to happiness and he kills because "within the great distress that filled him . . . his rebellion was the only true entity, whereas everything else was misery and obligation" ("dans la grande détresse qui l'emplissait . . . sa révolte était la seule chose vraie en lui et que le reste était misère et complaisance").[15] Mersault welcomes his rebellion as a positive force—a force that opposes alienation and, in contrast with Dostoevsky's *Crime and Punishment*, Zagreus's murder goes unpunished because Mersault does not believe in retribution.

Decapitation, however, will be Meursault's punishment for shooting the Arab. In *L'Étranger*, the symptoms of alienation are metaphysical strangeness and physical lethargy. Whereas Meursault's shooting of the Arab is an unconscious act of revolt against the forces of estrangement—be they social, political, or psychological—other Camusian characters perform lucid acts of rebellion against the dehumanizing forces of nature, society, and destiny. Thus, Mersault kills Zagreus in full cognizance of the consequences of his act, and Caligula, equally lucid, kills at random in order to affirm his imperial freedom. On the symbolic level, the narrative voice in *Noces* rejects the paternalism of Christianity (the heavenly Father) with its accompanying notions of sin, guilt, and hoped-for redemption, in favor of an immediate and hedonistic materialism: "Today the fool is king, and I call a fool whoever is afraid of bliss. We have heard so much about pride: you know, it's the sin of Satan" ("Aujourd'hui l'imbécile est roi, et j'appelle imbécile celui qui a peur de jouir. On nous a tellement parlé de l'orgueil: vous savez, c'est le péché de Satan").[16] In *Les Justes*, Dora becomes a terrorist in order to affirm human dignity and social justice, whereas in *Le Malentendu* Martha kills and robs the clients in her hotel so that she too will be able to "buy" a future happiness by the sea, where, like Mersault, she will bask in the warmth of a lost maternal presence: "The day when at last we will have reached the sea for which I have been longing, on that day you will see me smile" ("Le jour où nous serons enfin devant la mer dont j'ai tant rêvé, ce jour-là, vous me verrez sourire").[17]

Martha goes on to describe the symbolic death she feels in "the house of bitterness where one is exiled forever" ("la maison amère où l'on est exilé pour toujours").[18] After she kills her brother, Jan, she says that she is in the bitter realm (*amère*) in which loss of her mother's love is experienced as an intolerable exile. *Amère* denotes "bitter" but it connotes "distance," and the letter *a* in *a/mère* signifies this maternal severance. It is now futile, says Martha, to cry out toward the sea for love ("Pourquoi crier vers la mer ou vers l'amour?").[19] Once again, the homonymic *mer*, coupled with *l'amour*, veils the presence of Martha's desperate need—maternal love. Life by the seashore denotes physical happiness, as it did for Mersault, but it connotes the psychological happiness of a reunion. Martha desires a house of her own by the sea—a symbolic retrieval of the mother, whose value—metonymic substitute—is money which, after each murder and theft, she can acquire and hoard. Anticipating the future, Martha compares it to a rebirth: "It's as though I can hear the sea already. I feel a joy within me that is going to make me cry out" ("Il me semble que j'entends déjà la mer. Il y a en moi une joie qui va me faire crier").[20]

In *La Peste*, after weeks of life-sapping work and fatigue in the sanitary squadrons, Rieux and Tarrou take a rejuvenating swim in the sea and, again, it is this revivifying presence, contact with *la mer*, that enables them to face death once more and endure the long, bone-breaking hours of resistance to the plague. It is reassuring to know that the sea is there, and it explains why both Camus and Meursault prefer Algiers to the skies of Paris, because Algiers is a city open to the sea and from which the sea is visible from every street corner. "In Paris you can experience a nostalgia for space and the beating of wings. Here, at least, man is blessed and, assured of his desires, he can then measure his riches" ("A Paris, on peut avoir la nostalgie d'espace et de battements d'ailes. Ici, du moins, l'homme est comblé, et assuré de ses désirs, il peut alors mesurer ses richesses").[21] Compared to the maternal sea, the paternal skies of Paris are not to be desired. Indeed, Meursault says that Paris is dirty and full of pigeons—those messengers of the Holy Ghost.

In the Camusian system, man is in exile from the kingdom, but the kingdom is not the Father's, nor is the home a Christian one. Janine's recovery of the kingdom, in "La Femme adultère," is orgasmic and her fulfillment, although ephemeral, like all orgasms, is cosmic. It is an overwhelming reunion. It is a oneness and a bliss that abolish the Pascalian need for God, or the fear of "the eternal silence of these infinite spaces" ("le silence éternel de ces espaces infinis m'effraie").[22] Camus recreates Pascal's dehumanized landscape of universal space ("above the desert the silence was as vast as space"—"au-dessus du désert le silence était vaste comme l'espace"),[23] then contrasts it with anthropomorphized constellations that look like clusters of grapes. Finally, "Janine opened up a little more to the night . . . she felt as though she had recovered her roots" ("Janine s'ouvrait un peu plus à la nuit . . . il lui semblait retrouver ses racines").[24] She is the link between earth and sky, she is the metaphorical stem that connects the roots with the fruit. Instead of distance and fear, the gyrations of the stars have put her in touch with her deepest inner being, and it is the warmth of this oneness that expulses the chill of her exile and of the desert night. Until that moment, since she no longer loved her husband, she had felt alone, stifled, and oppressed. During several premonitory episodes, inscribed like hieroglyphs in the desert sand by distant configurations of dromedaries, the light of the sky crystallizes, time and the world seem to have stopped, and all of life, except for the beating of her heart, is as though suspended. During these special moments, Janine catches glimpses of the promised land ("The only paradises are the ones we have lost"—"Les seuls paradis sont ceux qu'on a perdus"),[25] and these moments fill her with a sweet sadness. This nostalgia goads her in the middle of the night to slip away from the bed of her husband's hard shoulder and to leave the hotel in search of something she vaguely apprehends and which, she feels, is waiting for her "out there," if only she can make the necessary gestures that will help her discover what it is. In *L'Été,* Camus says that "innocence needs sand and stones" ("l'innocence a besoin du sable et des pierres"),[26] the very landscape that precipitates Janine's adultery—the adultery of innocence and of recovery.

Janine's union with the starry night, alone on the ancient parapet under the sky, contrasts with the tired, quotidian familiarity of her husband's mendacious presence. Her adultery—bliss in contact with the world—is, admittedly, a very special kind of infidelity, but she too, like Mersault and the narrator of *Noces*, experiences the joy of symbolic retrieval:

> Then, with an unbearable sweetness, the water of the night began filling Janine, submerged the cold, rose little by little from the obscure center of her being and spilled over into her mouth and her moaning in one uninterrupted stream. A moment later, the entire sky stretched out above her as she lay on the cold earth, overwhelmed.

> Alors, avec une douceur insupportable, l'eau de la nuit commença d'emplir Janine, submergea le froid, monta peu à peu du centre obscur de son être et déborda en flots ininterrompus jusqu'à sa bouche pleine de gémissements. L'instant d'après, le ciel entier, s'étendait au-dessus d'elle, renversée sur la terre froide.[27]

The liquid warmth of Janine's orgasm—her epiphany—contrasts with the cold, windswept, and sand-blown desert of her voyage. Her nocturnal union is the climax to the internal struggle she has been waging between desire and exile, life and death, nature and her husband—a husband she has tolerated for many years because of her solitude and fear of dying. Only when he turns on the light in the room, after her return, does she begin to cry—tears of joy for her newly found self, tears of sadness for him, tears of insight caused by the light slapping her in the face. Her experience is one of innocence and joy coupled with knowledge but devoid of guilt. How could there be remorse when she has willingly submitted to the most overwhelming experience of her life. She has, literally, been bowled over—*renversée.*

Critics sensitive to the misogynistic connotations of Camus's works have given frequent negative readings of Janine's behavior based on moral condemnation for her infidelity and on her failure(s) to act independently during her marriage to Marcel. However, considering the historical marginalization of women virtually everywhere, Janine's actions, prior to her orgasmic epiphany, seem more typical than atypical. The desert has been a catalyst for her rediscovery of repressed desires and the rebirth of longings long buried. The veilings that have immobilized her for the past twenty-five years are phallocentric and her salvation (now that she has intimations of the kingdom) will come only because she responds to the call of the Other, that is, "the flood-wind" of her unconscious.

Despite the external realism of Janine's voyage, it is a voyage into the self and the unconscious. In addition to innocence, the cold rock-strewn desert is a landscape of repressed desire. Janine experiences it as the *concretization* of exile. It is a mirror of her forlornness. The alienating effects of Janine's trip are like a waking dream in which the manifest images of the desert correspond to the latent feelings of estrangement from youth, love, and happiness. "She dreamed of the straight and flexible palm trees, and of the young girl she had been" ("Elle rêvait aux palmiers droits et flexibles, et à la jeune fille qu'elle avait été").[28] She had once been a gymnastics champion, but now "she was suffocating under an immense weight, and she discovered suddenly that she had been dragging it for twenty years and was now struggling against it with all her strength" ("elle étouffait sous un poids immense dont elle découvrait soudain qu'elle le traînait depuis vingt ans, et sous lequel elle se débattait maintenant de toutes ses forces").[29] She realizes that she is overweight and that she needs deliverance from her present condition: deliverance from anguish, from the heaviness pressing against her heart, from fear of death, and the knowledge that she has neither lived nor loved.

Janine's "suspended moments" are like dreams whose desire (content) needs to be deciphered. Her symptom is unhappiness, and the symptom, says Lacan, is "the signifier of a signified repressed from the consciousness of the subject. A symbol written in the sand of the flesh" ("le signifiant d'un signifié refoulé de la conscience du sujet. Symbole écrit sur le sable de la chair")[30] where the combinatory power of language is also the mainspring of the unconscious.[31] Janine's angst is the symptom whose message we read in the desert runes formed by the herd of camels, in the hot sun-baked stones that burst at night from the cold, and in the horizon of expectations where, at dusk, the earth and the sky come together. Near the large black tents "a herd of dromedaries, motionless and small at this distance, formed on the gray earth the dark signs of a strange writing whose meaning had to be deciphered" ("un troupeau de dromadaires immobiles, minuscules à cette distance, formaient sur le sol gris les signes sombres d'une étrange écriture dont il fallait déchiffrer le sens").[32] Despite her sex, Janine's reunion with and recovery of the "lost breast" ("au sein d'une écriture du désert") within the configurations of desert hieroglyphs is consistent with the quest of Camus's male persona. Preceding the child's so-called mirror phase is the presymbolic world of the Imaginary—a world of unity in which mother and child are one and no separation is perceived between the self and the other. It is toward this unity with a presymbolic world that Janine seems to be moving—a preoedipal union with the mother.

Lacan insists that "where it was, there I must be" ("Wo Es war, soll Ich werden").[33] Indeed, Janine comes to the place where *it* was. Her orgasm is the union of the id and the ego, her self and the world as unconscious force—as primal generator—the earth and the sky as mother. This is the meaning of Janine's encounters on the parapet. The first time, in the afternoon with Marcel, she feels that something is waiting for her on the horizon where the earth and the sky meet. Suddenly, "in the heart of a woman brought there by pure chance a knot tightened by the years, habit, and boredom was slowly loosening" ("au coeur d'une femme que le hasard seul amenait là, un noeud que les années, l'habitude et l'ennui avaient serré, se dénouait lentement").[34] Janine is now face to face with the void, her fear, and her alienation. Her emerging awareness is, in Lacanian terms, a severing of the knot of misrecognition, because "the unconscious castration complex has the function of a knot" ("le complexe de castration inconscient a une fonction de noeud").[35] Janine is beginning to recognize the desire of the Other, and the reader understands that her desire for the phallus, that is, her autonomy, independence, happiness, and self-fulfillment, is a message that the Other has been inscribing on the desert landscape. And, as Janine's heart begins to loosen, it is in the place of the Other that she has access to the phallus as a signifier.[36] Like D. H. Lawrence's Christ, whose body, soul, and spirit were tied, Janine is beginning to realize that she must slice through the knot that binds and inhibits change.

Janine's unconscious has been responding to the messages of the landscape, and she eventually recognizes, as the surrealists did in their encounters with "objective chance," that the landscape is the image of herself. "What does the Other want of me?" ("Que me veut l'Autre?"), asks Lacan.[37] Janine's conscious self receives the message of the Other that has been concretized all around her in the desert. She sees herself and she listens to the message of the wind: "She sat up in bed and cocked one ear toward a call that seemed close by. . . . the waters of the wind dried up and she wasn't even sure she had heard anything except a muffled call . . . whose meaning she would never know if she didn't answer it immediately" ("Elle se dressa dans son lit et tendit l'oreille à un appel qui lui sembla tout proche. . . . les eaux du vent tarirent et elle ne fut même plus sûre d'avoir rien entendu, sinon un appel muet . . . dont plus jamais elle ne connaîtrait le sens, si elle n'y répondait à l'instant").[38] "The Law," says Lacan, "appears to be giving the order, '*Jouis!*,' to which the subject can only reply '*J'ouïs*' (I hear), the *jouissance* being no more than understood" ("La Loi en effet commanderait-elle: Jouis, que le sujet ne pourrait y répondre que par un: J'ouïs, où la jouissance ne serait que sous-entendue").[39] The wind is coming from the south where the desert and the night "were now again blending under the motionless sky, where life stopped, where no one ever grew old or died" ("se mêlaient maintenant sous le ciel à nouveau fixe, là où la vie s'arrêtait, où plus personne ne vieillissait ni ne mourait").[40] One by one Janine hears the message of these "suspended moments" and the message says *jouis*—enjoy. The erotic bliss (not unlike Marcel Proust's privileged moments that abolish time) that the wind's voice carries to Janine, and the knot she must untangle culminate in the midnight orgasm that bowls her over on the parapet under the starry sky.

Janine's ecstasy not only gives her the illusion that time has stopped and that death has been abolished, it also resolves life-long contrasts and contradictions. As it had for the surrealists, desire culminates in a harmony of opposites and dramatic oxymorons. Thus, the stars are both icicles and fire, the air Janine is breathing is icy and burning, she is filled with cold desire as well as the waters of the wind, and she experiences immobilized movement. She hears the message of the wind that has been liquefied, and although it is cold, it fills her with warmth.

Later, in her room, she hears and sees everything illuminated clearly in the light of the electric bulb. And the reader also sees and has been seeing the concretized landscape of her unconscious. Once again we feel the oneness of wind, sand, stones, and sky. Janine is now reunited with herself and mother earth—*it* and ego are one—she is fulfilled. Her newly found warmth is the answer to desire. The message has been received and understood. Janine, like her "cousin" Mersault, could also have said, in the innocence of her heart, that she "accepted this green sky and this love-moistened earth with the same trembling passion and desire" ("acceptait ce ciel vert et cette terre mouillée d'amour avec le même tremblement de passion et de désir").[41] Janine, Mersault, and the narrator of *Noces* (who is also *bouleversé* by his love affair with the world) find happiness in the embrace of a universal union. Martha, however, despite desire, remains alienated and bitter—the victim of her misunderstanding—a misunderstanding from which the play derives its title, *Le Malentendu*. Unlike Martha's wintry exile and rancor, Janine, despite the cold, is on the threshold of summer, and she basks in the inner warmth of her new being.

Yet another cousin, Meursault, achieves insight when the blinding glare of the sun overwhelms him; but it is too late because he has already shot the Arab. Nonetheless, early on, he too is haunted by the mother. "Today, maman died" ("Aujourd'hui, maman est morte"), is the novel's opening sentence—a sentence from which the word "maman" generates repetitions and traces that multiply, reverberating throughout the text. In part 1, the word "maman" and "mère," the syllable *ma*, as in *Marengo*, or the sound *ma* (*m'a*), as in "il m'a souri," "il m'a regardé et il m'a demandé," and so on, occur 101 times, for an average of 4.5 times per page, an extraordinary frequency, due in part to the use of the *passé composé*, but whose frequency also verges on the compulsive. In some instances it reaches eight *ma*s per page, thereby affirming an unconscious dissemination of meaning.[42] It is no doubt significant that the *ma* syllable is also contained in the word *dromadaires*, whose shapes form the writing in the sand and whose meaning needs to be deciphered. The traces of *ma* are everywhere: in the sand and in language, in the signifiers and the signified. They are the marks of loss and of desire that have been sown throughout Camus's works. The mother, homonymically and metonymically, is both present and absent. She is the sea, the source, and the warmth of mother earth, and Camus's protagonists carry within them the traces of this primal contact and repression.

For Camus, proximity to nature is a source of renewal and happiness—a happiness that overrides the consciousness of death and the absurd. *L'Été* is the antidote to Martha's and Janine's winter: "In the middle of winter, I learned at last that there was within me an invincible summer" ("Au milieu de l'hiver, j'apprenais enfin qu'il y avait en moi un été invincible").[43] The final essay in this collection, "The Running Sea" ("La Mer au plus près"), is a reworking of the nature motif and a renewed evocation of closeness. It is a sailor's log ("un journal de bord"), in this case a writer's log and a log of writing, since writing is the repetition of the *Fort!/Da!* game—the string of words that substitutes for and retrieves the loss. The essay is a philosophical and poetic record of experiences in, on, and above the sea. The transcription of a few key passages is revealing, particularly when we keep in mind the homonymic relationship between *mer* and *mère*, that is, between sea and mother. "I grew up in the sea . . . then I lost the sea." "What am I to do when I remember only one image?" "I know that the sea precedes and follows me." "Long days at sea, resembling each other like happiness." "Oh bitter bed, princely repose, the wreath is in the waters' depths!" . . . "we are sailing on a clear and muscled sea." "The open sea, always furrowed, always virginal, my religion with the night!" . . . "The sea would, at the final moment, flood into my cell, coming to sustain me beyond myself and to help me die without rancour." "I have always had the impression that I was living on the high seas, threatened, in the bosom of a royal happiness" ("J'ai grandi dans la mer . . . puis j'ai perdu la mer." "Que faire si je n'ai de mémoire que pour une seule image?" "Je sais que la mer me précède et me suit." "Journées en mer, toutes semblables comme le bonheur." "O lit amer, couche princière, la couronne est au fond des eaux!" . . . "nous filons sur une mer claire et musclée." "Grande mer, toujours labourée, toujours vierge, ma religion avec la nuit!" . . . "la mer, au dernier moment, emplirait ma cellule, viendrait me soutenir au-dessus de moi-même et m'aider à mourir sans haine." "J'ai toujours eu l'impression de vivre en haute mer, menacé, au coeur d'un bonheur royal").[44]

These excerpts, like Janine's voyage into the desert, reproduce descriptions of the sea that, like the desert, act as objective correlatives, as affective states, and as mirrors of the unconscious—manifest images of the sea that correspond to latent images of desire. Each excerpt may be read two ways: realistically and homonymically. With each substitution of the word *mère* for *mer*, the meaning of the word "mother" thickens and the connotations expand: gestation, loss, death, nostalgia, bed of desire, princely repose, muscled body that is furrowed and virginal, a royal but threatened happiness. The prince and the mother forever threatened by the Law. "O lit amer" is an exclamation in which *O* is the homonym for *eau(x)*—water(s)—and *amer* (denoting bitter) is the homonym for "belonging to the mother." Yet another reading produces *au lit à mère*, that is, "to the mother's bed." *Couche princière* (princely repose) denotes bed but it connotes a woman in labor, and a child's diaper, and *grande mer* connotes grandmother. The words and traces of an oedipal relationship persist and the reader need only scratch the surface of the text in order to discover a veiled presence underneath.

The combined effects of all these inscriptions confirm the notion that happiness in nature's bosom is, for Camus, linguistically and psychologically associated with retrieval. He prefers "la mer au plus près," in intimate contact, to flying over the sea and he compares the airplane to a barbaric coffin that keeps him away from the sea he would rather be on.[45] Camus's rebellious freedom overrides loss, even as desire and the passion for life affirm the energy of a lucid mind that refuses to submit to death. Contact is what matters and touch is essential so that the body of the text, the sea, and the mother will provide the missing *jouissance*—the bliss that overrides alienation.

Chapter 7

Albert Camus: *The Stranger*

If this event was recognized as being the cause of the symptom, it was because the putting into words of the event (in the patient's "stories") determined the lifting of the symptom.
—*Jacques Lacan, "The function and field of speech and language in psychoanalysis"*

Alienation, not bliss, is the dominant theme in Camus's first published novel, *The Stranger*. Nonetheless, there is a wor(l)d of difference between Meursault, the alienated narrator of part 1 of *L'Étranger*, and Meursault, the reconciled narrator of part 2. If the so-called primal scene is the cause of his symptoms—lethargy and indifference, coupled with anger and alienation—then putting the event into words (the killing of the Arab) enables Meursault to understand himself in relation to the "indifference" of the world. At the end of the novel he assumes the meaning of his life and the consequences of his death. However, before we proceed with this line of inquiry, that is, a Lacanian exegesis, we need to look briefly at the reception the novel has received since its publication in 1942.

Readers have offered many explanations for Meursault's character, his behavior, and his enigmatic shooting of the Arab. Meursault is sometimes viewed as indifferent, callous, and shallow—an individual who is alienated from society and from himself. At other times he is described as a person who is honest to a fault, a man who is unwilling to compromise with the system. René Girard says that "Meursault is the fictional embodiment of the nihilistic individualism expounded in *Le Mythe de Sisyphe* and commonly referred to as *l'absurde.*"[1] Robert Champigny, however, contends that the values expounded in *L'Étranger* and *Le Mythe de Sisyphe* are not the same.[2] Whereas Girard calls him a juvenile delinquent,[3] Germaine Brée refers to the "rigorous honesty" and "total sincerity" of a man without "sham or pretense."[4] Jean-Paul Sartre says that Meursault "is precisely one of those terrible innocents who shock society by not accepting the rules of its game."[5] Camus himself, echoing Sartre, says that Meursault is condemned "because he does not play the game" ("parce qu'il ne joue pas le jeu").[6] Champigny, like Sartre, sees Meursault as an innocent person who is "declared theatrically guilty by virtue of his innocence."[7]

Meursault has his defenders and his detractors. Monique Wagner is closer to Girard than to Brée, Sartre, and Champigny, when she writes that if Meursault does not "play the game" it is not because of his honesty, but because of his ineptness. She concludes that there is little evidence for Meursault's "love for truth" and that he "lets himself die" because he has no desire to go on living in a world whose meaning eludes him. Instead of a "joie de vivre," Wagner sees in Meursault a man who is "constantly dazed, drowsy, sleepy, hot, sweaty, or uncomfortable."[8]

Critics tend to side either with Meursault against the judges, or with the judges against Meursault. Indeed, the novel forces the reader to choose between Meursault and his accusers. Arguments abound both for and against the protagonist. Although the court magistrate calls him "Mr. Antichrist," Camus says that Meursault is "the only Christ we deserve" ("le seul christ que nous méritions")[9]—not exactly an endorsement of Meursault's character, but certainly also a deliberate slap at the society that will judge and execute him. Louis Hudon says that the murder of the Arab was an *accident,*[10] and many commentators agree with that interpretation. Girard, who is on the side of the judges, says that "the murder . . . in a novel otherwise rational and realistic, is a deux ex machina, or rather a *crimen ex machina.*"[11] Brée and Lynes say that the shooting lacks conscious motivation,[12] a theme that Camus's psychoanalytical critics pick up on and amplify. Following yet another tack, Albert Maquet writes that "the murder of the Arab is only a pretext; behind the person of the accused, the judges want to destroy the truth he embodies."[13] The truth, says Camus, is that "in our societies, every man who does not cry at his mother's funeral, runs the risk of the death penalty" ("dans notre société tout homme qui ne pleure pas à l'enterrement de sa mère risque d'être condamné à mort").[14] But that may not be the entire truth. Meursault *has* shot a man, and were it not for that fact, society would have taken little notice of him.

The murder of the Arab is no doubt necessary for dramatic conflict, but it unfolds with the rigorous determinism of Greek tragedy. Carl Viggiani, among others, rejects all rational interpretations of the event, attributing it to the same *Fatum* that presides over the lives of tragic heroes in ancient literatures.[15] Whereas, in another vein, Julian L. Stamm asserts that Meursault "was driven by the irrational homosexual forces within him,"[16] J. H. Matthews, less impressed by arguments for Meursault's unconscious motivations, writes, concerning the four additional shots, that "far from being the involuntary gesture of a brute, this is perhaps the first act in which the hero's will manifests itself" ("loin d'être le geste involontaire d'une brute, cette action est peut-être la première où la volonté du héros ait sa part").[17] This heightened consciousness on Meursault's part is foregrounded even further by Pierre-Louis Rey when he states that Meursault is not as innocent as he appears to be.[18] Brian T. Fitch, however, maintains that the only reasons for having Meursault shoot four more times are aesthetic and juridical. Camus, says Fitch, was determined to dramatize, and subsequently parody, Meursault's court trial at the expense of his accusers.[19] This is also the theatricality that Champigny refers to.

It would be impossible to comment on all the multifarious readings of *L'Étranger*. Nonetheless, it is interesting to note that fifty years after its publication, the novel continues to fascinate readers of different persuasions and to generate studies that, in volume, are sufficient to bury Camus's short work under a pyramid of paper. One thing is clear: the many contradictory readings of *L'Étranger* reveal not only the layered complexity of the novel but also the different preoccupations of its readers. Fitch has already summarized the various biographical, sociological, metaphysical, political, existentialist, ontological, and psychoanalytical readings of *L'Étranger* in order to highlight his aesthetic explication of the structural unity of the novel's internal contradictions. Alain Robbe-Grillet phrases it aptly stating that "*L'Étranger* c'est moi" . . . "each one of us has a tendency to create a history of literature that is one's own story" ("chacun d'entre nous a tendance à concevoir une histoire de la littérature qui est sa propre histoire").[20] If this is true, *L'Étranger* becomes an "open work," a work that reads the reader, because, in its overdetermined state, it allows commentators to project themselves into the silence of the narrative gap—the silence between the first shot and the four subsequent ones that Meursault pumps into the inert body of the Arab. Whereas Meursault fills the gap with the light of the sun, the magistrate fills it with his need to believe in a Christian God.

The death of the Arab always raises two fundamental questions: Why did Meursault kill him? And why, after the first shot, did he shoot four more times into the corpse? Meursault says that it was because of the sun, but his judges, not to mention many readers, do not understand how the sun could influence him to such a degree. Indeed, the question of his guilt or innocence hinges on each reader's reaction to Meursault's assertion. Those who believe him foreground his honesty, while those who doubt him devalue the sun's complicity. Everything depends on our interpretation of nature's role. However, before proceeding with a Lacanian reading of *L'Étranger*, a reading which, I believe, resolves the question of the sun's part in the death of the Arab, it will perhaps be useful to summarize the views of Freudian commentators.

Psychoanalytic studies of Camus's works in general and of *L'Étranger* in particular began with an article by Arminda A. de Pichon-Rivière and Willy Baranger. According to them Meursault's relations with his mother are marked by feelings of sadomasochism, while her death evokes in him reactions of guilt accompanied by schizophrenic symptoms. In order to escape this sadistic guilt and rejoin his mother in death, Meursault commits suicide. This, they say, is the meaning of the shooting of the Arab and of his failure to defend himself in court.[21] Julian L. Stamm interprets the murder of the Arab as a symptom of Meursault's unconscious homosexual sadomasochistic fantasies. The shooting is an ejaculation, and the four additional shots are a discharge of tension that is both aggressive and sexual. The entire scene, says Stamm, is analogous to the "orgiastic peak in the male and the gradual detumescence." Even the glare of the sun "expresses the seething homosexual desires within him [Meursault] . . . as well as his passive wish to be penetrated by these rays."[22] Whereas the magistrate fills the gap in the narrative with Christianity, Stamm fills the silence between the first shot and the others with homosexuality. Brée fills it with honesty; Girard with delinquency; Sartre with Meursault's refusal to play the game; Champigny with Epicurean heroism; Fitch with temporal distance; and Wagner with ineptness. We each read the book with our own unconscious desire.

Alain Costes provides the first Freudian analysis of Camus's work as a whole. Costes stresses the alleged origins of the schizophrenic symptoms that he finds in an early biographical piece, the one in which Camus describes an assault on his mother one evening by an unknown assailant.[23] The incident is interpreted by Costes as an oedipal phantasm whose reverberations reinforce the author's sadism, masochism, and guilt. Costes concludes that all of Camus's work is a projection of his unconscious longing for his mother, a need to transcend the void of her silence (she spoke little and seemed reluctant to show her feelings). Camus's discourse, says Costes, "emanates directly and unmistakenly from incestuous desire" ("émane directement du pur désir incestueux").[24]

Jean Gassin analyzes the underlying symbols and images in Camus's work, and, like Costes, he sees Camus's relationship with his mother as the key. For Gassin, however, the guillotine, like the Arab's knife flashing in the sun, and the piece of shrapnel that killed Camus's father during the war, is the essential symbol because it represents the image of primary castration and death. However, Gassin does not analyze the scene of the shooting of the Arab because he believes that everything about it has already been said.[25] A Lacanian reading does, nonetheless, cast a different light on the event and it is useful, therefore, to present the sun's complicity in the shooting of the Arab in Lacanian terms. Costes, while maintaining that a work of art should be interpreted as a dream or as a symptom, but seemingly unaware, in 1973, of Lacan's *Écrits*, wonders how conceptually to connect a spoken discourse with a written one ("La question demeure: Comment mener à bien cette transplantation massive de concepts, d'un matériel 'parlé' à un matériel 'écrit'?").[26] The exciting and perhaps not surprising aspect of Lacan's insights into the structure of language as a linguistic and semiotic system is that they confirm Freud's intuitions about the unconscious. All the Freudian analyses of Camus's works use a biographical approach to literature and they resemble Marie Bonaparte's exegesis of Edgar Allan Poe's "Purloined Letter," as opposed to Lacan's purely textual analysis of the short story.[27]

Different systems provide different foci of interpretation. Although my focus will be psychoanalytic, and Lacan's own readings *are* Freudian, the difference between earlier Freudian readings of *L'Étranger* and mine is that the previous ones, in their pursuit of teleological traumas and symbolic manifestations, have tended to devalue the text in order to privilege significant moments in

Camus's life. A Lacanian reading allows us to focus instead on the author's discursive weave, and on the relationship between the reader and the text. The orientation is in the direction of reader response and is not, strictly speaking, biographical. The author's life, although relevant, is secondary. Such a strategy allows us to discard the conjectures that Freudian critics sometimes use in order to shore up an analysis that is frequently speculative. For example, Costes, in explaining the shooting says: "I imagine that for years Camus must have repressed the inadmissible wish to kill this Arab" ("J'imagine que Camus a dû refouler pendant des années le souhait inavouable de tuer cet Arabe").[28] Although, in French, the words "must have repressed" can also mean "had to repress," the fact remains that the author can't know what was going on in Camus's mind. A Lacanian analysis, and this is the first of its kind for *L'Étranger*, bypasses such conjecture because the text itself, although in disguise, reveals the content of the author's unconscious.

Costes and Gassin are writing about an "incestuous" episode, when, after the attack on the balcony, Camus spent the night lying on the bed next to his mother. They both refer to this incident as a dramatization of the "primal scene." Gassin says that "within Camus's phantasm of the primal scene, once the aggressor had fled, it is the subject who found himself in bed with his mother" ("Dans le fantasme camusien de la scène primitive, l'agresseur s'étant enfui, c'est le sujet qui se retrouvait au lit avec sa mère").[29] Indeed, Camus's narrative describes with precision, the groans, the fever, the sweat, and the odors. It is difficult, says Gassin, "not to see the equivalent of a wedding night, but with his mother, a night during which the child discovers with satisfaction that he has triumphed over his rival" ("Il est bien difficile, dans une optique psychanalytique, de ne pas y voir l'équivalent d'une nuit de noces, mais avec la mère, et où l'enfant trouve la satisfaction supplémentaire de triompher de son rival").[30] Costes and Gassin both argue that Camus has triumphed over the intruder by substituting himself for the would-be assailant, and that he has also prevailed over his father by supplanting him in the mother's bed. Costes attributes significance to the fact that Camus, the family, and the people in the neighborhood were convinced that an Arab had attacked his mother.[31] According to Costes, Camus's repressed hostility toward the presumed Arab manifests itself, ultimately, as the shooting scene of the Arab on the beach in *L'Étranger*. Indeed, both Costes and Gassin endorse the idea of a double murder. There is meaning, says Costes, in the fact that the victim in *L'Étranger* is an Arab,[32] and that Meursault shoots him "in memory of the one who could have attacked the scriptor's mother" ("en mémoire de celui qui aurait agréssé la mère du scripteur").[33] All this is perfectly good, straightforward Freudian theory. I am suggesting, however, that readers need not go to *L'Envers et l'endroit*, or to Camus's biographers in order to find evidence in *L'Étranger* of the "primal scene."

Although they do not identify it specifically, Costes and Gassin both use Charles Mauron's psychocriticism, the methodological approach that emphasizes "significant" juxtapositions of words, sentences, and episodes in different texts (biographical and fictional). Such a methodology, when reinforced by word counts, such as Paul Fortier's unpublished collection, gives us insight into the author's psyche and his unconscious intentions. These studies are useful, but they do not explain the novel as text, and they certainly do not account for its impact on the reader. The shortcomings of conventional Freudian interpretations, that rely so much on biographical material, only serve to highlight the advantages of a Lacanian methodology that emphasizes metaphor and metonymy as tropes within the text's discursive weave. A Lacanian reading foregrounds metaphor and metonymy thereby, eliciting interpretive strategies based on the text's poetics rather than on the author's life.

It is not an accident that Freud erected his theory of the unconscious on the Oedipus myth, or that Lacan should find every man's history and destiny written metaphorically and metonymically in the discourse of the Other that derives from it. Because the unconscious is structured like a language the unfolding of each man's destiny occurs on the discursive side of the unconscious, where its pulsive forces are readable and audible. The murder of the Arab may look like a *crimen ex machina* to Girard, or, if we agree with Costes and Gassin, like Camus's subconscious hostility toward an aggressor, in this case the Arab, but a Lacanian analysis of the incident reveals that it is neither a pretext for the trial, nor a gratuitous event, nor specifically biographical. Although the shooting dramatizes Meursault's opposing personality traits and schizoid tendencies—traits that confirm and explain the many contradictory readings of the novel—it also foregrounds the discourse of the Other as the veiled workings of the unconscious, everybody's unconscious, including the reader's.

Although Pichon-Rivière, Baranger, Costes, and Gassin agree that the shooting symbolizes Meursault's killing of his parents,

Viggiani, in a mythical and religious context—says that the sea and the sun constitute religious symbols of the highest antiquity. Water is a primordial female substance from which all forms are born, while the sun is a fecundating element and male principle. Ra, the sun, was an Egyptian god, while the Apollo of ancient Greece drove his chariot across the sky. "A number of signs suggest that in Camus there is an unconscious identification of the mother and the sea who, like the father and the sun, are frequently recurring characters in his work" ("Plusieurs indices suggèrent chez Camus une identification inconsciente de la mère et de la mer, personnages omnipresents dans son oeuvre au même titre que le père et le soleil").[34]

These different studies have been circling Lacan's "Letter of the Unconscious" without actually putting their finger on it or on the role of metaphor in discourse. W. M. Frohock (1950) was perhaps the first to have noted that after having used only fifteen metaphors in eighty-three pages, Camus lavishes twenty-five metaphors on the four pages that describe the shooting of the Arab.[35] Meursault's intense metaphorical description of what is happening to him on the beach has exceptional dramatic value and Lacanian relevance. Robert de Luppé and Albert Maquet believe that this accumulation of metaphors represents an aesthetic lapse, a loss of control on Camus's part. Camus, they say, has given in temporarily to the exigencies of his character by abandoning the "style neutre" and the "écriture blanche" of the preceding pages.[36] Viggiani, however, believes that Camus is using a highly charged poetic language because Meursault has come up against "the unbridgeable mystery of the universe" ("l'indépassable mystère de l'univers"),[37] but Gassin is closer to the mark when he says that "the cymbals of the sun" belong to the category of obsessive metaphors.[38] Meursault, and even Camus, may be mystified by the proliferation of metaphor, but what is really at work is the symbolic manifestation of the "primal repression." For Lacan, the homologies of *la mère* and *la mer*, as well as "cymbals" and "symbols" are eruptions of the unconscious—tangible manifestations of latent content.

Camus had already used the "cymbals of the sun," his lyrical tribute to mother earth and to man's joyful contact with her.[39] In *Noces* (Nuptials) he personifies nature (mother nature), imbuing her with the same life-death duality that Meursault finds so disquieting. Meursault's "honeymoon" with the sea, with Marie, with the cool of the evening, like Camus's, opposes the harsh sun at noon. Indeed,

Meursault is acutely aware of the sun's extraordinary power. When the magistrate asks him why he shot the Arab, Meursault says it was because of the sun ("c'était à cause du soleil").[40] At first, this answer seems odd, and neither the magistrate nor the court can understand how the sun could have been responsible for such an implausible act. As an alibi, the sun elicits laughter in the courtroom. However, Robbe-Grillet gives the sun credence by calling attention to the language that Meursault uses in order to describe the event. Robbe-Grillet says that anthropomorphic metaphors are responsible for the homicide: Meursault pulls the trigger of the pistol because the language he uses to describe his feelings has humanized nature. He shoots because he is unable to keep the necessary distance between objects and himself:

> The absurd [says Robbe-Grillet] is therefore one aspect of tragic humanism. It is not an assertion concerning the separation of man and objects. It is a love quarrel that leads to the crime of passion. The world is accused of complicity in murder.
>
> (L'absurde est donc bien une forme d'humanisme tragique. Ce n'est pas un constat de séparation entre l'homme et les choses. C'est une querelle d'amour, qui mène au crime passionnel. Le monde est accusé de complicité d'assassinat.)[41]

Without actually identifying the father-mother relationship, Robbe-Grillet's analysis of the role of language is nonetheless apposite, because he calls it a "crime of passion" based on jealousy. The displaced object of Meursault's love is the world, since the absurd, as Camus defines it, is that irreparable rift between man and the world—between man's rage to live and the world's inability to fulfill that passion. The absurd is thus neither in man nor in things, but in the impossibility of establishing a relationship that is not estranged. This alienation is, in fact, endemic. It affects Meursault's relationship with nature, with society and its codes, and it also contaminates the language that the court will use in order to condemn him: Meursault does not recognize himself in the descriptions of the accused. Also, and unfortunately for him, he is an inarticulate nonconformist who refuses or is unable to defend himself and who is, literally, defined and imprisoned by encratic language, that is, the ideology of the society that will condemn him. His lawyer's defense is singularly ineffective against the arguments and intransigence of the state. If an anthropomorphized language is responsible for Meursault's shooting of the Arab, then surely it is the language of bourgeois ideology that condemns Meursault to death: "The magistrate told me in some weird formula that I would have my head cut off in a public square in the name of the French people" ("Le président m'a dit dans une forme bizarre que j'aurais la tête tranchée sur une place publique au nom du peuple français").[42]

The magistrate says that he cannot understand (nor is the reader given an explanation) why Meursault pumps four more bullets into an inert corpse. All he says is that they were "like four quick raps on the door of misfortune" ("c'était comme quatre coups brefs que je frappais sur la porte du malheur").[43] One bullet, as Meursault's narrative so strongly implies, is accidental, whereas four more, from the court's point of view, imply premeditation. There is a chasm between them. Indeed, it is this gap in Meursault's story and in the court's interpretation of it that raises so many questions and elicits such widely divergent interpretations. The hole in the text opens the door, so to speak, to a Lacanian analysis because Meursault's silence, and the court's dramatization of it, is the space in which the repressed material is hidden.

Meursault's discourse is a classical example of metaphor veiling the unconscious. It is so obvious, that had Meursault been the original Oedipus, he would have had to blind himself (had not nature, temporarily, done it for him) in order to expiate events that were, so to speak, staring him in the face, or, as in this instance, gouging his eyes. It is, as previous commentators have already pointed out, the classical oedipal triangle. The sun (*le soleil* in French is masculine) is the father, the sea (*la mer* in French is feminine, and is also the homonym for *la mère*, the mother) is the mother, and Meursault is the child. Indeed, Meursault is childlike in his "innocence" and need for immediate satisfactions. The sun, like the father, is sometimes harsh and authoritarian, and it punishes with a slap ("Le jour, déjà tout plein de soleil, m'a frappé comme une gifle").[44]

The sea offers Meursault pleasures he truly enjoys—swimming. But the sea is only one dimension of the earth's abundance. *Noces* (Nuptials) provides the backdrop for Meursault's honeymoon on earth. The earth is his true love, and other women, such as Marie, are but one of many satisfactions that constitute his "moveable feast." Meursault is willing to marry Marie, if she wishes, but he does not love her. What he does not say is that his real love is for "the mother"—for all the physical pleasures that mother-earth provides.

The Algerian beach is thus the metaphor for an atavistic relationship, one for which Martha, in the play *Le Malentendu* (The Misunderstanding), is willing to kill.

In *L'Étranger*, the 2:00 P.M. drama is generated not only by the searing heat of the sun. Far more disturbing for Meursault is the perceived *alliance* between the mother and the father. The mother, in collusion with the father, is no longer benign, but threatening. "The heat was pressing against me, opposing my advance" ("Toute cette chaleur s'appuyait sur moi et s'opposait à mon avance").[45] The sea (*la mer*), like the sun, is a sea of "boiling metal." Meursault's attempt to reach the source, that is, the cool spring, is thwarted by the blade of sunlight (metal) that strikes him on the forehead. The father has struck again, this time with the mother's complicity. The sea, the sun, the sky, and the beach, the *sources* of Meursault natural pleasures, are now one united and hostile force that impedes his advance and even threatens to destroy him. Meursault's walk on the beach toward the spring, in spite of the heat, can only be explained as an unconscious desire to find the mother, to slake his thirst at the source. In *Noces* Camus speaks of walking toward love and desire ("Nous marchons à la rencontre de l'amour et du désir"),[46] using words and connotations that adumbrate Meursault's walk along the beach toward the stream. The source, like the sea (*la mer/la mère*) also has latent signifieds as mother and as the origin of life. In the end, physical oppression by the heat and psychological frustration (the presence of the Arab is an obstacle to the source) combine, exploding as a defensive-aggressive act, the pulling of the trigger—the crime of passion and jealousy that Robbe-Grillet alludes to.

What is this crime of passion and where does the jealousy come from? Whereas Meursault's narrative is characterized throughout part 1 by its lean, sparse style virtually devoid of metaphors, the end of part 1, by contrast, as Frohock has pointed out, multiplies and anthropomorphizes them. We have "the ardent breath of the sea" ("La mer a charrié un souffle épais et ardent"), and "the rapid stifled breathing of the sea" ("la mer haletait de toute la respiration rapide et étouffée de ses petites vagues").[47] The sky opens up "in order to rain down fire" upon him ("Le ciel s'ouvrait sur toute son étendue pour laisser pleuvoir du feu"). Meursault's narration of events makes it clear that something extraordinary is happening to him. Indeed, by the time the sun "strikes" him on the forehead and "gouges" his eyes ("fouillait mes yeux douloureux"), he has come to believe that he is under attack. His description of these phenomena has given nature a volition that it does not and cannot have. The sun and the sea (nature) have become actors in the tragedy of Meursault's existence (the stage of his unconscious). However, this complicity between language and nature may not be enough to justify or explain the shooting. There is more than meets Meursault's blinded eyes ("mes yeux étaient aveuglés").[48]

A Lacanian reading demonstrates that, although there may be complicity in language, what Robbe-Grillet calls "tragic complicity" (*connivence tragique*),[49] the real complicity, as in the primal repression, is between father and mother, in this case, metaphorically, between the sun and the sea. Initially, the child's desire for the mother, due to the intervention of the father, is repressed, but the anger against the father and against the self remains. The repression of desire coincides with the child's accession to language. But in the realm of the repressed, the Imaginary (self), the Symbolic (father and mother), and the Real (which resists symbolization completely) continuously reenact the drama of death and desire. It is this language of the unconscious that surfaces and is rendered visible and audible as behavioral symptoms or as metaphorical discourse. The incidents immediately preceding the shooting are so traumatic for Meursault that metaphor is the only vehicle capable of conveying what he feels or what happens. However, even readers as perceptive as Robbe-Grillet are puzzled by the discrepancy in narrative tone between the events narrated just before the shooting and Meursault's earlier discourse, which is noteworthy for its absence of tropes. It is not narrative inconsistency, as some commentators maintain, but psychological necessity that dictates such an extreme use of figurative language.

Although the Arab's presence on the beach is a potential threat, Meursault's attention is riveted on the sun reflecting off the Arab's knife. The knife has been transformed into a blade of light, while the sweat that rolls down into Meursault's eyes, hurting them, is also, like the sea, salty. Metonymical slippage transforms sweat and light into a blade of fire. In French the word for blade (*la lame*) is also the word for wave.

> The light splashed on the steel and it was like a long shimmering blade [*lame*] transfixing my forehead. . . . Behind this curtain of tears and salt my eyes were blinded. I was conscious only of the cymbals of the sun clashing on my skull, and, less distinctly, of the blade of light flashing up from the knife, scarring my eyelashes and gouging my eyes with pain.

(La lumière a giclé sur l'acier et c'était comme une longue lame étincelante qui m'atteignait au front. . . . Mes yeux étaient aveuglés derrière ce rideau de larmes et de sel. Je ne sentais plus que les cymbales du soleil sur mon front et, indistinctement, le glaive éclatant jailli du couteau toujours en face de moi. Cette épée brulante rongeait mes cils et fouillait mes yeux douloureux.)[50]

Because this complicity of language is metaphorical, the word "*lame*" (blade) compresses the collusion between the sea and the sun. The wave of sweat that rolls into Meursault's eyes is also the blade of light that is gouging them. Although, on the manifest level, nature is blinding him, on the latent and repressed level, it is the mother-father complicity, that, once again, threatens Meursault's precarious identity, renewing his fears of death and castration. Instead of the wave "splashing" and the blade "gouging," the metaphor can also be read as the wave that "gouges" and the blade that "splashes." Whether wave or blade, the word, by synecdoche, elicits the whole, that is, the sea and the sun. At that point the sky opens up to rain fire on him and so the "fire" of the sun and the "boiling metal" of the sea become the blade that is blinding him. Meursault can no longer see and, in self defense, he pulls the trigger because the circumstances are perceived to be life threatening. Indeed, Meursault has reason to blame the sun for the shooting of the Arab and, when asked, he reports the events as he experienced them. What he does not and cannot know is that his metaphors veil the reenactment of the primal repression, namely, the complicity of the father and the mother, a complicity, that, once more, thwarts his desire for the source—the cool spring that will slake his thirst. His thirst is real, but it is also symbolic of his thirst for the mother and explains why, in spite of the heat, he should go walking along the beach looking for her. Physical thirst, by itself, does not explain why he left the cabin on the beach, since water was available there. The cabin was also a place of refuge from the sun. Therefore, compelling reasons must have existed for Meursault's quest. Although the cool spring may be signaling the purely imaginary character of his repressed thirst for his mother, it does so, on the linguistic level, by virtue of the fact that a signifier, in this case "the source," can have two signifieds.

If we keep in mind, once again that tropes represent a semantic slippage from a present sign(s), the blade (the sun and the sea), to an absent one(s) (the father and the mother), then a Lacanian reading of the events, reactions, and metaphors may be diagrammed as in Figure 7.1.

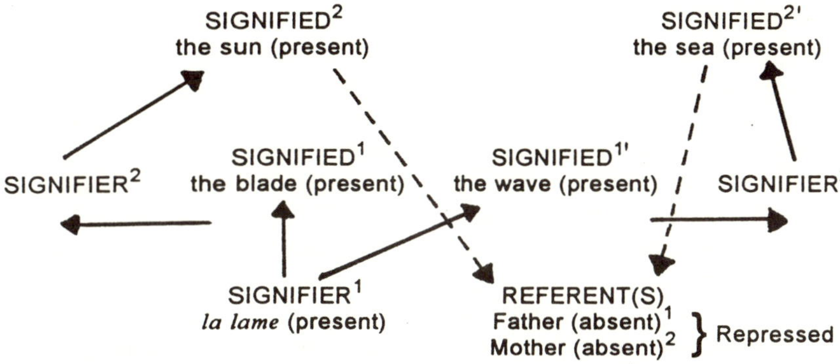

FIGURE 7.1

Reading a trope involves a series of operations that tend to occur simultaneously whenever denotations and connotations imply an overlapping of meaning. Thus, in the six circles in Figure 7.2, we

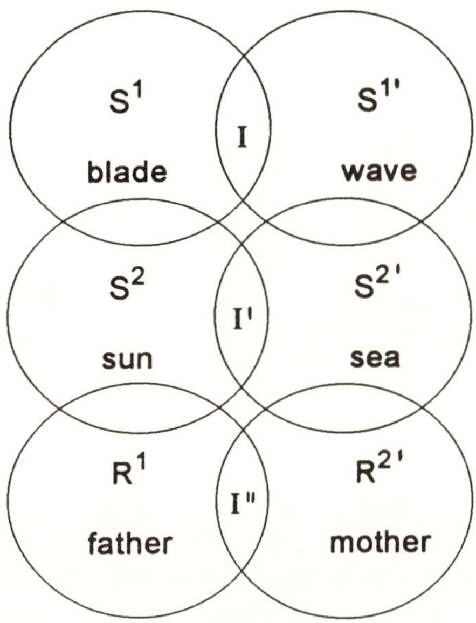

FIGURE 7.2

have S^1 (the blade, i.e., *la lame*) overlapping with $S^{1'}$ (the wave, i.e., *la lame*), with I as the intermediary. The two signifieds, (i.e., "blade" and "wave,") become the signifiers for two new signifieds (S^2 and $S^{2'}$), namely, the sun and the sea. The fire of the sun coincides with the boiling metal of the sea, and they overlap at I'. This overlapping is the metaphorical collusion between the two. The sun and the sea, in turn, become signifiers for the repressed referents, namely the father and the mother (R^1 and R^2). The overlapping of their complicity is expressed as I''. Three levels of meaning are expressed simultaneously, two of them present and one absent. The father and the mother are present in the unconscious, but absent from the beach where the tragedy of the unconscious is being played out.[51]

The tropic displacements with regard to *mer/mère* can be diagrammed here in exactly the same way as in the preceding chapter for David and Marita, because the sea, like the blade, represents a semantic transposition from a present sign to an absent one. Once again the referent dramatizes the presence of the repressed because the sea (*la mer*) is the "source" of all life as the mother (*la mère*) is the source of human life.

In this context Camus's use of the word *la source* reinforces the latent associative referents of *mother* and *beginning*. This relationship is diagrammed in Figure 7.3.

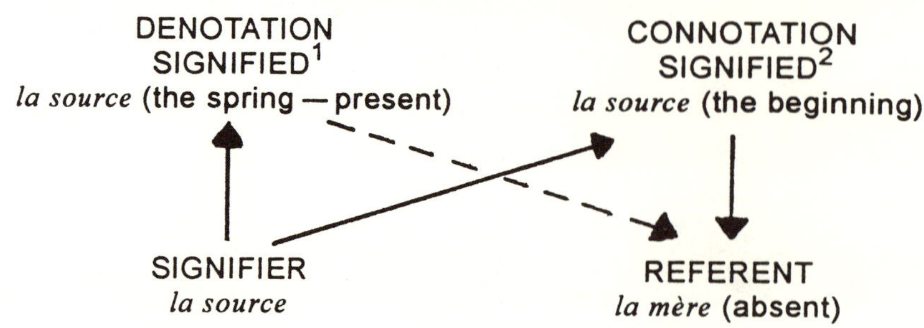

FIGURE 7.3

The text represses the reasons for Meursault's return to *the source*. Indeed, why did he return to the spring after lunch in the full heat of the day? Why did he not stay in the beach house with the others? He says he wanted to get away from the women's voices, but in fact, he has heard and felt the imperious call of the mother. And so, armed, he returns to the source to reclaim his lost rights.

Raymond's pistol, a potent male symbol, is still in Meursault's pocket. Moreover, it manifests the power of the phallus, because the sun (the father) appropriates it. "When Raymond gave me his revolver," says Meursault, "the sun glistened on it" ("Quand Raymond m'a donné son revolver, le soleil a glissé dessus").[52] With his phallus now firmly in place, Meursault runs the gauntlet on the beach (where the mother and the father together oppose his advance) toward the source in order to slake his "thirst," that is, his longing for the Edenic bond with the primal mother who is cool and perhaps at last potentially his. Once more the father (the sun) bars his way, there is a clash of cymbals/symbols (phalluses), the Arab falls, and "the exceptional silence of a beach on which I had been happy" is destroyed ("le silence exceptionnel d'une plage où j'avais été heureux").[53] Frustration, deception, and anger climax in the pulling of the trigger. The father has triumphed and the law condemns Meursault to the guillotine where his head will be severed—the ultimate castration.

But Meursault regrets nothing. Only hours before his execution, he thinks about his death and his mother's death, and he feels the cool night air, veined with smells of earth and salt. And he feels the marvelous peace of the sleep-bound summer night that floods through him like a tide ("Des odeurs de nuit, de terre et de sel rafraîchissaient mes tempes. La merveilleuse paix de cet été endormi entrait en moi comme une marée"). In death he will be united with his mother, and, like her, he now feels "ready to start life all over again" ("je me suis senti prêt à tout revivre").[54] With paradise in sight, Meursault looks forward to a crowd of spectators who, on the day of his execution, will greet him "with howls of hatred" ("avec des cris de haine").[55] At last he will have found the love and the peace of his mother's embrace—the incestuous encounter that we, the spectators, have been taught to execrate.

The earth-mother may be Meursault's true love, but he seems also not to have recovered from the castrating influence of the mythical father. Although he enjoys swimming with Marie in the sea and spouting water, he feels "his mouth burning from the bitterness of the salt" ("j'avais la bouche brûlée par l'amertume du sel").[56] This residual bitterness has connotations that go far beyond swimming. While sunning himself on the buoy with Marie, Meursault places his head on her abdomen, where he feels the pulsing of her being, sensations that adumbrate his quest for the mother as the source of life. Meursault's behavior reflects an ambivalence that has puzzled critics such as Fitch, who discern Camus's voice lurking behind Meursault's narrative. The problem, says Fitch, is that the reader has difficulty identifying with a character whose psychology and motivation he or she fails to grasp.[57] However, we can restore credibility to this apparent implausibility, if, instead of attributing the concealed voice to Camus, we center it within the discourse of the Other. A Lacanian reading gives us the key to an understanding of Meursault's psychological opacity. His discourse, whatever else it is, is also the discourse of the Other, and it is this concealment that Fitch defines as aesthetic distance.[58] A Lacanian reading explains Meursault's duality, not as Camus's loss of aesthetic control but as the surfacing of the unconscious, that is, of death and desire. The death wish then manifests itself in Meursault's actions as indifference, listlessness, and lack of ambition, even as desire prompts him, simultaneously, to seek out Marie, the symbolic mother.

Meursault spends Sundays on his balcony, a spectator to, not an actor in, the bourgeois activities in the street below. He is not interested in a job promotion or in going to Paris, and he does not cry at his mother's funeral. He is manipulated by the pimp Raymond, and it is, in part, this association that condemns him. Meursault says yes to Raymond's requests that he write a letter to Raymond's mistress because it is too much trouble to say no. Saying no requires more effort than a partially inebriated Meursault can muster, but he also always takes the path of least resistance. Meursault is like a cork bobbing in the sea, pushed this way and that by whatever social, emotional, and physical currents come his way. If we compare the significance of the words "yes" and "no" in Camus's *L'Homme révolté* (*The Rebel*), we begin to understand the distance that separates Meursault from Camus's metaphysical persona which, although rebelling, affirms a collective *cogito*—a reasoned affirmation of an essentialist attitude that gives meaning to their rebellion: "I rebel, therefore we are" ("Je me révolte, donc nous sommes").[59]

Meursault seems pathologically incapable of exercising his will (let alone of formulating the premises of collective rebellion or acting upon them), a symptom, surely, of psychological impotence, of a spirit broken by the name-of-the father (*le non/nom du père*). He is not a committed hero; he cannot defend himself in court, has nothing to say, although it is a matter of life and death, feels like a stranger at the proceedings, and has the impression that the court is talking about someone else, not him. Resistance, let alone rebellion, seems futile. He has not taken the leap into commitment, which is the second stage of the existential hero. Such is the meekness, humility, and poverty of mind of "the only Christ we deserve."

The trial mirrors the events as defined and described by the court, and the reader is, no doubt, as surprised as Meursault is, to learn that "he has buried his mother with a criminal heart" ("j'accuse cet homme d'avoir enterré une mère avec un coeur de criminel").[60] Is that possible? How could the court get away with so outrageous a statement, unless, of course, there were some truth to residual feelings of guilt that we all share. Are we not guilty of coveting our mothers and wishing for the death of our fathers? Fyodor Dostoevsky, adumbrating Freud and Lacan, may not have been the first to state that we all secretly desire the death of our fathers—hence the guilt. Camus himself sets up the parallelism between the man who is accused of patricide and Meursault's alleged matricide. Indeed, the magistrate implies that because Meursault is a heartless and soulless creature ("je n'en avais point, d'âme, et que rien d'humain, et pas un des principes moraux qui gardent le coeur des hommes ne m'était accessibles"),[61] he is as guilty of killing a father as he is of burying his mother with a criminal heart. Desire and guilt—two of the elements that Lacan refers to—implicate all of us, and, in the context of the primal repression, we are all guilty. *L'Étranger* is a novel that mirrors the Other in all of us, and that is the reason, I believe, for its fascination and haunting endurance.

In part 2, after Meursault is condemned to die, he finds his tongue and, instead of only describing objects and events from the outside, as he had in part 1, he begins to reason like a philosopher. He accedes to language in another classical illustration of the Lacanian concept of the primal repression. The child discovers language along with desire and death. The Law denies the infant's desire for the mother, thereby symbolically castrating the child. This castration and repression is internalized as a death wish directed at the father and as a death of the self. Meursault's indifference to everything except mother-earth is the symptom of the death of the self from which he has never recovered.

So Meursault is condemned to die, and, like the child acceding to language, even as it represses the death of the self, Meursault's discourse assumes a giant epistemological and ontological leap. He discourses on life, death, freedom, and the self. Whereas in part 1 he was living the "absurd," in part 2 he describes it. Whereas in part 1 he was living as a free man, in part 2 he describes what it means not to be free. Whereas in part 1 he seemed indifferent to his mother's death, in part 2 he accepts death calmly but not indifferently. When questioned by the priest about life after death, he says that he would like to be able to remember this one ("Une vie où je pourrais me souvenir de celle-ci").[62] Meursault says that he has no regrets, that he accepts the consequences of his acts (these characteristics define him as an authentic being), and he *assumes* the Other in himself. While waiting to die he looks up at the starry sky:

> I opened myself to the tender indifference of the world. To feel it so like me, indeed, so brotherly, made me realize that I'd been happy, and that I was happy still.
>
> (Je m'ouvrais pour la première fois à la tendre indifférence du monde. De l'éprouver si pareil à moi, si fraternel enfin, j'ai senti que j'avais été heureux, et que je l'étais encore.)[63]

Meursault is calm after his stormy encounter, after venting his anger at the priest who has tried to talk to him of God, repentance, and the afterlife—the very concepts that Meursault rejects—because, for him, they have no significance. But Meursault's anger is significant because it is only the second time in the novel that it has exploded. The first time was on the beach, when he pumped the four extra bullets into the Arab. Is there a connection to be made between a priest who calls Meursault "my son," and asks him to call him "father," and Meursault's reaction to the sun (the mythical father and the repressed father) on that fateful afternoon when he shot the Arab? When the heat is on, so to speak, whether it is physical or metaphysical, Meursault's anger surfaces. His anger is the symptom that identifies the father as the source of his disturbance. It also proves that there is one fundamental exception to his fatigue, listlessness, and indifference: the prohibition of the father.

The law of nature is death, and death is the essential meaning of an absurd world: "Men die and they are not happy" ("Les hommes meurent et ils ne sont pas heureux"), says Camus's crazed although lucid Caligula.[64] However, the law of the father is also death—the symbolic death of the self—and that is the meaning of the primal repression. Society's laws can also be lethal, and criminals are executed in the name of the law. Camus's works synthesize the natural, social, and psychological laws of existence into one irrepressible principle: death. Except for those privileged moments when

Meursault comes in contact with the mother and is happy, he is the puppet of the father. By using the code words "father" and "son"—by invoking the law—the priest unwittingly opens the sluice gates to Meursault's repressed anger, frustration, and resentment. This anger, directed at the father and the law illuminates the unconscious impulses that goad him to shoot the sun, which is the "mythical father," if not "our Father in heaven."

The unusual quality of Meursault's narrative with which part 1 ends, with its atypical metaphors, is thus not inconsistent with his state of mind and emotional turmoil. Since the latent content of the unconscious can manifest itself as discourse only in disguised form, Meursault's metaphors are the symptoms of a profound disturbance. He is reenacting the trauma of the primal repression when the unity in the mirror between mother and infant was cleaved by the father. The father asserts his rights, claims the mother, and forces the child to recognize an identity that will forever be alienated. The strangeness of this Other and its relationship to the superego will also determine the degree of alienation each man feels within himself and from society. Meursault's alienation from society, as his behavior clearly shows, is extreme. The murder of the Arab forces society to take note of his action and, consequently, in order to understand it, to examine his other actions. The magistrate does not like what he discovers. Meursault's values are perceived as disruptive, antisocial, and destabilizing. This is why he is accused of burying his mother with the heart of a criminal. A paternalistic society, emphasizing law and order, cannot abide a man who appears to be subverting that order. Meursault's penchant for living in the present, his inability to resist immediate satisfactions will offend the court, which places such heavy emphasis on decorum. The magistrate says that "'the emptiness that one discovers in this man's heart is a chasm ready to engulf society'" ("'le vide du coeur tel qu'on le découvre chez cet homme devient un gouffre où la société peut succomber'").[65] He smokes a cigarette at his mother's funeral, drinks café au lait, and does not cry. He goes to a Fernandel film and laughs, and he begins a liaison with a woman when he should have been in mourning. The murder of the Arab is indeed the pretext that will allow the law to proscribe behavior that subverts its structures. Barthes uses the term *arrogance* to describe the self-assurance of an ideology that is arbitrary, but which, nonetheless, believes in its inviolability.[66]

Meursault's hedonism (he is responsive to physical pleasures such as swimming, eating, lovemaking) places him in the mother's camp, not the father's. The father represents the harshness of the law—striving, ambition, convention, obedience—virtues to which Meursault is indifferent. He marches to another drummer: he is attuned to nature's rhythms, not society's expectations. He is in harmony with a mother who tends to be permissive, tolerant, and giving. Camus's references to man's honeymoon on earth are not gratuitous.[67] They are the yearning of a child who longs for the pleasures and comforts of the mother's body. As a metaphor, *Noces* is the disguised image of the mother and the nostalgia of a child's desire. At night, Meursault's behavior, patterned after the mother's ("je m'ouvrais pour la première fois à la tendre indifférence du monde"),[68] opposes the harshness of paternalistic authority—the sun at noonday. No wonder Barthes calls *L'Étranger* a solar novel.

For millennia the rule of the father has been responsible for feelings of castration, death, and inadequacy: indeed, the incest taboo is one of many legacies. Meursault's accusers may denounce him, but the "cymbals" of the sun suggest that the blade of the guillotine, like the Arab's knife, will have to flash once more in order to punish him for violating, even unconsciously, the taboo of incest. Incest is the latent and repressed content of Camus's novel, and it continues to fascinate readers who, as in a mirror ("this is you"), recognize in Meursault's actions the image of oedipal desire.

Chapter 8

Toward Bliss: Roland Barthes and Alain Robbe-Grillet Autobiography as Fiction

The mirror stage *is a drama whose internal thrust is precipitated from insufficiency to anticipation—and which manufactures for the subject, caught up in the lure of spatial identification, the succession of phantasies that extends from a fragmented body-image to a form of its totality that I shall call orthopaedic.*

—*Jacques Lacan, "The mirror stage as formative of the function of the I"*

Lacan's theories show how an unconscious and decentered discourse parallels conscious narration and imbues it with the voice of the Other. A decentered and tropical discourse enables Barthes and Robbe-Grillet to write autobiography in the guise of fiction. Their two works, *Roland Barthes* and *Le Miroir qui revient*, foreground the discourse of the Other while also deconstructing the text.

I propose to embed the *Roland Barthes* and *Le Miroir qui revient* in a Lacanian matrix. The oedipal connotations of the words "embed" and "matrix" are evident, as is the fact that Lacan's formulation of the Law—the source of authority—constitutes the father. If the French language is the mother (tongue) and ideology is the father, then Barthes and Robbe-Grillet react as a son might whenever they oppose the *non/nom du père*—ideology encoded in language. Their manhandling of language enables them to experience the bliss (*jouissance*) of contact with the forbidden, that is, with the mother. Each writer projects his body as text onto the operational field (the matrix) where the textual (sexual) game is played. Their act of writing is a transgression, an act that is all the more audacious, because each man consciously impresses himself as body and text on the mother tongue.

Every text contains repressed material that structures a never-ending dialog with the Other—a fictitious self made up of the confluence of the Symbolic, the Imaginary, and the Real. The Symbolic is the Law, the restrictive role of the father, eventually all *doxa*. *Doxa*, says Barthes, is "public Opinion, the Mind of the majority, the Consensus of the petit-bourgeois, the Voice of the Natural, the Violence of Prejudice" ("l'Opinion publique, l'Esprit majoritaire, le Consensus petit-bourgeois, la Voix du Naturel, la Violence du Préjugé").[1] The Imaginary is that displaced self that has to come to terms with the postponement of satisfaction, the repression of desire, and the nurturing of discontent. The Imaginary reinforces the individual's desire for union with the mother while also enabling the subject to define himself or herself in relation to others. This is the *imago*. The Real, in terms of discourse, is the individual's unconscious relationship with death. The Real corresponds to primitive and instinctive levels, to whatever lies behind the effects of socialization.

If all discourse, including autobiography, is fiction, then a conscious manipulation of the text—a text that includes Freudian and Lacanian components—foregrounds the unconscious. Such a discourse unveils and deconstructs the presence of the Other by calling the reader's attention to it.

For Lacan, the act of writing, and the repetition of writing, posits the enticement of textuality, thereby acknowledging, unconsciously, the child's "wound" and alienation. To produce a text, whatever its conscious modes and operations, is also to relive the process by which an affective charge—a cathexis—is released from its generating poles. The writer, and eventually the reader, directs this charge, imbuing it with the Reality that both produces and attracts it. Fiction (fantasy) and autobiography thus have the power to link the conscious and unconscious systems which, in turn, constitute the discourse of the self. The writer's need to repeat, rather than simply remember repressed material, illustrates the need to reproduce and work through painful events from the past as if they were present. Like psychoanalysis, writing repeats the discontent of what never took place during that "time-event" referred to as the primal scene. The so-called fantasy of desire, incest, castration, death, and repression reenact not what took place, but what did not. Nonetheless, it is this scene that is replayed and reenacted on the stage of discourse as the metaphorical actors put on their masks and perform (repeat) their ritual. This discourse of the self, which is always a discourse of desire, seeks to retrieve the lost object, be it breast or mother, and because language manifests the presence of the mother tongue, writing recovers an absence. "We write with our desire," says Barthes, "and I have never stopped desiring" ("On écrit avec son désir, et je n'en finis pas de désirer").[2]

Barthes alludes to the mother tongue as the language with which he, like every author, has an incestuous relationship: "The French language is for him," says Barthes, referring to himself in the third person, "essentially the umbilical language" ("La langue française n'est rien d'autre pour lui que la langue ombilicale").[3] In fact, the text of the *Roland Barthes* has a certain corporeality: it is Barthes himself striving to reconstitute an identity out of the textual fragments that compose it. By using the pronoun "*il*" Barthes is, in effect, writing the Other. These fragments, connected by "*il*" are the incestuous comingling of his body with the mother tongue. These fragments are the body of the text (himself) without the father and beyond the Law: "The fragment," says Barthes, ". . . implies immediate bliss: it is a phantasm of discourse, an opening of desire" ("Le fragment . . . implique une jouissance immédiate: c'est un fantasme de discours, un baillement de désir").[4] This gap in the text, this interstice of silence, is the focus of desire unable to speak its longing but, nonetheless, signaling its presence. This tattered body, like the unconscious, is also structured like a language. It is, in fact, the language of the unconscious. Indeed, Barthes has given the text and the photographs that precede the written portion of it a Lacanian flavor, nudging his informed reader to seek out the discourse of the Other. There are photographs of the boy with his mother, references to the death of his father, Barthes's oedipal frustration at not having had a father to oppose his monopoly of the mother, allusions to the absence of the Law, an emphasis on desire and on the bliss of writing—preferably orgasmic—all incorporating elements of the Symbolic, the Imaginary, and the Real.[5] Barthes, like Robbe-Grillet, derives pleasure, if not bliss, from the subversion of the name-of-the-father and of the bourgeois order for which it stands.

Barthes and Robbe-Grillet, in addition to their allusive writing, also incorporate direct references to Lacan. Barthes uses a photograph of himself as a baby in his mother's arms with the caption "The mirror stage: 'this is you'" ("Le stade du miroir: 'tu es cela'"),[6] and Robbe-Grillet, in an interview with Jean-Pierre Salgas entitled "I have never spoken of anything but myself" ("Je n'ai jamais parlé d'autre chose que de moi"), says that "*Le Miroir qui revient* corresponds to Lacan's mirror stage: the child reglues the fragments on the mirror and discovers that the image of itself is another!"[7] He also describes *Le Miroir qui revient* as the first panel of a series that might have been entitled *Romanesques*, a term that Barthes uses to define the fictional dimension of his own autobiography. Lacan's theories set the stage, so to speak, for both writers' works.

Opposite from a drawing of the human circulatory system entitled *Anatomie*, Barthes's caption reads: "To write the body. Neither the skin, nor the muscles, nor the bones, nor the nerves, but the rest: a clumsy id, fibrous, fluffy, and frayed, the cloak of a clown" ("Écrire le corps. Ni la peau, ni les muscles, ni les os, ni les nerfs, mais le reste: un ça balourd, fibreux, pelucheux, effiloché, la houppelande d'un clown").[8] The text is, literally, the body of the Other that struts and frets on the stage of language. Barthes's writing, therefore, in addition to its theoretical thrust, has a fictional component, whereas, in Robbe-Grillet's writing, which is almost always fictional, our attention focuses on the play within the text—a form of play that foregrounds the text's metaphorical connotations as a body. The women in Robbe-Grillet's texts are indeed metaphors for language, and language, like the women, submits to the assaults of an author who dismembers it/them in order to reveal the secrets of the id or of ideology (encoded in language and therefore functioning as a repressed superego). *Projet pour une révolution à New York* and *Souvenirs du triangle d'or* contain many such scenes—scenes that foreground the creative process, the body as text, the play of language, and the transgression of codes. Meaning, as such, is less important to Robbe-Grillet than the fact that something is circulating. The circulation of these different components is comparable to the "fibrous, fluffy, and frayed" *Anatomie* of Barthes's illustration.

Barthes's and Robbe-Grillet's discourses reenact ongoing acts of desire in which the name-of-the-father is deconstructed, ridiculed, and downgraded. Both autobiographies invite the reader to read them as fiction. "All this must be viewed as spoken by a character in a novel" ("Tout ceci doit être considéré comme dit par un personnage de roman"), says Barthes in his epigraph on the inside cover of the *Roland Barthes*. Thus, each work projects the discourse of the Other (as fiction) into the text where the play of characters, pronouns, and signifiers foregrounds the Other's presence. Barthes's autobiography is written in the third person, whereas Robbe-Grillet interweaves biographical events and imaginary happenings in a manner that blurs the boundaries between the two.

Since Barthes maintains that all his writings are a form of autobiography—an intellectual autobiography—he prefers, in the *Roland Barthes*, to minimize the importance of birthdates, names, progenitors, diseases, and so forth. Indeed, he opposes his civil status (*état civil*) to the corpus of his work. Pictures of his mother, his birthplace, and of grandparents (without identifying names) replace the details of the customary written ancestry. The headings of succeeding passages follow, sometimes in alphabetical arrangement, thereby calling attention to the arbitrariness of their placement, as well as to the letters themselves—A, B, C, . . . T, from which every written text is composed. These characteristics remind us of Saussure's arbitrariness of the sign that forms the basis of the signifying chain.

In addition to posing as fiction, both men's autobiographies deconstruct bourgeois ideology and the myth of nature. They focus on language, using linguistics and psychoanalysis, in order to demonstrate that everybody's mother tongue is a repository of unconscious values. "Nature," says Barthes, "is sociality in its most oppressive form, immobilized . . . in 1963, *the imaginary* was a vaguely Bachelardian term (*EC* [*Essais Critiques*], 214); but in 1970 (*S/Z*, 17), it has been rebaptized and its meaning has become entirely Lacanian (deformed even)"; ("la *Nature*, c'est la socialité dans ce qu'elle a d'oppressif, d'immobile . . . *imaginaire*, 1963, n'est qu'un terme vaguement bachelardien (*EC*, 214); mais en 1970 (*S/Z*, 17), le voilà rebaptisé, passé tout entier au sens lacanien (même déformé)").[9]

Bourgeois ideology has always claimed to be natural, that is, the logical outgrowth of language and nature—a nature whose representation is alleged to be transparent, whereas, in fact, language, nature, and things are always opaque. Whereas Barthes's works deconstruct the myth of the natural (*Mythologies*), Robbe-Grillet's works strive to duplicate nature's opacity even as they devalue the simplistic currencies of bourgeois values and of the ready-made. "Consciousness," says Robbe-Grillet, "is structured like our language" ("la conscience est structurée comme notre langage").[10] To say this is perhaps to assert the self-evident, because, in essence, our perception of reality depends on the sign-system that is used to describe it. In the final analysis, both men demonstrate that all values are man-made, that all sign-systems oppose nature, and, that, therefore, the language of autobiography is as removed from reality as the language of fiction. Robbe-Grillet's critiques of bourgeois order and of the myth of nature echo Barthes's distaste for the sticky insidiousness of ideology and its pervasive arrogance. "It is not very useful to say 'dominant ideology,'" says Barthes, "because it is a pleonasm: ideology is nothing more than an idea in its dominant form. . . . But, from a subjective point of view I can improve on it by saying: *arrogant ideology*" ("Il n'est pas très utile de dire 'idéologie dominante,' car c'est un pléonasme: l'idéologie n'est rien d'autre que l'idée en tant qu'elle domine. . . . Mais je puis renchérir subjectivement et dire: *idéologie arrogante*").[11]

Like the *Roland Barthes, Le Miroir qui revient* contains childhood reminiscences and adult commentaries. Robbe-Grillet juxtaposes fragments of memory, myth, history, and the imagination in order to define himself and his values by referring, among other things, to the quasi-fictitious life of a certain Henri de Corinthe—a mythical character whose presence can be traced to the legend of "la fiancée de Corinthe" that Jules Michelet describes in *La Sorcière*, a historical fiction of witchcraft from the Middle Ages to the mid-eighteenth century.[12] In fact, Henri de Corinthe becomes an alter ego and a mythical Other for Robbe-Grillet. It is apposite to note, in passing, that Barthes's book on Michelet and *La Sorcière* are books that Robbe-Grillet greatly admires. Moreover, in asserting that he has never spoken of anyone but himself, Robbe-Grillet maintains that fiction is a truer portrait of the writer than autobiography: "In the final analysis, fiction is an expedient that is more *personal* than the alleged sincerity of confession" ("Le biais de la fiction est, en fin de compte, beaucoup plus *personnel* que la prétendue sincérité de l'aveu").[13] Robbe-Grillet believes that his work consists in relating fables and in replacing the elements of his biography with figural motifs which he calls *des opérateurs*, a thematics that is a more accurate reflection of an author's self than a consciously projected and therefore distorted portrayal could be.[14] "Once again," says Robbe-Grillet, "it is within fiction that I venture forth." ("C'est encore dans une fiction que je me hasarde ici").[15]

A recurring mirror may be viewed as the code image of reflexive writing, of an art that mirrors itself. "As soon as it thinks itself," says Barthes, "language becomes corrosive," ("Dès qu'il se pense, le langage devient corrosif").[16] Reflexive art, which is nonmimetic, undermines the alleged realism of the natural world and of the mimetic art that claims to mirror it. Indeed, Robbe-Grillet's fictions devalue the real in favor of imaginary constructions, because fiction, as a metalanguage, enables us to understand the autobiographical language of the self. Since no sign-system is the reality it purports to signify, its analogical signs and images enable us to apprehend the artist's self projected on the mind-screen of his fantasy world. One aspect of this fantasy world is the materiality of language, of the text as body and the body as text. It is, on the one hand, the construction of the self, and, on the other, an incestuous game played with the mother tongue. Desire motivates the game, pleasure sustains it, and bliss rewards it. Barthes's "pleasure of the text," like Robbe-Grillet's "recurring mirror," is the voice and the muzzle that cuts and grates and comes. The text is not only reflexive, it is a metaphorical Other playing with the mother while acknowledging, albeit rejecting, the name-of-the-father. The Law and its prohibitions, be they sexual, social, or artistic, are transcended by embedding the Other and the mother together as text, united and indissoluble—beyond taboo—where they speak as though one, united in a blissful and enchanting embrace.

Barthes's fragmented texts and Robbe-Grillet's discontinuous fictions reflect their concerted endeavor to subvert mimesis and encratic language. Their systematic deconstruction of the arrogance of ideology and their devaluation of *doxa* are a rejection of paternalistic thinking and the alleged authority of nature with which such thinking buttresses itself. They repudiate the castrating influence of the Law, advocating pleasure in its place—the pleasure of a transcendence through which the repressive power of the *non/nom du père* is discarded so that the self can assert a new and untrammeled identity. "This imagery encompasses the entire parental field," says Barthes, "and, acting as a medium, puts me in contact with my body's 'id'" ("Embrassant tout le champ parental, l'imagerie agit comme un médium et me met en rapport avec le 'ça' de mon corps").[17]

Robbe-Grillet's works consistently subvert the Law. The forms of his fiction oppose the normative and the content of his novels regularly offends certain readers. The polysemia of his writing replaces characters, plot, and suspense with generative themes, discontinuity, and play. He devalues mimesis in favor of autonomous sign-systems whose purpose is to rival nature, not copy it. Robbe-Grillet believes that to play with language and its encoded values is to assert a modicum of freedom. To break the constraints of the literary canon is to attack the Law. Order, he says, encourages rigidity in thinking and fascism in politics, whereas disorder is a source of freedom, ferment, and originality. When forced to choose between order and disorder, Robbe-Grillet always comes down on the side of disorder.[18]

> I came to realize quite naturally [says Robbe-Grillet] that experimenting with the problematic materials of fiction and its contradictions was, for me, . . . the most propitious arena in which to foreground, in its permanent state of disequilibrium, the fatal struggle between order and freedom, that is, the insoluble conflict between rational classification and subversion, otherwise known as disorder.
>
> Mais l'expérimentation problématique de la matière romanesque et de ses contradictions s'imposait à moi tout naturellement . . . comme le champ le plus propice pour mettre en scène dans son déséquilibre permanent cette lutte à mort de l'ordre et de la liberté, ce conflit insoluble du classement rationnel et de la subversion, autrement nommée désordre.[19]

For Barthes, as for Robbe-Grillet, "incoherence is preferable to an order that deforms" ("l'incohérence est préférable à l'ordre qui déforme").[20] The emergence of disorder within an oppressive or deforming order is a source of pleasure, and it is the pursuit of such pleasure that generates works such as *Fragments d'un discours amoureux* and *La Belle captive.* The body of the text—*la belle captive*—and the mother tongue are metaphors, the veiled projections of the Other that enable the author to indulge in fantasies of the imaginary. This knotty (naughty) discourse asserts its independence from the father, by flaunting literary canons and normative codes by, in effect, indulging in metaphorical and linguistic incest.

Homonyms, as metaphors, as we have already noted, are useful agents that enable us to unveil the workings of the unconscious. If we play with the word "knot," meaning a tangle, and the word "naughty," meaning bad, we can approximate the dual function of metaphor in discourse. Our knotty joke is indeed an incestuous one, and it enables us to understand that language veils the impulses of the unconscious, that is, desire.

Freud formulated "the pleasure principle" then countered it with *Beyond the Pleasure Principle.* Indeed, as a Freudian, Lacan saw in "the death instinct" the manifestation of the injurious and castrating presence of the primal repression. Barthes's and Robbe-Grillet's works assimilate these premises and limitations. For them a "readerly text" is paternalistic, whereas a "writerly" one is incestuous. For example, *S/Z*, a "writerly text," is Barthes's rewriting of the father text, a rejection of castration—the projection of a voice that thwarts the once inviolate determinism of the Law and of the knot of castration. The letter "*Z*," says Barthes, is the letter of deviance.[21] It is the deformed mirror image of the letter *S*, the sign of castration and, in Honoré de Balzac's *Sarrazine*, of the castrato. "Writerly texts" incorporate the presence of the Other, thereby transcending the "death instinct." They become a source of bliss, and bliss, says Barthes, "is not what *answers* the call of desire (or satisfies it), but whatever astonishes it, excedes it, baffles and diverts it" ("la jouissance, ce n'est pas ce qui *répond* au désir (le satisfait), mais ce qui le surprend, l'excède, le déroute, le dérive").[22]

If the "readerly text" provides pleasure, and the "writerly text," in astonishing us, is a source of bliss, then the projection of the Other, as text, has to be incestuous because this union with the mother is a deliberate flaunting and exorcism (catharsis) of the trauma of the primal repression. By regluing the fragments of the self on the mirror and calling them "another," we recognize our inherent duality, the presence of the unconscious, of desire, and of death.[23] This reenactment of the primal scene, as a transgression, moves "beyond pleasure" and "the death-wish" into realms of play and consciousness where new, unexpected, and productive encounters act as defamiliarizing agents. In writing the body and in acknowledging desire, the play of the text and of language deconstructs itself and the unconscious. This freedom is astonishing and its bafflement is bliss.

Chapter 9

Alain Robbe-Grillet: Fantasy as Discourse of the Other

The fact that the phallus is a signifier means that it is in the place of the Other that the subject has access to it. But since this signifier is only veiled, as ratio of the Other's desire, it is this desire of the Other as such that the subject must recognize, that is to say, the other in so far as he is himself a subject divided by the signifying Spaltung.

—*Jacques Lacan,*
"The signification of the phallus"

Because every conscious narration veils an accompanying discourse that is unconscious, all speech is fantasy. If tropes veil a reality that lies hidden beneath the subject's utterances, be they verbal or written, then the Real is that unverbalized and repressed dimension of every discourse that accompanies its overt expression. Accordingly, the conscious portion of narration, in relation to its unconscious dimension, can only be a fanciful and, at best, approximate excrescence of the ego. This is what Barthes means by style, that is, the attempt by the writer to assert an identity through idiosyncratic writing. Barthes prefers the terms *écriture* and *scripteur* because they engage us in conscious narrative processes, whereas the words "style" and "author" *imply* unconscious emanations of the self that pass for discourse but do nothing to unite the conscious self with the unconscious one.[1] As long as the two remain separate, the manifest discourse must, by definition, remain a discourse of fantasy.

The discourse of D. H. Lawrence's Christ in *The Escaped Cock* strives for a melding of the id and the ego, an ego that is illumined by "the dark sun" of the unconscious. And Hemingway's *Garden of Eden* concludes with the flawless narration of the subject who experiences the coalescing of the two voices. Indeed, Barthes's *Roland Barthes* consciously exploits the discourse of the Other, thereby demonstrating that all language is fiction. In a similar context Derrida speaks of the gap between the signifier and the signified and of the play of language, even as J. Hillis Miller alludes to its "lateral dance."[2] Indeed, poststructuralists refer to the autonomy of language, to the self-contained nature of the signifying chain, to the fact that words are not the objects, people, places, and concepts they are supposed to represent. The lateral play within words and meanings, as well as their connotations and slippages, suggest that language has an internal dynamism that transgresses the semantic expectations of grammar and syntax. These syntactical transgressions also challenge the Law, but such challenges are, at best, sporadic. In emphasizing man's dependence on language Nietzsche once said that God was not dead because we still believe in grammar, and Derrida has accused Lacan of relying on a transcendental signifier because his "letter of the Law" is contained within "the letter of the unconscious."[3] Lacan, however, is probably not referring to the transcendence of the *non/nom du père*, but only to the presence of this Law as a symptom—the manifestation of things as they are, not as they should be.[4] The fact that Barthes's autobiography overrides the discourse of the Other by engaging in its conscious subversion demonstrates the possibility of moving beyond the transcendence of the phallus. Barthes, however, is an exception to the rule. He incorporates allusions to Lacan while playing with Lacanian concepts, his own autobiography, and images of the unconscious. Whereas most writers and readers do not address the Other directly, a hyperconscious Barthes manipulates this discourse in order to make us aware of its determining presence.

If language is fantasy because reality is elsewhere, and the signifier is not the signified, then language, although it veils the Other, also denotes itself. But its representational value is, at best, approximate, and, at worst, suspect. If suspect, the reality of the world is an illusion because the signifying systems we use to apprehend it determine our perceptions of it. Saussurian linguistics enables us to study language and the values encoded in language, even as Freudian theory enables us to speak of the unconscious in ways that were not possible before his time.

Freud's exploration of dreams reveals that the dream work is fantasy verging on the fantastic because we see and experience people, places, time, images, relationships, and situations that contradict the reasoned and rational continuity of our waking lives. Indeed, dreams fulfill the various definitions of fantasy and the fantastic that have proliferated in the past several decades. W. R. Irwin says that we dream the impossible, Eric S. Rabkin says that there are 180-degree reversals from reality, and Rosemary Jackson says that there are subversive episodes that get by the "censor."[5] Tzvetan Todorov states that dreams enable us to suspend disbelief in order to "live" realistically within the fantastic, as though it were true.[6] While dreaming we feel that experience is real (hence the suspension of disbelief), and it isn't until the nightmare awakens us or we remember the dream that we acknowledge its distance from the realism of consciousness because the events in the dream are perceived as impossible, reversed, subversive, and unbelievable.

The alleged incoherence of dreams is said to violate the norms of realism that regulate our waking lives. It may be interesting to note in passing, as Kathryn Hume points out, that realism in literature is a relatively recent phenomenon that began with the Enlightenment, culminated in the nineteenth century with the rise of science, and is now on the wane because the certainties of science are themselves uncertain.[7] The theory of relativity, quantum physics, Heisenberg's uncertainty principle, and chaos theory suggest that the laws of nature are often random, haphazard, and unpredictable. Doubt, discontinuity, chance, polysemy, play, plurivocalism, transgression, circularity, abyssal effects, and self-conscious reflexivity are all at work in contemporary writing and postmodern thinking. Marginality is stressed even as metafiction focuses on the story of telling instead of on the telling of a story. As language is foregrounded, plot is devalued and writing (the exploration of the creative process) becomes increasingly self-conscious.

It is this heightened awareness of the writing process that Bruce Kawin defines as "the mind of the novel," that is, works that mime the workings of the mind because they are hyperconscious of their internal generative dynamics.[8] The study of the uses of language in art, film, linguistics, and writing, provides insights into the unconscious organization of the creative act. Reflexive writing is frequently a mirror of the mind—a mind that is conscious of the fact that it is thinking. Specular effects, the present tense, and the subversion of the canon of realism suggest that storytelling is not the prime concern of metafiction. Its incessant babble and compulsion to engage in discursive genres is one of the symptoms of the *Fort!/Da!* Whenever a narrative weave manifests itself, be it realistic or reflexive, we may be sure that the Other is always also speaking.

Linguistics, psychoanalysis, and postmodern writing all focus on language. In many contemporary fictions, such as Robert Coover's *Spanking the Maid*, language, to the exclusion of expected order, character, and suspense, is both hero and heroine, master and servant. Indeed, many postmodern writers are more interested in exploring the creative process than in fabricating plots. Samuel Beckett's trilogy is one example among many that devalues realism. Robbe-Grillet's generative themes in *Topology of a Phantom City*, Italo Calvino's aborted plots in *If on a Winter's Night a Traveler*, in addition to his medieval fantasies, and his "cosmicomics," blend the detective genre with science fiction in order to explore new worlds of fantasy, thereby simultaneously emphasizing ontology and epistemology. Brian McHale asserts that modernism, the detective novel as a genre, and ontology belong together and that postmodernism, science fiction, and epistemology form another triad; but the works themselves display no such exclusive categories.[9] Robbe-Grillet's *Djinn*, for example, is a detective novel that is also science fiction. Although this novel is reflexive, parodic, and postmodern it also addresses ontological and epistemological concerns. The most revealing feature in all this is that reflexive writing and fantasy manifest a natural affinity.

In the postmodern era it is language that has become fantastic. Fantasy is interesting not because it renders implausible worlds plausible, but because, as in Jorge Luis Borges's work, it explores the metaphysical labyrinths of language. "Pierre Menard, Author of the Quixote" maintains that it is possible to rewrite this celebrated novel word for word in the twentieth century and, in doing so, make it a richer work.[10] This achievement, were it possible, would be fantastic, but that is perhaps not the point. The point is that language changes and that we can now have two simultaneous readings, the later one being the richer of the two. The shift here is away from authorial intention to reader response, a shift that also fits the Lacanian mold. The role of the audience is not to worry whether fantasy is realistic, or plausible, or intended, or reversed, or subversive, or impossible but whether it can reveal something about death and desire and freedom and the cry of a lost Eden. Such are the affective states that prompt the creative imagination to weave the strands of the unconscious into carpets of fantasy.

However, without desire bliss would be impossible because the discourse of the Other is a generative system spinning metaphorical worlds out of the magma of the primal repression. For Lacan, repression is the origin of unconscious desire—a desire that manifests itself in the language of fiction. In this context, Sheherazade is the archetypal storyteller whose tales, night after night, like the genie emerging from the lamp, performed an extraordinary task: they kept death at bay. For Lacan, keeping death at bay is the function of all discourse. As long as Sheherazade keeps telling stories, her life is secure. Even as they prolong her life, her tales are also a demonstration of language at work, of the law of the phallus (the Vizir who reigns over her), of language veiling death, and of repetition that is designed to keep her alive. She, like the rest of us, talks incessantly, speaking of desire, so that death—the ultimate encounter—will not prematurely silence the cry, the babble, the discourse, the dialog, the sound, the fury, the nothing.

Fantasy, as discourse, is the manifestation of the presence of the Other. Discourse fills the void, and it is language—the ongoing, incessant stream of tropological veilings—that reveals the latent content of desire. This discourse, by nature, is subversive, discontinuous, reversed, and impossible. Fantastic worlds, however, are not a prerequisite. Even ordinary language can reveal the presence of the Other. All that is required, in order to transform a realistic or "readerly" text into a fantasy or "writerly" text (using Barthes's terminology) is that the reader transmute its manifest realism into its latent fantasy.[11] The reader liberates the text from its realistic constraints and produces meaning by tapping into the text's veiled desire. The reader's desire and the text's desire, together, provide the orgasmic bliss to which Barthes refers. It's an encounter which, like the one on Lautréamont's dissecting table, is unpremeditated, but always beautiful, because the surrealist's aesthetic strategy posits the supremacy of dream and the play of metaphor. Nothing is more beautiful, they said, echoing Lautréamont, than the fortuitous encounter on a dissecting table of an umbrella and a sewing machine. The sexual connotations of these seemingly unrelated objects—metaphors of death and desire—are quintessential examples of Lacanian theory at work. To assert that such objects can generate a spark of excitement or even ecstasy is indeed marvelous, and the shock effect of the marvelous is what the surrealists wanted to achieve.[12]

Reality is elsewhere because the manifest discourse hides a latent desire. If the manifest discourse mirrors Reality, then, as a projected fantasy of desire, it necessarily veils the Other. The juxtapositions of surrealism demonstrate that, within the realm of the unconscious, opposites coexist, continuously: dream and reality, life and death, past and present. It is this blend of contradictory impulses that makes language fantastic because the presence of the Other always asserts itself as fantasy.

In the postmodern era we don't know whether to believe in the representational possibilities of language or not. We hesitate between its mimetic properties and language as a closed, self-contained system that can signify only itself. We hesitate because we are uncertain. If we assimilate an event and explain it by natural causes it ceases to be fantastic, but if we can no longer explain what happens because it defies our experience or the laws of nature—because in passing over into the world of the supernatural, it either defies credulity or it persuades us that unusual happenings are the result of unknown or superior forces—then our hesitation gives the fantastic a designated space.[13] This moment or this space of hesitation between the real and the unreal, between belief and disbelief, between knowing and not knowing corresponds to Todorov's definition of the fantastic, but with one important difference: he applies it to so-called real fictional events whereas I am applying it to language and to metafiction.[14]

Robbe-Grillet's novels destroy classic realism because they fulfill Rabkin's requirement for a 180-degree reversal from reality. It is not only the structural circularity and timeless simultaneity that give Robbe-Grillet's fictions a fantastic aura, it is also the denial of mimesis that defines them as metafiction, giving them the status of an artifact. They are artifacts that flaunt their independence by calling attention to themselves instead of to the world they seem to be representing. Instead of imitating nature, they rival it. Despite its artificial status, metafiction, like realism, functions on two simultaneous levels. Realism believes in mimesis and defines departures from it as fantastic, whereas metafiction subverts mimesis. Its first level denies realism thereby ushering in fantasy whereas the second level addresses the discourse of the Other. Contrary to Irwin's assertion that fantasy is playing "the game of the impossible,"[15] metafiction is playing the game of the possible. In the world of metafiction the fantastic is the norm and the writer's freedom is a source of poetic license. Furthermore, once we accept the possibility of reversal and the freedom of the artist to write with desire in pursuit of bliss (Barthes's *jouissance*), we also eliminate Todorov's hesitation. We abolish it with one stroke because language is arbitrary (Saussure), metafiction is artifact (Waugh), and its characters are not real and do not pretend to be.

Donald Barthelme's *Dead Father* is one example among many of a character in a novel who does not fulfill the reader's expectations of conventional flesh and blood realism. However, on the second level (desire), language's connotations propel us away from metafiction (the first level) into ourselves (which is the world of so-called realism). On this level, the discourse of the Other functions metaphorically and continues to arouse uncertainty: do we read it on the discursive level of mimetic denial and reversal (metafiction), or do we dwell on the repetitive imagery in order to uncover the Real, which is the discourse of the Other? These are not mutually exclusive strategies, but two different ways of reading desire, and both are subversive. The subversion of realism, as Jackson reminds us, is one of the cornerstones of the fantastic.

Metafiction is subversive because it undermines the ideology of realism, *doxa*, and encratic language (the arrogance of ideology), whereas the discourse of the Other is subversive because it foregrounds desire and the imagery of the unconscious. Both are by definition fantastic, but before analyzing language as the decentered artifact of the Other, let us look at the devices of Robbe-Grillet's metafiction that subvert the language of realism. For example, the detective genre requires that a murder occur at the beginning of the novel and that the murderer be apprehended before it ends. In *Les Gommes* Robbe-Grillet denies these expectations by having the murder take place at the end instead of at the beginning.[16] The reader's expectations are again denied in *Le Voyeur* because parts 2 and 3 contest part 1 in order to emphasize imaginary structures and the creative process.[17] They reorder and nullify the sequence of events developed in part 1, thereby erasing guilt, realism, and representation. The realism of events in *La Jalousie* is contradicted by circularity and simultaneity and the text contests itself as it foregrounds the creative process.[18]

Robbe-Grillet's works subvert the codes of classic realism even as they exaggerate, parody, and undermine cultural clichés, myth, nature, and essentialist thinking. Readers conditioned to expect conventional story-telling may consider his devices fantastic, but this is true only in relation to realism. Once we accept the subversion and reversal of realism, we read Robbe-Grillet's novels as metaphorical artifacts and we situate their fantasies within a context that is both corrosive and a manifestation of desire. The reversal is not without its perils because, despite the metafictionists' endeavors to construct a separate fictional reality, the connotations of words, sentences, and paragraphs drag us, sometimes screaming, back into the world of personal experience. This emphasis on autofiction, as the preceding chapter demonstrated, is a new dimension in Robbe-Grillet's projected series of *Romanesques* (*Le Miroir qui revient*, *Angélique ou l'enchantement*, *Les Derniers jours de Corinthe*, and perhaps the ones to follow). He is now tracking the *analogons*, the tropes of psychic experience that seem to explain the persistence of certain metaphorical structures in his writings and in his films.

Death, desire, and the Other are always embedded in language because tropical language veils the unconscious. Even such highly self-conscious writing as metafiction is not impervious to the unconscious connotations of metaphor and metonymy. However, if all discourse, including autobiography, is fiction—particularly autofiction—then a conscious manipulation of the text's unconscious foregrounds the discourse of the Other. This discourse deconstructs itself by calling the reader's attention to the way metafiction foregrounds language and desire.

Fiction (fantasy), when coupled with autobiography, has the power to link the conscious and unconscious systems. Besides, Robbe-Grillet's need to repeat, rather than simply remember repressed material, illustrates the need to reproduce and work through events from the past as if they were present. There is an obsession with sado-erotic scenes in which young women are tortured, tender flesh is violated, and mythical virgins are assaulted. In *Le Voyeur* the reader is led to presume that Jacqueline/Violette is tied, burned with cigarettes, drowned, and her body mutilated by crabs. In *Projet pour une révolution à New York* a giant saw rips through the vagina of a naked woman. In *Topologie d'une cité fantôme* all but one of the virgins swimming in the sea are killed with arrows. In *Souvenirs du triangle d'or* burning candles are stuffed up a woman's vagina. *La Belle captive* is carried off to a secret room where the narrator performs clandestine experiments on her body. In *La Maison de rendez-vous* a young woman is cut up and her flesh served in an exotic Chinese dish, and so on.

Robbe-Grillet is not unaware of this obsessive motif, but he is surprised that feminists are upset with his constant maiming of women's bodies, arguing that not all of his women are victims. A . . . the heroine in *La Jalousie* is a force to be reckoned with. Lady Ava runs the Blue Villa in *La Maison de rendez-vous*, the metaphorical house of the imagination with which she structures the novel's diegesis as she lies dying. Robbe-Grillet's female vampires are formidable creatures who subjugate men. Sara Zeitgeist, in the film *La Belle captive*, is a free and powerful woman who rides a motorcycle dressed in black leather, and she directs the actions of men dressed in black uniforms who obey her orders. In *Glissements progressifs du plaisir* Alice's fantasies generate the film's imagery, narrative structure, and discontinuity. One by one she seduces the lawyer, the policeman, and the cleric, thus asserting her power over men and women and her ability to disrupt social codes. Clearly Robbe-Grillet's women can be very assertive, but typically they occupy dual roles, symbolized perhaps in *La Belle captive* (the novel) by Vanadé who is both "victorious" and "vanquished." Robbe-Grillet borrows the theme of the victorious and vanquished woman from Michelet who asserts that historically women have been both virgins and whores, healers and witches, victims and vampires.[19] Although Robbe-Grillet also exploits the clichés of male fantasies and cultural violence as metafictional tropes there is a repetitive sado-erotic pattern that is not without its affective charge.

I have argued elsewhere that such scenes are not realistic because the devices of metafiction that take them out of the mimetic frame are a subversion of realism.[20] On the metafictional level these scenes exaggerate and parody the conventions of horror realism. Nonetheless, many readers find it difficult, sometimes impossible, to distance themselves critically in order to read a text as metafiction. If, however, we read these scenes as the discourse of the Other, then, despite Robbe-Grillet's parody and conscious manipulation of sado-erotic themes, the repetitions suggest that he is wrestling with desire, the symbolic *Fort!/Da!*

Because desire and the discourse of the Other respond to the pleasure principle, it is appropriate that we turn next to the sado-erotic imagery of Robbe-Grillet's tropological discourse in order to pursue its manifestations. His tropes are so charged with eroticism and violence and so offensive to some readers that we must surmise that he wants to shock the sensibilities of a bourgeois audience. The covert sexual violence of *le nouveau roman* becomes progressively overt in *le nouveau nouveau roman*. Explicit scenes of abduction, rape, torture, and murder (although canceled by the strategies of metafiction) remain nonetheless, hauntingly vivid. Indeed, Robbe-Grillet's introduction to the complete works of the Marquis de Sade reveals more than casual interest in such matters, particularly when we compare Sade's writings to his.[21] It is as though Robbe-Grillet were determined to liberate the images of erotic violence from the dungeons of our unconscious. Although he has argued that exposure to such images will free us from our nightmares and obsessions,[22] the sado-eroticism in his novels and films is so persistent that we wonder about the latent meaning of these repetitions.

The manifest content focuses on women's bodies: flesh, blood, sex, torture, and death. Although the virgin/vampire, victorious/vanquished themes dramatize stereotypes of myth, literature, and culture, things get more complicated, particularly in the realm of autofiction. In *Le Miroir qui revient* Robbe-Grillet remembers a pet bat that his mother kept inside her blouse and which, occasionally, when guests were present, crawled into plain view on her neck. As a small boy he had long curls and his mother dressed him in girl's clothes. He also recounts the episode when he refused to drink his milk saying he wanted to drink mother milk (*lait Maman*).[23]

Robbe-Grillet also writes that as a child he had nightmares of the sea and he stresses "the phonetic resemblance between wave (*la vague*) and vagina (*le vagin*): and also the etymology of the word 'nightmare' (*cauchemar*), whose root (*mare*), in Latin, signifies the sea (*la mer*), but which, in Dutch, designates the phantoms of the night."[24] In French *la mer* (the sea) is a homonym for *la mère* (the mother). Ironically, his mother would comfort him when he awoke screaming from his nightmares—nightmares that seem to have been generated at least in part by her (*la mer*) and by the "vagina" (the latent meaning of the manifest images of the sea and the waves). How is a boy child to cope with the ambivalent feelings elicited by the presence of the comforting yet threatening mother?

We should also note that Robbe-Grillet's father is not cast in the role of authoritarian figure. He manufactured cardboard boxes for dolls and, Robbe-Grillet tells us, his earliest erotic fantasies were with doll-like figurines.[25] Catherine, his young bride is described as a doll-like woman whom strangers persisted in misidentifying as his daughter—a variant on the nymphet syndrome that Irina Ionesco's photographs illustrate in their collaborative volume *Temple aux miroirs*. Despite this trail which, in theory, is an unconscious one, the ambiguous and repetitive imagery of Robbe-Grillet's adult fantasies confirms the traces we find in *Le Miroir qui revient*. However,

Robbe-Grillet is too sly an artist not to have inserted these passages into the book deliberately. Like Michelet, he is fascinated with blood, and, throughout his works, he strives to give this liquid its appropriate mythical resonance: woman, nature, the tides, lunar cycles.[26] For both men blood connotes the sea, but for Robbe-Grillet the seashore also connotes freedom and woman. The sea and the seashore are thus privileged if ambivalent places, on the one hand connoting nightmares and death and, on the other, purity and freedom. This ambivalence is dramatized on the sandy beach of the film *La Belle captive* as the free-spirited and ethereal woman dances in a gown of white lace and is then violated by the men in black.

Robbe-Grillet is also fascinated by Michelet's description in *La Sorcière* of the recurring episode of "la fiancée de Corinthe," first narrated by Phlégon, the freed slave of Hadrian (A.D. 76–138). The story surfaces again in the twelfth and the sixteenth centuries. Michelet describes a young Athenian, a pagan, who goes to Corinth to meet his fiancée, unaware of the fact that since his betrothal her family has become Christian and her mother has promised her virginity to God. Despite this vow, the young couple's passion overcomes the bride's reticence and she succumbs to the man's amorous advances. A fourth-century Roman variant of this encounter describes a young Corinth weakened and emasculated by the impure blood of his once pure and now deflowered fiancée.[27]

"La fiancée de Corinthe" is no doubt the backdrop for Robbe-Grillet's description, in *Angélique ou l'enchantement*, of precocious sexual games in an old barn by the Brittany seashore—games that rehearse the now familiar ritual and reversible roles of dominance/submission. A naked and vulnerable Angélique requests that she be bound hand and foot. She then asks the boy to stick a finger into her vagina, and when, after exploring the orifice, he withdraws his finger covered with menstrual blood, she says he has deflowered her. After the boy unties her hands and feet she threatens to denounce him. She coerces him into licking the blood off his fingers, saying that there is a curse on it and that he will be impotent forever.[28] In view of the striking similarities with the legend of "la fiancée de Corinthe," Corinthe as the projection of Robbe-Grillet's persona, and his allusions to blood, the sea, and lunar cycles, are we to believe this account of early sexuality? Is the trauma of this initiation to be taken seriously? Should we graft Angélique's threat of impotence onto the impotence of the primal repression? Are Robbe-Grillet's repeated scenes describing the abuse of women's bodies in an eroticized context designed to overcome this double trauma? Are the vampire/victim scenes of his adult fantasies the composite images of fear and lust, and of nightmare and desire? Did these juvenile games really occur, or is Robbe-Grillet fabricating an episode with a twelve-year-old girl in order to duplicate and foreground the mythical episodes that Michelet, Goethe, and others refer to? The details of his autofiction read like desire—the "enchantment" of *Angélique*'s subtitle.

Such speculations are both tantalizing and titillating, but there is more. Several days after the episode of the children's clandestine sex games in the ancient barn, Angélique is recovered from the sea, drowned and naked. Foul play, accident, suicide? Why naked? If it was murder, who did it?[29] The parallels between Jacqueline/Violette, the thirteen-year-old girl of *Le Voyeur* and the Angélique of Robbe-Grillet's autofiction are all too clear. Indeed, part 1 of *Le Voyeur* recreates one possible hypothesis for Angélique's death: the murderer was a traveling watch salesman, a hypothesis obliterated in parts 2 and 3 as Mathias retraces the figure eight in the passage known as *"le double circuit."* The reality of murder is short-circuited even as the blank, enigmatic white page at the end of part 1 leaves the space between fiction and reality unsolved. Whatever happened, Angélique's death, when combined with her erotic games, and Robbe-Grillet's childhood nightmares and remembrances, provides the leitmotif against which he generates his adult fantasies. It is strange, perhaps, that the need to symbolically recover the "lost breast" (the mother) should elicit such violence. Still, the bicycle of desire, "la belle machine" of *Le Voyeur* and *Glissements progressifs du plaisir*, follows the circuitous traces of the Imaginary which, in *Le Voyeur* gives us an exaggerated movie poster of a colossus bending a submissive woman toward his desire. But the ambivalence remains, and the image of a seductive, dominant, and vampiric woman coexists with the image of her frailty. The reversals of desire—the fragmented image of the Other—are no less a theme of the fantastic than the formal reversal that transforms realism into metafiction.

The language and imagery of Robbe-Grillet's fiction connote both woman as vampire and woman as victim—Vanadé, victorious and vanquished. When language is foregrounded and when fiction becomes conscious of its own creative processes, that is, when it becomes reflexive, it develops characteristics that downgrade the traditional roles of character, conflict, psychology, story, and denouement. It is the generative themes, the proliferation of stories, the textual polysemy, and the paronomasia that, in subverting the coded conventions of fiction, push it toward fantasy. The writer no longer tells stories, rather, he explores the story of telling, and it is this reversal of the canon that engenders the fantastic. However, the story of telling goes hand in glove with the exploration of the creative process which, in turn, unveils the discourse of the Other.

Robbe-Grillet's metaphorical discourse focuses obsessively and repetitively on woman, both as fictive body and as sexual object, and it is this reenactment of his preferred imagery, within the scene of writing, that displaces realism and replaces it with fantasy. The irony is that the *analogons* become the new reality, and this new realism—Breton's surrealism—may, as the surrealists claimed it would, help to resolve life's contradictions. This is the context within which Robbe-Grillet develops the notions of freedom and bondage, inside and outside, victim and assassin. He structures a dialectic of opposites, a dialogue of contradictions that are, nevertheless, profoundly related. If the *langue* of bourgeois interrogators imprisons, then the artist's *parole* has a liberating force. Says Robbe-Grillet:

> It is not a question of closing my eyes to sex and violence, nor to condemn them, but to organize them within a living *parole* . . . what's needed . . . is not to speak about these matters, but to *voice them,* i.e., to invent a discourse that will control the pulsive forces, the images . . . of violence which, without our knowing it, threaten to overwhelm us. It is the organization of these images that structures the space within which my freedom asserts itself.[30]

To voice these stereotypes in fictional form is to provide an outlet from the cultural prisons that govern our thinking. To loosen the grip of social taboos on our daily lives is to provide alternative, perhaps freer, ways of dealing with them. Robbe-Grillet believes that the dramatization of this repressed material is a form of catharsis that will reverse the sexist attitudes of paternalism.

Subversion and catharsis are thus two essential facets of Robbe-Grillet's discourse. Metafiction subverts the canon because it draws our attention to its own internal self-regulating machinery. This subversion also depends on cultural stereotypes that are inflated and then parodied. Robbe-Grillet foregrounds units of establishment ideology and undermines them through exaggeration and distortion, thereby generating a discourse of fantasy. He plays with cultural myths striving for a reversal that will fragment the reader's perception of a unified whole. His images violate normative codes even as diegesis turns plausibility and verisimilitude upside down. Robbe-Grillet's ritual violence, like Sade's, uses the wrong side of things and the wrong side of words. It is because ideology is securely fixed that this overthrow has meaning. To play with sex and violence, to parody phallocentrism, as Robbe-Grillet does, is to subvert and at the same time to reinvent reality. An artist interested in fantasy and play derives his strength, his freedom, and his pleasure from such parodic acts. Robbe-Grillet's writing thus casts desire and fantasy as metaphorical actors on the scene of writing staging the discourse of metafiction as a discourse of the Other.

CONCLUSION: BETWEEN THE FOLDS OF METAFICTION AND MIMESIS (OR) WRITING THE READER WITH POSTMODERN VESTMENTS

Who will allege then that the Clothes *do not put the truth itself onstage? that is, the possibility of the true as a denuding? and as a denuding of the king, the master, the father, the subjects?*
—Jacques Derrida, "Le Facteur de la vérité"

Barthes foregrounds the pleasure of the text as an acoustical function of the reader's ear. The reader must hear him- or herself writing in order to savor the material delights of intervocalic substance—a substance that cuts, grates, and comes, generating the bliss of a quasi-incestuous relationship with the mother tongue—the umbilical cord and link to the body of the text that nurtures and sustains desire.[1] The reader imprints desire onto language (his or her utterance is desire) and produces meaning with his or her *parole*, like a seamstress modeling a pattern from the whole cloth of *langue*.

The couturier, the model, the pattern, and the fabric. The joy of writing the reader is like the practice of shaping cloth to the model's form. The process covers and it exposes, simultaneously. It reveals flesh while concealing the object of desire. There is pleasure in the fold that hides and that implies the unseen. The seam is the shadow of desire. It unfolds around the quest while obscuring its direction. Scissors cut, the needle sews, and the thread of an idea hems with stitches of design. Intention governs form. But whose form and whose intention? Is it the simple, utilitarian peasant garb made for work in the fields where form and function are subordinate to sweat and toil? Or is it the fanciful and perhaps also utilitarian design of unique high fashion where the whimsy of cost and seduction play important roles? Is it the sari of India and the delicate silken wrap of color, the grass skirt of tropical islands, or the black garb of Muslim countries that often hides everything but the seduction of eyes?

Language, like the vestments of different cultures, like their clothing that conceals and reveals, is also shaped by ideology. Language may be plain, colorful, religious, profane, good, bad, and indifferent. It forms the body and it transmits the message worn by its users. Indeed, it is frequently a worn message, but I am now speaking of metaphorical language, of tropological discourse, of desire, and the veils of desire. There is also hunger, thirst, love, hate, and death. Hunger for the unknown, thirst for the afterlife, love of truth, hate of tyranny or, on a more elemental level, the urgent images of struggle in those countries oppressed by famine or political repression. The daily strategies for survival in countries where people are dying, or in which their lives are threatened, may seem unrelated to my vestimentary metaphor, but if language (the mother tongue) determines our perception of the world, then the kinds of clothing people wear and display, whether real or metaphorical, are influenced not only by climate and geography, but also by the ideology of culture.

Language, like clothing generally, is opaque, and its folds are designed to hide. Only the eyes of children may perhaps see through the obfuscations of the adult world, and only children, as both Freud and Lacan have noted, may sometimes have the naïveté to say that the king is wearing no clothes. Language, by design, tells us what to see and even how to see it. Language is the ideology of power, and it is this power, as Foucault points out, that subordinates the subjects of a culture and its language.[2] The subject of desire who is ruled by language and who wears the colors of its ideology finds it difficult to escape from the hegemony of its control. Why then did the mythic courtiers clothe the king in the transparency of illusion and why did they let him ride forth naked on his horse? Is this tale a metaphor of power and if so why was the king made to look like a horse's ass?[3]

Language, like clothes, has degrees of opacity, and it is the pretense of transparency that obscures the relationship between the word and the wor(l)d. The letter *l* creates a word of difference and it is this difference, as Saussure first argued, that alerts us to the presence of the sign. What does the king's nakedness signify and why the pretense of absent finery? Why the lure of a translucence that exposes the body, since disrobing the king, although it emphasizes the relationship, alters neither the word nor the world. His nakedness, like the letter *l*, remains phallic and erect. The phallus is there and it is useful to remember that it functions whether we see it or not. Disrobing the king is a reminder that metaphors of language hide his potency—a reminder that we are ruled by the letter of his law and the ideology of his body politic. The Law prescribes obedience and it proscribes desire.[4] It is the obedience of the king's subjects that clothes his nakedness, and only the innocence of desire sees through the cultural dissimulation. Desire, although subversive, can afford to be ingenuous. Its voice rises above the imposed and accepted blindness of convention. Desire sees the king as he is: naked, riding the horse of obedience down the streets of encoded values where the people wave their mimetic banners and the guards draw the canon of realism. Desire, however, burns the banners and explodes the canon, focusing on language as a body and on the pleasure of the text, thereby foregrounding the relationship between illusion and insight, transparency and blindness.

Language is both the mirror and the mother of desire and it produces two kinds of writing: mimetic and reflexive, if only we have eyes and ears. Eyes with which to see the colors and ears with which to hear the sounds that snuggle in the muzzle of rhetorical bliss.[5] The language of obedience (mimesis) represses the urges of felicity, whereas a language of desire (metafiction) is a force that liberates. Desire is the spark that asserts its independence. It subverts the king's secret police, his executioners, and the men who run the torture chambers of his linguistic inquisition. For the clairvoyant the king will always be naked, even when clothed. Only obedient and ignorant subjects will say that he is clothed when he is not; yet today, despite the works of Saussure, Lacan, Derrida, and others, many still believe in the transparency of language and the king's ideology.

Desire rides the naked truth but it does not move forward on the transparency of language. The nature of the signifier, the ambiguity of the signifying chain, supplementary transgressions, and the dissemination of meaning all veil the illusion of a diaphanous oneness.[6] The mimesis of classic realism—a manifestation of regal power—is now a corrupt ideology and it fails to account for the current epistemological and ontological disruptions of the king's authority. His reign is booby-trapped and the vision of linguistic truth or scientific objectivity is a minefield that only the blind would traverse. Nonetheless, those equipped with the instruments of metavision (Freud's analysis of dreams or Lacan's eliptical discourse) and the strategies of deconstruction, reader-response theory, and metafiction as a creative impulse—the process of exploring the theory of fiction through the practice of writing it—are engendering fresh insights and a new praxis that seem dystopian to many because they disrupt the expectations of mimetic clarity and the conventions of classic realism, but which, in fact, pose a utopian, albeit difficult, challenge.[7]

Utopian, because they allow us to identify encratic thinking, isolate the ideologies of power, and counter them with discourses that resist the coercive agendas of paternalism. Foucault's and Derrida's works, among others, attest their resistance to and deconstruction of logocentrism. Consequently, the arbitrary albeit motivated nature of language now allows marginalized groups to assert their solidarity, their needs, and their dreams. The new discourses are utopian insofar as new social, political, and aesthetic orders can be envisioned, ones that give disfranchised groups a higher degree of autonomy.

The monarch says "conform," "believe in God," and "imitate nature" and his subjects quickly and obediently fall in line, strive to copy reality, and listen to his word. Resistance to *doxa* has always been difficult because the philosophical systems were unequal to the task. However, postmodern discourses suggest that language and the world are both one and the same, not because language is transparent, on the contrary, but because language determines our perception of the world. The letter *l*, has always been there and it is the simultaneous sign of obedience and transgression which, like a remedy and poison (Socrates' *pharmakon*, for example), may function together, in opposition, depending on the dosage.[8] Indeed, the letter *l*, as the phallic trace of the king's authority is everywhere—the inscribed presence of his Law that regulates both ideology and the unconscious. Ideology speaks us and it speaks to us through the internalized voice of the superego, whereas the unconscious voice of the Other (Lacan's capital *O*) manifests desire in its metaphorical and metonymical disguises.[9] Today, we see the authorial subject and the subject of authority as a fragmented and decentered presence, an entity speaking in tongues that transmit the conflicting messages of authority and subservience on the one hand, and of freedom and desire on the other.

Desire, however, speaks only of itself. It has no ulterior goal and it mistrusts mimesis. Desire is ambiguous, decentered, and circular. Desire is language caught in the labyrinth of its exploratory sign-system. Desire is playful, reflexive, plurivocal, and simultaneous. Desire plays with the body of the text, clothing it (like this one) in opaque vestments. Paronomasia is a source of pleasure—a pleasure that transcends the Logos of univocal sense in favor of plurivocity.

I may already be writing the reader, inviting your collaboration, providing a context with which to generate meaning by inscribing a text whose point of departure is desire and whose goal is bliss—a text in which the slippages of pleasure have no meaning except that meaning is circulating, elliptically and circuitously, eschewing the linearity, continuity, and unity of the Idea. Desire is antiessentialist, it subverts authority, and it revels in dissemination. The *glas* and the *glue* of the glyph are everywhere, sowing/sewing their seeds with *o*'s and *e*'s and modeling their forms in the textual fields and patterns of endeavor.[10]

These enumerations will perhaps help to foreground some of the strategies of metafiction that also write the reader: the mistrust of authority, the subversion of the law, an emphasis on language as a form of free play drawing on ambiguity, traces, fragmentation, and discontinuity; the belief that meaning can be multiple, simultaneous, and reflexive; that it circulates, slipping and sliding this way and that, following the tracks of desire, pursuing obscure pleasures, listening to multiple voices, crying out that the king has no clothes, happy that the mirror of realism has been shattered, unhappy that the self has been decentered, happy that the veils of illusion are gone, unhappy that the new clothes may also be illusory.

Patricia Waugh says that "*metafiction* is a term given to fictional writing which self-consciously and systematically draws attention to its status as an artefact in order to pose questions about the relationship between fiction and reality."[11] In contrast to the canon of classic realism the practitioners of metafiction, such as the *nouveaux romanciers* in France, innovative writers in the United States, and, to a lesser degree, the authors of "magical realism" in Latin America have been accused of dehumanizing the novel, when not killing it outright. The now familiar litany of grievances concerns the lack of plot, flat characters, discontinuity, plurivocity, indeterminacy, and so forth. It is alleged that metafiction's most egregious failure is its refusal to reflect the real world. Critics of metafiction, such as Fredric Jameson, dismiss its apparent self-centered nature, its lack of historical context, and its decadence, all of which, they say, reveal a preoccupation with form that remains indifferent to world problems.[12] As far as they are concerned, you can stick metafiction in your ear and rotate it, never mind the acoustical pleasure of Barthes's text.

However, it might be useful to remember that metafiction, like a number of Picasso's paintings of Dora Maar, or *Les Demoiselles d'Avignon*, distorts reality in order to reshape our awareness of the possible. Such artistic license allows the artist and the audience to escape the death-grip of the ready-made and the cultural straitjackets of convention. If flesh-and-blood characters, plot, and setting are only artificial props for the play of language, as, for example, in Coover's *Spanking the Maid*,[13] in which the beginning of the novel repeats itself endlessly in a variety of comic permutations, then by contorting language and bending the conventions of realistic fiction, the scriptor establishes language as the central concern. Indeed language—the interplay of *langue* and *parole*—becomes the main character rather than some imaginary person or persons. Insofar as the reader also uses language, there is an inevitable link with the world outside the text and this is what I mean, in part, by writing the reader. In forcing this awareness of the text's use of language and the reader's, metafiction affirms a mimetic function, but differently. Some works do it better than others, for example Beckett's *Company* or *How It Is*,[14] but I think it is a mistake to try to recuperate meaning the old-fashioned way instead of deconstructing mimesis, because mimesis, as Vladimir Nabokov has noted, is just one more totalitarian system.[15] It believes in the transparency of language, it arrogates the truth of God and nature to itself, it is authoritarian, coercive, and pervasive and its symptoms are cliché, the best-seller list, the bottom line, plot, the status quo, common sense, and reality (objectively speaking, of course). Mimesis is also the house of classical humanism with its dream of reason which has animated Western society since Plato and Aristotle. However, as George Steiner puts it, this utopian house is breaking apart: "Ideas of cultural development, of inherent rationality held since ancient Greece and still intensely valid in the utopian historicism of Marx and the stoic authoritarianism of Freud . . . can no longer be asserted with much confidence."[16]

Surrealism was a reaction to the failure of reason and the intellect in preventing the calamity of World War I. Metafiction in the postmodern period, a genre that had been brewing in the modernist pots of James Joyce, Raymond Roussel, and many others is, in part, a reaction to World War II and the holocaust, but also an attempt, in concert with surrealism, to link the conscious and unconscious systems. Metafiction is thus profoundly subversive of a canon that often wears the clothes of reason but which, like the king, displays its foolish nakedness. This subversion of the king's authority pushes realism toward fantasy and it is this fantasy that helps to overthrow the old regime. Although metafiction is generally apolitical, it does have the inherent power to revise perception. In calling attention to itself as a signifying system it foregrounds the contingency of reality—the fact that meaning cannot exist outside of the signifying chain. The language we use to describe what we experience, whatever we may think about its inadequacy to do so, is, for others, the only reality of that experience. Insofar as language, as a ready-made system, also determines how we perceive experience, metafiction can nudge us away from bias, *doxa*, encratic thinking, and all the truisms that lock us into culturally conditioned behavior patterns.

To emphasize the prison-house of language is an invitation to escape from its confines. Mimetic fiction gives us the illusion that the prison is freedom, whereas metafiction imprisons us in its form(s) in order to demonstrate how arbitrary form is (any form, including mimesis). Although the intentions of metafiction are not utopian—metafiction has no agenda, since its emphasis is on the creative process, the play of language, and the freedom to oppose convention—its presence is utopian because it subverts logocentrism, deriding univocal vision, short-circuiting ideology, and mocking the serious.

The courtiers who need the transparency of mimesis and who believe in logocentrism will object to this subversion of the king's reign. They will emphasize the need for authority and tragedy, whereas in our postmodern era comedy is on the ascendance because only parody and the comic vision are able to cope with the complexity of "things falling apart," as the title to Chinua Achebe's novel suggests.[17] In this context, *Lolita*, as Lance Olsen points out, is a Janus-text.[18] It is both modern and postmodern, looking forward and backward, simultaneously, dramatizing the opposition between mimesis and fantasy through parody and destabilization. This clash of mutually exclusive worlds that turns the text into a joke illustrates Foucault's idea of a heterotopia,[19] the clash of mutually exclusive worlds that Barthelme, in *The Dead Father*, highlights by means of linguistic games, incongruities (the father is as alive as any other character), and play.[20] In such texts discursive slapstick undermines the stability of language even as the power of words to mean falls under erasure. These are the signs of Derrida's radical subversion of logocentrism and Western metaphysics. Surely, the children who mocked the king's nakedness would have believed in Derrida's derision because he is the ultimate derider. He rides the horse of deconstruction with new pomp and ceremony, hailed by approbation, but he also derides in the face of much public anger. Derrida may have redressed the king but his critics would love to redress him. He may have abolished the transparency of language but his detractors still believe in representation, and mimesis is everywhere despite the opacity of the sign.

Metafiction, like Socrates' *Pharmakon*, is one person's poison and another's remedy. For Jameson it is a symptom of indifference to history and a sign of decadence. For others, although it is a symptom of the ontological decentering of man, it is welcomed as a necessary aesthetic and philosophical discourse. For its critics, metafiction is dystopian, whereas for believers metafiction is capable of generating an epistemological force that has utopian value. Mimetic frames are transgressed through parody, reversal, and comedy. The king is ridiculed and his rule is subverted so that farce may reign. The role of puns, jokes, and wordplay in unveiling the discourse of desire cannot be overestimated, because the slippages of language reflect the configurations of desire. The unconscious—an autonomous force in search of satisfactions—veils itself in metaphor and metonymy and its horseplay is inevitable. Fantasy and the fantastic sabotage the king's canon, and desire, in alliance with the pleasure principle, ushers in a new era of the possible. Postmodernism and metafiction thus represent an interim period and texts such as *Lolita*[21] and Robbe-Grillet's *La Jalousie*[22] are Janus-like because they look backward at modernism and forward to the utopian possibilities of *L'Homme nouveau*—the new man that Robbe-Grillet and Jacques Leenhardt both allude to.[23]

None of this would be possible without the participation of the reader or her willingness to collaborate in order to produce meaning from texts that are overdetermined, circular, discontinuous, and contradictory. Because desire circulates throughout the labyrinthine streets of fiction, whenever it sees a naked king it cries out: "Look,

Ma, no clothes!" As a discourse of desire, metafiction inscribes the reader within the text, inviting him or her, as Barthelme says, to join "the ongoing circus of the mind in motion. Give me the odd linguistic trip, stutter and fall, and I will be content."[24] I hope this book will, in some future civilization, if not in the present one, or the past, allow you, dear audience, to hear bliss and to wear with pleasure the clothes of metafiction without too much self-conscious discontent.

Notes

Introduction

1. Jacques Lacan, *Écrits II* (Paris: Seuil, 1971), 112, 158–59, 232–33.

2. James M. Mellard, *Using Lacan, Reading Fiction* (Urbana: University of Illinois Press, 1991), 56.

3. Ellie Ragland-Sullivan, "The Magnetism Between Reader and Text: Prolegomena to a Lacanian Poetics," *Poetics* 13 (1984): 381.

4. Mellard, *Using Lacan*, 36.

5. Anika Lemaire, *Jacques Lacan*, trans. David Macey (London: Routledge and Kegan Paul, 1977), 54.

6. Juliet Flower MacCannell, *Figuring Lacan: Criticism and the Cultural Unconscious* (Lincoln: University of Nebraska Press, 1986), 14.

7. Jacques Lacan, *Écrits I* (Paris: Seuil, 1966), 136, 183. Subsequent references will appear as *Écrits I*.

8. Robert Con Davis, "Introduction," in *Lacan and Narration: The Psychoanalytic Difference in Narrative Theory* (Baltimore: The Johns Hopkins University Press, 1983), 848.

9. Marie Bonaparte, *The Life and Works of Edgar Allan Poe: A Psychoanalytic Interpretation*, foreword Sigmund Freud, trans. John Rodker (London: Imago, 1949).

10. Ernest Jones, *Hamlet and Oedipus* (New York: Norton, 1976).

11. For a discussion of the terms "intrinsic" and "extrinsic" see Austin Warren and René Welleck, *Theory of Literature*, 3rd rev. ed. (London: Cape, 1966).

12. Sigmund Freud, *The Interpretation of Dreams*, vol. 4 in *The Standard Edition of the Complete Psychological Works*, vols. 1–23, trans. James Strachey (London: Hogarth, 1953), 277–338.

13. MacCannell, *Figuring Lacan*, 39.

14. Raymond Federman, *Critifiction: Postmodern Essays* (Albany: State University of New York Press, 1993), 48–64.

15. See Roman Ingarden, *The Literary Work of Art: An Investigation on the Borderlines of Ontology, Logic and Theory of Literature*, trans. with an introduction by George Grabowicz (Evanston: Northwestern University Press, 1973); see also Eugene Falk, *The Poetics of Roman Ingarden* (Chapel Hill: University of North Carolina Press, 1981).

16. Mellard, *Using Lacan*, 55.

17. Peter Brooks, "The Idea of a Psychoanalytic Criticism," *Critical Inquiry* 13 (1987): 345. See Jacques Lacan, *The Four Fundamental Concepts of Psycho-Analysis*, trans. Alan Sheridan (New York: Norton, 1981), where, in addition to transference, the three other fundamental concepts of psychoanalysis are discussed, namely the unconscious, repetition, and the drive.

18. Brooks, 345.

19. Norman Holland, "The 'Unconscious' of Literature," in *Contemporary Criticism*, eds. Norman Bradbury and David Palmer (New York: St. Martin's, 1970), 131–54.

20. For a more detailed listing see Mellard, *Using Lacan*, 221–32.

21. Ferdinand de Saussure, *Cours de linguistique générale*, 3rd ed. (Paris: Payot, 1967).

22. Jacques Lacan, *Écrits: A Selection*, trans. Alan Sheridan (New York: Norton, 1977), 175. Lacan, *Écrits I*, 289. Subsequent references to these editions will appear as *Écrits*, *Écrits I*, and *Écrits II*.

23. Ibid., *Écrits*, 50–51; *Écrits I*, 136–37.

24. Ragland-Sullivan, 382.

25. Mellard, *Using Lacan*, 16–17.

26. Lacan, *Écrits*, 69; *Écrits I*, 160.

27. Roland Barthes, *Le Plaisir du texte* (Paris: Seuil, 1973), 105.

28. Lacan, *Écrits*, 156; *Écrits I*, 264.

29. Ibid.

30. Ibid., 154; 260–61.

31. Ibid., 154; 261.

32. Sigmund Freud, *Beyond the Pleasure Principle,* vol. 18 in *The Standard Edition of the Complete Psychological Works,* vols. 1–23, trans. James Strachey (London: Hogarth, 1953), 25.

33. Vincent B. Leitch, *Deconstructive Criticism: An Advanced Introduction* (New York: Columbia University Press, 1983), 209.

34. Jacques Lacan, "Seminar on 'The Purloined Letter,'" trans. Jeffrey Mehlman, in *The Purloined Poe: Lacan, Derrida, and Psychoanalytic Reading,* eds. John P. Muller and William J. Richardson (Baltimore: The Johns Hopkins University Press, 1988), 32; "Le séminaire sur 'La Lettre volée,'" in *Écrits I,* 24.

35. Jacques Derrida, "Le Facteur de la vérité," in *The Post Card,* trans. Alan Bass (Chicago: The University of Chicago Press, 1987), 443.

36. Lacan, *Écrits,* 85; *Écrits I,* 180.

37. Ibid., *Écrits,* 287; *Écrits II,* 110.

38. Freud, *Beyond the Pleasure Principle,* 39.

39. Charles Baudelaire, "Correspondances," in *Les Fleurs du mal* (Paris: Gallimard, 1961), 22.

40. Albert Camus, *Carnets I,* May 1935–Feb. 1942 (Paris: Gallimard, 1962), 25.

41. Jacques Derrida, *La Vérité en peinture* (Paris: Flammarion, 1978), 183.

42. Lacan, *Écrits,* 65; *Écrits I,* 155.

43. Ibid.

44. Sigmund Freud, *Jokes and Their Relation to the Unconscious,* vol. 8 in *The Standard Edition of the Complete Psychological Works,* vols. 1–23, trans. James Strachey (London: Hogarth, 1953), 22.

45. Ernest Hemingway, *The Sun Also Rises* (New York: Scribner, 1954), 239.

Chapter 1

1. D. H. Lawrence, *The Escaped Cock,* ed. Gerald M. Lacy (Los Angeles: Black Sparrow, 1973), is out of print. In 1959, Vintage reprinted the novella as *The Man Who Died,* despite the fact that *The Escaped Cock* was

Lawrence's preferred title. See Lacy's introduction for details. All page references are to the Vintage edition.

2. D. H. Lawrence's *Psychoanalysis of the Unconscious and Fantasia of the Unconscious* (New York: Viking, 1960), alert us to his knowledge of Freudian and Jungian theory and his attempts to accommodate the unconscious within his writings. Indeed, in 1918, Lawrence wrote Katherine Mansfield that he had sent her the Jung book, probably *The Psychology of the Unconscious* (translated in 1916), in which, chapter six, "The Battle for Deliverance from the Mother," reflects many of Lawrence's attitudes concerning incest and the devouring mother. "This Mother-incest idea," he says, "can become an obsession. But it seems to me there is this much truth in it: that at certain periods the man has a desire and a tendency to return unto the woman, make her his goal and end, find his justification in her. In this way he casts himself as it were into her womb, and she, the Magna Mater, receives him with gratification. This is a kind of incest" (301–02). In *Fantasia of the Unconscious*, however, Lawrence denies that incest craving is a component of the unconscious and he affirms instead an incest-aversion. Judith Ruderman, in *D. H. Lawrence and the Devouring Mother: The Search for a Patriarchal Ideal of Leadership* (Durham, N.C.: Duke University Press, 1984), notes that Lawrence wrote his essays on psychology "in order to define scientifically the 'kind of incest' that he wrote of incessantly and obsessionally in his letters, poetry, and narrative prose—a pre-oedipal, pre-genital desire to merge with the caretaker mother" (24). Daniel J. Schneider, in *D. H. Lawrence: The Artist as Psychologist* (Lawrence: University Press of Kansas, 1984), asserts that Lawrence recognized the desire in himself for the bliss of Nirvana in the womb/tomb of the female, but "fought against it, insisting that the healthy power impulse counters the desire for a regressive submission" (250). From 1930 to the present, as Ruderman observes, writers who have discussed Lawrence's psyche, have shown a marked oedipal bias, looking toward mother-love to explicate his work. The main differences in their approach, according to Ruderman, and I agree with her, stem from two separate but related issues: "whether Lawrence retained his obsessional love for his mother or grew away from it, and whether his mother fixation was emotionally and artistically crippling or emotionally and artistically ennobling" (7).

3. D. H. Lawrence, *St. Mawr* and *The Man Who Died* (New York: Vintage, 1959), 208.

4. Lawrence's "quarrel with Freud," as well as the congruences of the ideas of both men, have been examined by a number of scholars, notably by Frederick J. Hoffman, *Freudianism and the Literary Mind* (Baton Rouge: Louisiana State University Press, 1957); Philip Rieff, "The Therapeutic as Mythmaker," in *D. H. Lawrence: Modern Critical Views*, ed. Harold Bloom (New York: Chelsea House, 1986), 31–58; James C. Cowan, "Allusions and

Symbols in D. H. Lawrence's *The Escaped Cock,*" *Critical Essays on D. H. Lawrence,* eds. Dennis Jackson and Fleda Brown Jackson (Boston: G. K. Hall, 1988), 174–88; Daniel A. Weiss, *Oedipus in Nottingham: D. H. Lawrence* (Seattle: University of Washington Press, 1962). Weiss refers us to the oedipal level in *The Escaped Cock,* and to Ruderman, and Schneider, among others. Only recently have Lacanian studies of Lawrence's work begun to appear: see Ed Jewinski, "The Phallus in D. H. Lawrence and Jacques Lacan," *The D. H. Lawrence Review* 21 (1989): 7–24, and Jane A. Nelson, "The Familial Isotopy in *The Fox,*" in *The Challenge of D. H. Lawrence,* eds. Michael Squires and Keith Cushman (Madison: University of Wisconsin Press, 1990), 129–43.

5. See Jacques Lacan, "The Agency of the letter in the unconscious or reason since Freud," in *Écrits: A Selection,* 146–78; "L'instance de la lettre dans l'inconscient ou la raison depuis Freud," in *Écrits I,* 249–89.

6. See "The mirror stage as formative of the function of the I" (*Écrits,* 1–7); "Le stade du miroir comme formateur de la fonction du Je" (*Écrits I,* 89–100).

7. Lawrence, *Psychoanalysis and the Unconscious,* 42.

8. Ibid., 13.

9. Lacan, *Écrits,* 166; *Écrits I,* 277.

10. Lacan, *Écrits I,* 284, 227; *Écrits,* 171, 129. In this passage, Lacan is referring to the English translation of Freud. It should not be confused with Sheridan's translation of Lacan.

11. Lacan, *Écrits,* 128–29; *Écrits I,* 226–27.

12. See Jane Gallop, *Reading Lacan* (Ithaca: Cornell University Press, 1985). According to Gallop, "Freud's discovery, as Lacan casts it, is that the center of the human being is not the ego, as we have long supposed, but what Lacan calls the subject, which sometimes but not always corresponds to what Freud called the id" (96). See also Jean Laplanche, "The Ego and the Vital Order," in *Life and Death in Psychoanalysis,* trans. Jeffrey Mehlman (Baltimore: Johns Hopkins University Press, 1976), 48–65.

13. Lacan, *Écrits,* 141; *Écrits I,* 242.

14. Lacan, *Écrits,* 312. *Écrits II,* 176.

15. Lawrence, *The Man Who Died,* 179.

16. Ibid., 174.

17. Ibid., 172.

18. Ibid., 178.

19. Ibid., 181.

20. Ibid., 180.

21. Ibid., 175.

22. Ibid., 178.

23. Ibid., 167.

24. Ibid., 193.

25. Ibid., 172.

26. Ibid., 196.

27. Ibid., 201.

28. Ibid., 202.

29. Ibid., 204.

30. Ibid., 206.

31. Ibid., 207.

32. Ibid.

33. Ibid., 208.

34. Ibid.

35. Ibid.

36. Ibid.

37. Ibid., 170.

38. D. H. Lawrence, *Apocalypse* (Cambridge: Cambridge University Press, 1980), 149.

39. Lawrence, *Psychoanalysis and the Unconscious*, 15.

40. Ibid., 16.

41. D. H. Lawrence, *The Complete Poems of D. H. Lawrence*, vol. 2, eds. Vivian de Sola Pinto and Warren Roberts (New York: Viking, 1964), 611.

42. Lawrence, *The Man Who Died*, 165.

43. Ibid., 164.

44. Gallop, *Reading Lacan*, 156. Lacan begins his essay, "The signification of the phallus," with the following statement: "We know that the unconscious castration complex has the function of a knot" ("On sait que le complexe de castration inconscient a une fonction de noeud"), *Écrits*, 281; *Écrits II*, 103.

45. Lawrence, *The Man Who Died*, 165.

46. Ibid., 166.

47. Jacques Derrida, *The Post Card: From Socrates to Freud and Beyond*, trans. Alan Bass (Chicago: The University of Chicago Press, 1987), 411–96.

48. Lawrence, *The Man Who Died*, 193.

49. Derrida, "Freud's Legacy," in *The Post Card*, 292–337.

50. Lawrence, *The Man Who Died*, 166.

51. Ibid., 184.

52. Lawrence, *Psychoanalysis and the Unconscious*, 120.

53. Lawrence, *The Man Who Died*, 171.

54. Ibid., 194–95.

55. Ibid., 185.

56. Ibid., 186.

57. Ibid., 191.

58. Ibid., 193.

59. Ibid., 187.

60. Ibid.

61. Ibid., 198.

62. Ibid., 186.

63. Ibid., 187.

64. Ibid., 193.

65. The following passage from "The Man of Tyre," in Lawrence's *Complete Poems* gives the word "maidenhair," in conjunction with *The Escaped Cock*, its appropriate connotation:

> Oh lovely, lovely with the dark hair piled up, as she
> went deeper, deeper down the channel, then rose
> shallower, shallower,
> with the full thighs slowly lifting of the wader wading
> shorewards
> and the shoulders pallid with light from the silent sky
> behind
> both breasts dim and mysterious, with the glamorous
> kindness of twilight between them
> and the dim notch of black maidenhair like an indicator,
> giving a message to the man— (693)

66. Lawrence, *The Man Who Died*, 191.

67. Ibid., 207.

68. Ibid., 203.

69. Ibid., 208.

70. In 1927, Lawrence discovered the Etruscan tombs and he records his impression of the oneness of all life in *Etruscan Places* (New York: Viking, 1963): "To the Etruscan all was alive; the whole universe lived; and the business of man was himself to live amid it all. He had to draw life into himself, out of the wandering huge vitalities of the world. The cosmos was alive, like a vast creature. The whole thing breathed and stirred" (83).

71. Lawrence, *The Man Who Died*, 196.

72. Ibid., 201.

73. Ibid., 189.

74. Ibid., 204.

75. Ibid.

76. Ibid., 189.

77. Lawrence, *Psychoanalysis and the Unconscious*, 21.

78. Ibid., 32.

79. Lawrence, *The Man Who Died*, 206.

80. Ibid.

81. Ibid.

82. Ibid., 207.

83. Ibid., 208.

84. Lacan, *Écrits*, 285; *Écrits II*, 108.

85. Lacan, *Écrits*, 128; *Écrits I*, 226.

86. Lawrence, *The Man Who Died*, 208.

87. Ibid., 211.

88. Ibid., 208.

89. See Daniel A. Weiss, *Oedipus in Nottingham: D. H. Lawrence* (Seattle: University of Washington Press, 1962). My conclusion contradicts Weiss's belief that *Lady Chatterley's Lover* "represents the total dilapidation of Lawrence's Oedipal longings . . . [that] Along with the heroic contempt for the mother image in absolute decay comes the full identification with the once-despised father" (109). In this context Weiss reads *The Escaped Cock* as "the spiritual abstract" of a novel that was written just before the composition of the novella (107). However, if *The Escaped Cock* is the spiritual abstract of *Lady Chatterley's Lover*, then it too must mirror a contempt for the mother, whereas, in fact, the opposite is true, because the images of nature, Isis, and the mother assume cosmic proportions that belie any dilapidation of oedipal longings. Lawrence's conscious manipulation of metaphorical structures suggests that his so-called mother-fixation, even near the end of his life, was artistically ennobling rather than crippling because the tropological weave works both artistically and psychologically.

90. See Leigh Travis, "D. H. Lawrence: The Blood-Conscious Artist," *The American Imago* 25 (1968): 163–90. Travis maintains that Lawrence has produced characters driven by mind- and blood-consciousness who are caught in a rite de passage that should have been more human. It is the mechanical patterns of his fictions, she argues, that produce "the rigid, only slightly varied plot structure, and the constant feeling that the cast of characters from story to story are actors who first played in *Sons and Lovers*" (190). Travis believes that this recurring pattern in Lawrence's works means that the "material has gotten the best of him" (190), whereas from a Lacanian point of view the recurring pattern is inevitable and must, perforce, surface in all discourse. Nonetheless Travis believes that the "other inward sun" is the symbol for the male organ, sensuality, and blood-consciousness (183), and her view is consistent with Lacan's use of the phallus as a symbol of the Law and of the repressed.

Chapter 2

1. W. S. Marks III, "The Psychology of the Uncanny in Lawrence's 'The Rocking-Horse Winner,'" *Modern Fiction Studies* 11 (1965–66): 381.

2. George F. Freije, "Equine Names in 'The Rocking-Horse Winner,'" *CEA Critic* 51 (1989): 82.

3. Janice Hubbard Harris, *The Short Fiction of D. H. Lawrence* (New Brunswick: Rutgers University Press, 1984), 225.

4. Ibid.

5. W. D. Snodgrass, "A Rocking-Horse: The Symbol, the Pattern, the Way to Live," in *D. H. Lawrence: A Collection of Critical Essays*, ed. Mark Spilka (Englewood Cliffs, N.J.: Prentice Hall, 1963), 121.

6. Ibid., 117.

7. Ibid., 122.

8. Harris, 226.

9. Marks, 382–86. The essays in the *Collected Papers* that Marks focuses on are the following: "A Special Type of Object-Choice," "Obsessive Acts and Religious Practices," "The 'Uncanny,'" "From the Neurosis of Demoniacal Possession in the Seventeenth Century," "The History of an Infantile Neurosis," and "A Phobia in A Five Year Old Boy." According to Marks, "Paul's ability to make lucky predictions by riding himself into a trance on his totemic hobbyhorse is principally suggested by Freud's paper 'The "Uncanny,"' where this phenomenon is defined as a product of narcissistic regression to a primitive belief in animism" (384). . . . Paul's self-destructive act of rocking comes under the heading of Freud's *repetition-compulsion*: '. . . a principle powerful enough to over-rule the pleasure-principle, lending to certain aspects of the mind their daemonic character, and still very clearly expressed in the tendencies of small children' (IV, 391)" (Marks, 384).

10. D. H. Lawrence, "The Rocking-Horse Winner," in *Love Among the Haystacks and Other Stories* (New York: Viking Penguin, 1960), 82.

11. Ibid.

12. Ibid., 92.

13. Ibid., 89.

14. Ibid., 82–83.

15. Ibid., 83.

16. Ibid., 96.

17. Freud, *Beyond the Pleasure Principle*, 15.

18. Lawrence, "The Rocking-Horse Winner," 83.

19. See Harris, who states that the mother has given her son a murderous education because she represents a society that runs on a money ethic: "the tale reads as a satire on the equation of money, love, luck, and happiness" (225).

20. Ibid., 119.

21. Freud, *Jokes and Their Relation to the Unconscious*, 94.

22. Ibid., 120.

23. Ibid., 121.

24. Lawrence, "The Rocking-Horse Winner," 82–83.

25. Freud, *Jokes and Their Relation to the Unconscious*, 118.

26. Lawrence, "The Rocking-Horse Winner," 83.

27. "The Law," says Lacan, "appears to be giving the order, 'Jouis!,' to which the subject can only reply 'J'ouïs' (I hear), the *jouissance* being no more than understand" ("La Loi en effet commanderait-elle: Jouis, que le sujet ne pourrait y répondre que par un: J'ouïs, où la jouissance ne serait que sous-entendue." Lacan, *Écrits*, 319; *Écrits II*, 184.

28. Freud, *Jokes and Their Relation to the Unconscious*, 95.

29. Ibid., 28.

30. Ibid., 166.

31. Ibid., 44.

32. Ibid., 34.

33. Eric Partridge, *Origins: A Short Etymological Dictionary of Modern English* (New York: Macmillan, 1958), 239.

34. See Jacques Derrida, *L'Écriture et la différence* (Paris: Seuil, 1967), trans. Alan Bass, *Writing and Difference* (Chicago: University of Chicago Press, 1978); *De la grammatologie* (Paris: Minuit, 1967), trans. Gayatri Chakrovorty Spivak, *Of Grammatology* (Baltimore: Johns Hopkins University Press, 1976); *La Dissémination* (Paris: Seuil, 1972).

35. See Snodgrass, who states that Paul is demonic and has compacted with evil (119).

36. Lawrence, "The Rocking-Horse Winner," 96.

37. Ibid., 81.

38. Ibid., 92.

39. Ibid., 95.

40. See Freije, who states that the *bar* of Malabar, according to the *OED*, "is a proper term for a part of a horse's mouth, a section of the hoof, and a piece of the bridle bit used in controlling the horse. . . . the psychoanalytic interpretations of the story (whether they discuss the oedipal quest . . . or the rocking horse as allegory of self-abuse) make it difficult to avoid seeing *bar* as a symbol of Paul's destructive sexuality" (82). In legal matters, again according to the *OED*, *bar* is a "hindrance to the achievement of a goal or a right." But Malabar is also interpreted as one of a series of names within a floral motif—the culmination of a sequence that began with Daffodil. Freije: "Sansovino suggested the garden deity as punisher of those who distort love. Mirza differentiated between virtue and corrupt striving, flowery paradise and shrouded hell. Blush of Dawn and Lively Spark recalled the expulsion from the garden. Singhalese introduced the demonic intruder." Malabar is a toxic plant, a member of the nightshade family, and the poison's symptoms are characteristic of Paul's madness and fever (81–82). There is also an Oriental motif. Freije believes that Mirza can be interpreted in light of Eastern fantasy (78). Snodgrass sees two British colonial regions named Singhalese and Malabar: "For years Malabar and Singhalese were winners for British stockholders and for the British people in general" (121). The Singhalese (Cinglese in Frazer's *The Golden Bough*) are the largest group of people in Shri Lanka. Freije cites Frazer and the fact that the Cinglese believed their world to be populated by infinite numbers of demons (81).

41. Lawrence, "The Rocking-Horse Winner," 96.

42. Jacques Lacan, "The agency of the letter in the unconscious or reason since Freud," 146–78; "L'instance de la lettre dans l'inconscient ou la raison depuis Freud," in *Écrits I*, 249–89.

43. Lacan, *Écrits*, 87; *Écrits I*, 183. Occasionally, my translation will appear without reference to Sheridan.

44. See Marks, who states that Paul "becomes a scapegoat who atones for the sins of his house—the material, social, and intellectual ambitions that corrupt normal affection, dislocate the proper authority of the father, and disintegrate the moral ties of the family, replacing them with the cash-nexus" (385).

45. Lawrence, "The Rocking-Horse Winner," 94. See *Fantasia*, which reinforces the devouring mother syndrome. Lawrence says: "In becoming the object of great emotional stress for her son, the mother also becomes an

object of poignancy, of anguish, of arrest, to her son. She arrests him from finding his proper fulfillment on the sensual plane" (168).

46. Lacan, *Écrits*, 147; *Écrits I*, 251.

47. Lacan, *Écrits I*, 35.

48. Lacan, *Écrits*, 149–50; *Écrits I*, 253–54.

49. Jean-Luc Nancy and Philippe Lacoue-Labarthe, *The Title of the Letter: A Reading of Lacan*, trans. François Raffoul and David Pettigrew (Albany: State University of New York Press, 1992), 39.

50. François Raffoul and David Pettigrew, "Translators' Preface," in *The Title of the Letter*, 42.

51. Lacan, *Écrits I*, 35.

52. Ibid., 258.

53. Lacan, *Écrits*, 155; *Écrits I*, 262.

54. Ibid.

55. Ibid.

56. Nancy and Lacoue-Labarthe, *The Title of the Letter*, 67.

57. Lacan, *Écrits II*, 233. My translation.

58. Raffoul and Pettigrew, "Translator's Preface," xii–xiii.

59. Freud, *Jokes and Their Relation to the Unconscious*, 176.

60. Ibid., 177.

61. Nancy and Lacoue-Labarthe, *The Title of the Letter*, 81.

62. Lacan, *Écrits I*, 33.

63. *The Holy Bible*, 2 Corinthians 3:6.

64. Lacan, *Écrits I*, 267.

65. Lawrence, "The Rocking-Horse Winner," 92.

66. Lacan, *Écrits*, 310; *Écrits II*, 173.

67. See Marks, 383. "Fixated at a narcissistic stage of development, Paul's libido is precisely objectified in the rocking-horse. Lawrence's young hero gives a first indication of his symptomatic preoccupation with riding (which later becomes obsessional) when he asks his mother "Why don't we

keep a car of our own? Why do we always use uncle's, or else a taxi?' Her reply, 'Because we're poor members of the family,' fatally impresses Paul with the association between money and the power to 'ride,' precipitating his short but sensational career as a gambler." It is worth remembering, as Snodgrass points out (122), that "riding" was once a common sexual verb. Therefore, riding, be it the hobbyhorse or in Uncle Oscar's car, brings everybody into the family romance.

Chapter 3

1. There are some 300 essays, articles, and book chapters devoted to Hemingway's first novel, *The Sun Also Rises.* Two books, Frederic Joseph Svoboda's *Hemingway and* The Sun Also Rises: *The Crafting of a Style* (1983) and Michael S. Reynolds's The Sun Also Rises: *A Novel of the Twenties* (1988) chronicle the novel's genesis and historical context, respectively. Not surprisingly there is a lack of unanimity among commentators concerning the novel's central character or what that centrality means. Opinions range from Jake Barnes, the narrator, to Robert Cohn, the romantic antihero, to Pedro Romero, the code-hero, to Bill Gorton as code-hero, to Brett Ashley as love Goddess. There are essays on Count Mippipopolous, Mike Campbell, Wilson-Harris, money, values, manners, humor, France, Spain, bullfighting, irony and pity, tragedy, comedy, terror, art, travel, religion, the beginning, the ending, and Pamplona, to name the more frequent ones. Perhaps adumbrating this lack of unanimity, Hemingway himself viewed the earth as the novel's abiding hero.

2. George Plimpton, "An Interview with Ernest Hemingway," reprinted in *Hemingway and His Critics: An International Anthology,* ed. Carlos Baker (New York: Wang and Hill, 1962), 29.

3. Ernest Hemingway, *Selected Letters, 1917–1961,* ed. Carlos Baker (New York: Scribner, 1981), 29. In a letter dated December 9, 1951, Hemingway explained to a Rinehart editor that the genesis of *The Sun Also Rises*

> came from a personal experience in that when I had been wounded at one time there had been an infection from pieces of wool cloth being driven into the scrotum. Because of this I got to know other kids who had genito urinary wounds and I wondered what a man's life would have been like after that if his penis had been lost and his testicles and spermatic cord remained intact. I had known a boy that had happened to. So I took him and made him into a foreign correspondent in Paris, and, inventing, tried to find out what his problems would be when he was in love with someone who was in love with him

> and there was nothing that they could do about it. . . . But I was not Jake Barnes. My own wound had healed rapidly and well and I was quit for a short session with the catheter. (239–40)

4. Susan Sontag, *Against Interpretation* (New York: Doubleday, 1986), 3–14.

5. Ernest Hemingway, *The Sun Also Rises* (New York: Scribner, 1954).

6. Freud, *Beyond the Pleasure Principle,* 15.

7. Jacques Derrida, *La Dissémination* (Paris: Seuil, 1972).

8. Michael S. Reynolds, The Sun Also Rises: *A Novel of the Twenties* (Boston: G. K. Hall, 1988), 40. In *Metafiction: The Theory and Practice of Self-Conscious Fiction* (New York: Methuen, 1984), 2, Patricia Waugh defines metafiction as

> a term given to fictional writing which self-consciously and systematically draws attention to its status as an artefact in order to pose questions about the relationship between fiction and reality. In providing a critique of their own methods of construction, such writings not only examine the fundamental structures of narrative fiction, they also explore the possible fictionality of the world outside the literary fictional text.

9. Reynolds, 39.

10. John Atherton, "The Itinerary of the Postcard. Minimal Strategies in *The Sun Also Rises,*" *ELH* 53 (1986): 215.

11. Lacan, *Écrits*, 55. *Écrits*, I, 143.

12. Nina Schwartz, "Discourse in *The Sun Also Rises*: A Cock and Bull Story," *Criticism: A Quarterly for Literature and the Arts* 26 (1984): 49–69; Atherton, 199–218; Robert B. Jones, "Mimesis and Metafiction in Hemingway's *The Garden of Eden,*" *The Hemingway Review* 7 (1987): 2–13; Elizabeth D. Vaughn, "*In Our Time* As Self-Begetting Fiction," *Modern Fiction Studies* 35 (1989): 707–16.

13. Joseph Frank, "Spatial Form in Modern Literature," in *Criticism: The Foundations of Modern Literary Judgment*, eds. Mark Schorer, J. Miles, and G. McCenzie (Berkeley: University of California Press, 1958), 73.

14. Frederic Joseph Svoboda, *Hemingway and* The Sun Also Rises: *The Crafting of a Style* (Lawrence: University Press of Kansas, 1983), 112.

15. Murray Krieger, *Words about Words about Words: Theory, Criticism and the Literary Text* (Baltimore: Johns Hopkins University Press, 1988), 11.

16. Ibid., 13.

17. Kostas Axelos, *Vers la pensée planétaire* (Paris: Minuit, 1964), 15.

18. Hemingway, *The Sun Also Rises*, 28.

19. Ibid., 31.

20. Ibid., 58.

21. Freud, *Beyond the Pleasure Principle*, 15–16.

22. Hemingway, *The Sun Also Rises*, 63.

23. Ibid., 26.

24. Ibid., 148.

25. W. M. Frohock, "Violence and Discipline," in *Ernest Hemingway: The Man and His Work*, ed. John K. M. McCaffery (Cleveland: World Publishing Company, 1950), 286.

26. James Hinkle, "What's Funny in *The Sun Also Rises*," in *Ernest Hemingway: Six Decades of Criticism*, ed. Linda W. Wagner (East Lansing, Michigan: Michigan State University Press, 1987), 77.

27. Atherton, 213–14.

28. Hemingway, *The Sun Also Rises*, 239.

29. Jacques Derrida, *The Post Card: From Socrates to Freud and Beyond*, 286.

30. Hemingway, *The Sun Also Rises*, 35.

31. Ibid., 183–84.

32. Ibid., 239.

33. Roland Barthes, *Roland Barthes* (Paris: Seuil, 1975), 119.

34. Derrida, *The Post Card*, 343.

35. See Shoshana Felman, "On Reading Poetry: Reflexions on the Limits and Possibilities of Psychoanalytic Approaches," in *The Purloined Poe: Lacan, Derrida and Psychoanalytic Reading*, eds. John P. Muller and William J. Richardson (Baltimore: The Johns Hopkins University Press, 1988), 147–48.

36. Hemingway, *The Sun Also Rises*, 190.

37. Ibid., 72.

38. Ibid., 75–76.

39. Ibid., 73.

40. Jacques Derrida, *L'Écriture et la différence,* 315–17.

41. Lacan, *Écrits,* 281.

42. Ibid., 282.

43. Hemingway, *The Sun Also Rises,* 239.

44. Maurice Blanchot, *Arrêt de mort* (Paris: Gallimard, 1977).

45. Derrida, *The Post Card,* 285–86.

46. Derrida, *La Dissémination,* 146–53.

47. See Jacques Derrida, "To Speculate on 'Freud,'" in *The Post Card,* trans. Alan Bass (Chicago: University of Chicago Press, 1987), 257–409.

48. Reynolds, 24.

49. Roland Barthes, "The Death of the Author," reprinted in *Modern Criticism and Theory,* ed. David Lodge (New York: Longman, 1988), 167–72.

CHAPTER 4

1. Gerry Brenner, *Concealments in Hemingway's Works* (Columbus: Ohio State University Press, 1983), 35.

2. Michael S. Reynolds, *Hemingway's First War: The Making of* A Farewell to Arms (Princeton: Princeton University Press, 1976), 207.

3. Carlos Baker, *Ernest Hemingway: A Life Story* (New York: Scribner, 1969), 78.

4. Ibid., 81.

5. Robert W. Lewis, Jr., *Hemingway on Love* (Austin: University of Texas Press, 1965), 48–49.

6. Ray B. West, Jr., "The Biological Trap," in *Hemingway: A Collection of Critical Essays,* ed. Robert P. Weeks (Englewood Cliffs, N.J.: Prentice-Hall, 1962), 139–51.

7. Scott Donaldson, *By Force of Will: The Life and Art of Ernest Hemingway* (New York: Viking, 1977), 155–56.

8. Faith Pullin, "Hemingway and the Secret Language of Hate," in *Ernest Hemingway: New Critical Essays*, ed. A. Robert Lee (Totowa, N.J.: Barnes & Noble, 1983), 172–92.

9. Jackson J. Benson, *Hemingway: The Writer's Art of Self-Defense* (Minneapolis: University of Minnesota Press, 1969), 84–85, 110–11.

10. Robert Penn Warren, "Ernest Hemingway," in *Modern Critical Views: Ernest Hemingway*, ed. Harold Bloom (New York: Chelsea, 1985), 35–62.

11. Reynolds, *Hemingway's First War*, 43.

12. Edmund Wilson, "Hemingway: Gauge of Morale," in *Modern Critical Views: Ernest Hemingway*, ed. Harold Bloom (New York: Chelsea, 1985), 17–34.

13. Lacan, *Écrits I*, 264–67; see also Jacques Lacan, *Le Séminaire: Livre II. Le moi dans la théorie de Freud et dans la technique de la psychanalyse*, ed. Jacques-Alain Miller (Paris: Seuil, 1978); see also Lacan, *Écrits: A Selection*, 156–59.

14. Freud, *The Interpretation of Dreams*, 277–338.

15. Reynolds, *Hemingway's First War*, 283. Brenner's *Concealments* was published in 1983. Reynolds's book was published in 1976.

16. Reynolds. *Hemingway's First War*, 136.

17. Ibid., 170.

18. Ibid.

19. Ibid., 283.

20. Ibid., 15–16.

21. Ibid., 281.

22. Ibid., 104.

23. Ibid., 282.

24. Ibid., 46.

25. Ibid., 175.

26. Benson, *Art of Self-Defense*, 82.

27. Ernest Hemingway, *A Farewell to Arms* (New York: Scribner, 1957), 300.

28. Marcel Proust, *Du Côté de chez Swann*, vol. 1, in *A la recherche du temps perdu* (Paris: Gallimard, 1954), 188–383. "Swann in Love" is a clinical case description of jealousy and the vicissitudes of love.

29. Hemingway, *A Farewell to Arms*, 54.

30. Ibid., 91.

31. Ibid.

32. Ibid., 87.

33. Ibid., 106.

34. Brenner, *Concealments*, 34.

35. Hemingway, *A Farewell to Arms*, 289.

36. Bernard Oldsey, *Hemingway's Hidden Craft: The Writing of* A Farewell to Arms (University Park: The Pennsylvania State University Press, 1979), 66.

37. Hemingway, 299.

38. Ibid., 251.

39. Ibid., 232–33.

40. Ibid., 243.

41. Ibid., 323.

42. Ibid., 327.

43. Ibid., 149.

44. Ibid., 218.

45. Ibid., 222.

46. Ibid., 228.

47. Ibid., 31.

48. Ibid., 34. Reynolds (*Hemingway's First War*, 64) prefers one of the rejected working titles, namely *A Separate Peace*, in lieu of *A Farewell to Arms*, because the homonym of the word "peace," that is, "piece," "would have been a sardonic statement about the love affair." The word "peace," like the word "arms," also connotes war and love, but unlike the caring resonance of "arms," a "piece of ass" has a pejorative meaning that radically alters the reading of the novel.

49. Hemingway, *A Farewell to Arms*, 224–25.

50. Ibid., 223.

51. Ibid., 332.

52. Ibid., 249.

53. John Killinger, *Hemingway and the Dead Gods: A Study in Existentialism* (Lexington: University of Kentucky Press, 1960). In *Hemingway's First War* Reynolds reproduces pages cut from the published version of *A Farewell to Arms*. These passages clearly reveal the existential dimensions of "the biological trap" (40–41).

54. See Jean-Paul Sartre, *L'Existentialisme est un humanisme* (Paris: Nagel, 1952); see also Albert Camus, *Le Mythe de Sisyphe* (Paris: Gallimard, 1942).

55. Albert Camus, *Caligula and Three Other Plays*, trans. Stuart Gilbert (New York: Random, 1958), 112.

56. William Wasserstrom, "*A Farewell to Arms*: Radiance at the Vanishing Point," in *Ernest Hemingway: New Critical Essays*, ed. A. Robert Lee (Totowa, N.J.: Barnes and Noble, 1983), 64–78.

57. Brenner, *Concealments*, 28.

58. Philip Young, "Adventures of Nick Adams," in *Hemingway: A Collection of Critical Essays*, ed. Robert P. Weeks (Englewood Cliffs, N.J.: Prentice-Hall, 1962), 95–111.

59. Benson, *Art of Self-Defense*, 74.

60. See John Barth, *Letters* (New York: Putnam, 1979); see also Robert Coover, *Spanking the Maid* (New York: Grove, 1982); see also Alain Robbe-Grillet, *La Maison de rendez-vous* (Paris: Minuit, 1965). Although James Joyce is considered a modernist writer, works such as *Ulysses* and *Finnegans Wake* adumbrate the linguistic play of postmodernist writing.

61. Lewis, *Hemingway on Love*, 41–42.

62. Sophocles, "Oedipus at Colonus," scene 3 in *The Complete Greek Tragedies*, vol. 1, trans. David Grene, eds. David Grene and R. Lattimore (Chicago: University of Chicago Press, 1954), 105.

63. Lacan, *Le Séminaire: Livre II*, 269.

64. Shoshana Felman, "Beyond Oedipus: The Specimen Story of Psychoanalysis," in Robert Con Davis, ed., *Lacan and Narration: The Psychoanalytic Difference in Narrative Theory* (Baltimore: Johns Hopkins University Press, 1983), 1029.

65. Hemingway, *A Farewell to Arms*, 149.

66. Ibid., 38.

67. Ibid., 44.

68. Ibid., 231–32.

69. Ibid., 232.

70. Ibid., 320–21.

71. Ibid., 115.

72. Barthes, *Roland Barthes*, 119.

Chapter 5

1. Barbara Probst Solomon, "Where's Papa?," *The New Republic* (March 9, 1987): 34.

2. Ibid., 31.

3. Ernest Hemingway, *The Garden of Eden* (New York: Scribner, 1986).

4. Ibid., 159.

5. Ibid., 201.

6. Ibid., 199.

7. Ibid., 201.

8. Ibid., 223.

9. Ibid., 190.

10. Ibid., 203.

11. Ibid., 156.

12. Ibid., 241. My translation.

13. Ibid.

14. See Donald Rice and Peter Schofer, *Rhetorical Poetics: Theory and Practice of Figural and Symbolic Reading in Modern French Literature* (Madison: University of Wisconsin Press, 1983), 19–34.

15. *The Garden of Eden*, 84.

16. Ibid., 183.

17. Ibid., 247.

Chapter 6

The translations in the text of Camus's works are my own.

1. Albert Camus, "Le Mythe de Sisyphe," in *Essais*, vol. 2 (Paris: Gallimard [Pléiade], 1965), 145–46.

2. Albert Camus, "Noces," in *Essais*, vol. 2 (Paris: Gallimard [Pléiade], 1965), 76. Camus is referring to Pandora's box in which were to be found all the evils of humanity. The most terrible of all was hope and it was the last scourge to come out. "I know of no symbol more moving because hope, contrary to what people believe, is the same as resignation. And to live is not to resign oneself" ("Je ne connais pas de symbole plus émouvant. Car l'espoir, au contraire de ce qu'on croit, équivaut à la résignation. Et vivre, c'est ne pas se résigner").

3. Ibid., 57–58.

4. Albert Camus, "Caligula," in *Théâtre, récits, nouvelles*, vol. 1 (Paris: Gallimard [Pléiade], 1962), 16.

5. Ibid., 100.

6. Camus, "Noces," in *Essais*, 2: 56.

7. Albert Camus, "L'Envers et l'endroit," in *Essais*, vol. 2 (Paris: Gallimard [Pléiade], 1965), 44.

8. Albert Camus, "L'Été," in *Essais*, vol. 2 (Paris: Gallimard [Pléiade], 1965), 881.

9. Alain Costes, in *Albert Camus ou la parole manquante, étude psychanalytique* (Paris: Payot, 1973), stresses Camus's literary sublimation through the use of "incestuous language" (132). Jean Gassin, in *L'Univers symbolique d'Albert Camus: Essai d'interprétation psychanalytique* (Paris: Minard, 1981), also highlights incestuous elements in Camus's oeuvre. In "Entre oui et non," an early autobiographical essay first published in *L'Envers et l'endroit* in 1937, Camus ardently elicits the son's longing for union with the mother. See Camus, "L'Envers et l'endroit," in *Essais*, 2: 23–30.

10. See Vicki Mistacco, "Nomadic Meanings: The Woman Effect in 'La Femme adultère,'" in *Albert Camus'* L'Exil et Le Royaume: *The Third Decade*, ed. Anthony Rizzuto (Toronto: Paratexte, 1988), who says that "the

sea, especially in French through homonymic association (*mer/mère*), is a conventional symbol for the mother. Camus's personal associations of water and sea imagery with the figure of the mother are also well known" (77).

11. Camus, "Noces," in *Essais*, 2: 57–58.

12. Ibid., 60.

13. Albert Camus, *La Mort heureuse* (Paris: Gallimard, 1971), 125.

14. Ibid., 121.

15. Ibid., 88.

16. Camus, "Noces," in *Essais*, 2: 58–59.

17. Albert Camus, "Le Malentendu," in *Théâtre, récits, nouvelles*, vol. 1 (Paris: Gallimard [Pléiade], 1962), 117.

18. Ibid., 178.

19. Ibid., 179.

20. Ibid., 163.

21. Camus, "Noces," in *Essais*, 2: 67.

22. Blaise Pascal, *Les Pensées* (Paris: Éditions du Cerf, 1982), 152.

23. Albert Camus, "La Femme adultère," in *Théâtre, récits, nouvelles*, vol. 1 (Paris: Gallimard [Pléiade], 1962), 1562.

24. Ibid., 1572.

25. Camus, "L'Envers et l'endroit," in *Essais*, 2: 23.

26. Camus, "L'Été," in *Essais*, 2: 829.

27. Camus, "La Femme adultère," in *Théâtre, récits, nouvelles*, 1: 1573. Mistacco, in "Nomadic Meanings: The Woman Effect in 'La femme adultère,'" prefers maternal incest to adultery: "Rather than adultery as the title would lead us to believe, is it not *maternal incest* that Janine's illicit *jouissance* evokes? What we witness in this transgressive moment is a massive return of the repressed, a *jouissance* related to the desire of the mother's body, a displacement of adultery, and a displacement of mother/son incest onto this female figure" (80).

28. Camus, "La Femme adultère," in *Théâtre, récits, nouvelles*, 1: 1563.

29. Ibid., 1571.

30. Lacan, *Écrits*, 69; *Écrits I*, 160.

31. Ibid., 59; 147.

32. Camus, "La Femme adultère," in *Théâtre, récits, nouvelles*, 1: 1567.

33. My translation; Lacan, *Écrits II*, 229.

34. Camus, "La Femme adultère," in *Théâtre, récits, nouvelles*, 1: 1568.

35. Lacan, *Écrits*, 281; *Écrits II*, 102.

36. Ibid., 288; 108.

37. Ibid., 316; 180.

38. Camus, "La Femme adultère," in *Théâtre, récits, nouvelles*, 1: 1571.

39. Lacan, *Écrits*, 319; *Écrits II*, 184.

40. Camus, "La Femme adultère," in *Théâtre, récits, nouvelles*, 1: 1571.

41. Camus, *La Mort heureuse*, 186.

42. See Vicki Mistacco, "Mama's Boy: Reading Woman in *L'Étranger*," in *Camus's* L'Étranger: *Fifty Years On*, ed. Adele King (London: Macmillan, 1992), 152–69.

43. Camus, "L'Été," in *Essais*, 2: 874.

44. Ibid., 879–80, 882, 884, 886.

45. Ibid., 884.

Chapter 7

The translations in this chapter are my own.

1. René Girard, "Camus's Stranger Retried," *PMLA* 79 (1964): 519.

2. Robert J. Champigny, *A Pagan Hero: An Interpretation of Meursault in Camus' "The Stranger"* (Philadelphia: University of Pennsylvania Press, 1969), 106.

3. Girard, 531.

4. Albert Camus, *L'Étranger*, eds. Germaine Brée and Carlos Lynes, Jr. (New York: Appleton, 1955), 7–8.

5. Jean-Paul Sartre, "An Explication of *The Stranger*," in *Camus: A Collection of Critical Essays*, ed. Germaine Brée (Englewood Cliffs, N.J.: Prentice-Hall, 1962), 111.

6. Albert Camus, "Préface à l'édition universitaire américaine," in *Théâtre, récits, nouvelles*, vol. 1 (Paris: Gallimard [Pléiade], 1962), 1920.

7. Champigny, *A Pagan Hero*, 106.

8. Monique Wagner, "Physical Malaise and Subconscious Death-Wish in *L'Étranger*," *Michigan Academician* 11 (1979): 331–41.

9. Camus, "Préface à l'édition universitaire américaine," 1921.

10. Louis Hudon, "*The Stranger* and the Critics," *Yale French Studies* 25 (1960): 61.

11. Girard, 524.

12. Brée and Lynes, "Introduction," in *L'Étranger*, 12.

13. Albert Maquet, *Albert Camus ou l'invincible été* (Paris: Debresse, 1956), as quoted by Girard, 521.

14. Camus, "Préface à l'édition universitaire américaine," 1920.

15. Carl A. Viggiani, "*L'Étranger* de Camus," in *Configuration Critique d'Albert Camus*, ed. J. H. Matthews, *La Revue des Lettres Modernes* 8 (1961): 103–36.

16. Julian L. Stamm, "Camus' *Stranger*: His Act of Violence," *American Imago* 26 (1969): 285.

17. J. H. Matthews, "L'Oeil de Meursault," in *Configuration Critique d'Albert Camus*, ed. J. H. Matthews, *La Revue des Lettres Modernes* 8 (1961): 149.

18. Pierre-Louis Rey, *L'Étranger Camus: Analyse critique* (Paris: Hatier, 1970), 50.

19. Brian T. Fitch, L'Étranger *d'Albert Camus. Un texte, ses lecteurs, leurs lectures* (Paris: Larousse, 1972), 105–16.

20. Alain Robbe-Grillet, "Monde trop plein, conscience vide," in *Albert Camus: Oeuvre fermée, oeuvre ouverte?*, eds. Raymond Gay-Crosier and Jacqueline Lévi-Valensi (Paris: Gallimard, 1985), 214.

21. Arminda A. de Pichon-Rivière, and Willy Baranger, "Répression du deuil et intensification des mécanismes et des angoisses schizo-paranoïdes. Notes sur *L'Étranger* de Camus," *Revue Française de Psychanalyse* 3 (1959): 409–20.

22. Stamm, 286–88.

23. Albert Camus, "L'Envers et l'endroit," in *Essais*, 2: 26.

24. Alain Costes, *Albert Camus et la parole manquante* (Paris: Payot, 1973), 132.

25. Jean Gassin, *L'Univers symbolique d'Albert Camus: Essai d'interprétation psychanalytique* (Paris: Minard, 1981). "Sur cette scène de *L'Étranger* et sur le rôle meurtrier qu'y joue le soleil, tout a été dit" (26).

26. Costes, 16.

27. See Marie Bonaparte, "Selections from *The Life and Works of Edgar Allan Poe: A Psycho-analytic Interpretation*," in John P. Muller and William J. Richardson, eds., *The Purloined Poe: Lacan, Derrida, and Psychoanalytic Reading* (Baltimore: Johns Hopkins University Press, 1988), 101–32.

28. Alain Costes, "Le double meurtre de Meursault," in *Albert Camus: Oeuvre fermé, oeuvre ouverte?*, eds. Raymond Gay-Crosier and Jacqueline Lévi-Valensi (Paris: Gallimard, 1985), 73.

29. Gassin refers to Camus's account of the incident in "L'envers et l'endroit." See Camus, *Essais*, 2: 27.

30. Gassin, 88.

31. Costes, "Le double meurtre de Meursault," 68.

32. Ibid., 56.

33. Ibid., 69.

34. Viggiani, 114–21.

35. W. M. Frohock, "Camus: Image, Influence and Sensibility," *Yale French Studies* 4 (1950): 93–94.

36. Robert de Luppé, *Albert Camus* (Paris: Editions Universitaires, 1952); Albert Maquet, *Albert Camus ou l'invincible été* (Paris: Debresse, 1956).

37. Viggiani, 127.

38. Gassin, 130.

39. Camus, "Noces," in *Essais*, 2: 58.

40. Albert Camus, "L'Étranger," in *Théâtre, récits, nouvelles* (Paris: Gallimard [Pléiade], 1962), 1: 1196.

41. Alain Robbe-Grillet, "Nature, humanisme, tragédie," *Pour un nouveau roman* (Paris: Minuit, 1963), 58.

42. Camus, "L'Étranger," in *Théâtre, récits, nouvelles*, 1: 1199.

43. Ibid., 1166.

44. Ibid., 1158.

45. Ibid., 1165.

46. Camus, "Noces," in *Essais*, 2: 56.

47. Camus, "L'Étranger," in *Théâtre, récits, nouvelles*, 1: 1165–66.

48. Ibid., 1166.

49. Robbe-Grillet, "Nature, humanisme, tragédie," 45–68.

50. Camus, "L'Étranger," in *Théâtre, récits, nouvelles*, 1: 1166.

51. I am indebted in my analyses of metaphor and metonymy to Donald Rice and Peter Schofer, *Rhetorical Poetics: Theory and Practice of Figural and Symbolic Reading in Modern French Literature* (Madison: University of Wisconsin Press, 1983).

52. Camus, "L'Étranger," in *Théâtre, récits, nouvelles*, 1: 1164.

53. Ibid., 1166.

54. Ibid., 1209.

55. Ibid., 1210.

56. Ibid., 1149.

57. Fitch, 115, 137.

58. Ibid., 155.

59. Albert Camus, "L'Homme révolté," in *Essais*, vol. 2 (Paris: Gallimard [Pléiade], 1965), 432.

60. Camus, "L'Étranger," in *Théâtre, récits, nouvelles*, 1: 1192.

61. Ibid., 1195.

62. Ibid., 1208.

63. Ibid., 1209.

64. Camus, "Caligula," in *Théâtre, récits, nouvelles*, 1: 16.

65. Camus, "L'Étranger," in *Théâtre, récits, nouvelles*, 1: 1195.

66. Barthes, *Roland Barthes*, 51.

67. See the two essays, "Noces" and "L'Été" in *Essais*, vol. 2.

68. Camus, "L'Étranger," in *Théâtre, récits, nouvelles*, 1: 1209.

Chapter 8

1. Barthes, *Roland Barthes*, 51. This and all subsequent translations are my own.

2. Ibid., 193.

3. Ibid., 119.

4. Ibid., 98.

5. Ibid., 119.

6. Ibid., 25.

7. Alain Robbe-Grillet, "Je n'ai jamais parlé d'autre chose que de moi," interview with Jean-Pierre Salgas, in *La Quinzaine littéraire* (16 to 31 Jan. 1985): 6.

8. Barthes, 182–83.

9. Ibid., 129.

10. Alain Robbe-Grillet, *Le Miroir qui revient* (Paris: Minuit, 1984), 17.

11. Barthes, 51.

12. Jules Michelet, *La Sorcière* (Paris: Garnier-Flammarion, 1966).

13. Robbe-Grillet, *Le Miroir qui revient*, 17.

14. Ibid., 18.

15. Ibid., 13.

16. Barthes, 71.

17. Ibid., 5.

18. Robbe-Grillet, 132.

19. Ibid., 133.

20. Barthes, 97.

21. Roland Barthes, *S/Z* (Paris: Seuil, 1970), 94.

22. Ibid., 116.

23. Robbe-Grillet, *Le Miroir qui revient*, 6.

Chapter 9

1. See Roland Barthes, "Qu'est-ce que l'écriture," in *Le Degré zéro de l'écriture* (Paris: Seuil, 1953), 17–30.

2. J. Hillis Miller, "Fiction and Repetition: *Tess of the d'Urbervilles*," in *Forms of Modern British Fiction*, ed. Alan Warren Friedman (Austin: University of Texas Press, 1975), 58–59. "The reader," says Miller, "must execute a lateral dance of interpretation to explicate any given passage, without ever reaching, in this sideways movement, any passage that is chief, original, or originating, a sovereign principle of explanation."

3. See Derrida, "Le Facteur de la vérité," in *The Post Card: From Socrates to Freud and Beyond*, 413–96.

4. See MacCannell, *Figuring Lacan: Criticism and the Cultural Unconscious*, 20–21. "Lacan emphasized . . . the awesome power—for him, the power of life and death—of the signifier, the phallus, to shape our existence. But this does not necessarily make him its partisan, although the fact that so brilliant and sophisticated a reader as Derrida at first responds to him in this way shows how effective Lacan's proof of this power is. In short, the critique does not, ultimately, apply to Lacan. Lacan calls for a 'limping truth' . . . The phallic truth is precisely that against which Lacan re-writes every line—in its metaphoric hegemony, its fiction of unity, its creation of 'oneness'" (21).

5. William Robert Irwin, *The Game of the Impossible: A Rhetoric of Fantasy* (Urbana: University of Illinois Press, 1976), 9; Eric S. Rabkin, *The Fantastic in Literature* (Princeton: Princeton University Press, 1976), 12; Rosemary Jackson, *Fantasy: The Literature of Subversion* (New York: Methuen, 1981), 175.

6. Tzvetan Todorov, *Introduction à la littérature fantastique* (Paris: Seuil, 1970), 30, 165.

7. See Kathryn Hume, "Historical perspectives on fantasy and realism," in *Fantasy and Mimesis: Responses to Reality in Western Literature* (New York: Methuen, 1984), 29–51.

8. Bruce F. Kawin, *The Mind of the Novel: Reflexive Fiction and the Ineffable* (Princeton: Princeton University Press, 1982), 13–15, 228.

9. Brian McHale, *Postmodernist Fiction* (New York: Methuen, 1987), 16.

10. Jorge Luis Borges, "Pierre Menard, Author of the Quixote," in *Labyrinths: Selected Stories and Other Writings*, eds. Donald A. Yates and James E. Irby (New York: New Directions, 1962), 36–44.

11. Roland Barthes, *S/Z*, trans. Richard Miller (New York: Hill and Wang, 1974), 3–6.

12. See Lacan, *Écrits: A Selection*, 157. According to Lacan, the conjunction of two signifiers may constitute a metaphor. However, its creative spark does not spring from the presentation of the two disparate images, that is, the juxtaposition of the umbrella and the sewing machine. "It flashes between two signifiers one of which has taken the place of the other in the signifying chain." The occulted signifier remains by virtue of "its (metonymic) connexion with the rest of the chain." The umbrella, in addition to its denotation, signifies something absent, fantastic even, namely *man*, and the sewing machine, in addition to its denotation, signifies something absent, namely *woman*. The spark generated arcs between the two absent signifieds. It is the spark of desire and love on the dissecting table of death. The imagery of this discourse is fantastic because each signifier has two signifieds: one that is denoted and one that is absent and repressed. As referents, the man and the woman emerge from the spark of recognition that illumines this famous paradigm of surrealist endeavor.

13. Todorov, *Introduction à la littérature fantastique*, 29–30, 46.

14. See Patricia Waugh, *Metafiction: The Theory and Practice of Self-Conscious Fiction* (New York: Methuen, 1984), 2.

15. Irwin, *The Game of the Impossible*, 9.

16. Alain Robbe-Grillet, *Les Gommes* (Paris: Minuit, 1953).

17. Alain Robbe-Grillet, *Le Voyeur* (Paris: Minuit, 1955).

18. Alain Robbe-Grillet, *La Jalousie* (Paris: Minuit, 1957).

19. Michelet, *La Sorcière*.

20. Ben Stoltzfus, *Alain Robbe-Grillet: The Body of the Text* (Rutherford: Fairleigh Dickinson University Press, 1985), 76.

21. Alain Robbe-Grillet, "L'Ordre et son double: Érotisme et littérature dans les oeuvres du Marquis de Sade," reprinted as "Order and Its Double:

Eroticism and Literature in the Works of the Marquis de Sade," *The Bennington Review* 3 (1969): 3–6.

22. Alain Robbe-Grillet, "Le Sadisme contre la peur," interview with Guy Dumur, in *Le Nouvel observateur* 310 (19 October 1970): 48.

23. Alain Robbe-Grillet, *Le Miroir qui revient*, 181.

24. Ibid., 14–15.

25. Ibid., 180.

26. See Roland Barthes, *Michelet* (Paris: Seuil, 1954), 129–61.

27. Michelet, *La Sorcière*, 49.

28. Alain Robbe-Grillet, *Angélique ou l'enchantement* (Paris: Minuit, 1987), 237–45.

29. Ibid., 245.

30. Robbe-Grillet, "Le Sadisme contre la peur," 48.

Conclusion

1. Barthes, *Le Plaisir du texte*, 105.

2. Michel Foucault, *The History of Sexuality*, vol. 1, trans. Robert Hurley (New York: Pantheon, 1978), 96.

3. See H. C. Andersen, "The Emperor's New Clothes," in *The Complete Fairy Tales and Stories* (New York: Doubleday, 1974).

4. Jacques Lacan, "La Signification du phallus," in *Écrits II*, 103–19.

5. Barthes, 105.

6. Jacques Derrida, "La Structure, le signe et le jeu dans le discours des sciences humaines," in *L'Écriture et la différence*, 409–28.

7. See Jacques Derrida, *De la grammatologie* (Paris: Minuit, 1967) and *L'Écriture et la différence*; Wolfgang Iser, *The Implied Reader*: Patterns of Communication in Prose Fiction from Bunyon to Beckett (Baltimore: Johns Hopkins University Press, 1974); Patricia Waugh, *Metafiction: The Theory and Practice of Self-Conscious Fiction* (New York: Methuen, 1984).

8. Jacques Derrida, "La Pharmacie de Platon," in *La Dissémination*, 69–198.

9. Lacan, "L'Instance de la lettre dans l'inconscient, ou la raison depuis Freud," in *Écrits I*, 249–89.

10. Jacques Derrida, *Glas* (Paris: Galilée, 1974), 137–38, 178, 261–63.

11. Waugh, *Metafiction*, 2.

12. Fredric Jameson, *The Political Unconscious: Narrative as a Socially Symbolic Act* (Ithaca: Cornell University Press, 1981).

13. Robert Coover, *Spanking the Maid* (New York: Grove, 1982).

14. Samuel Beckett, *Company* (New York: Grove, 1980); *How It Is* (New York: Grove, 1964).

15. Alfred Appel, Jr., "An Interview with Vladimir Nabokov," in L. S. Dembo, ed., *Nabokov: The Man and His Works* (Madison: University of Wisconsin Press, 1967), 19–44.

16. George Steiner, *Language and Silence: Essays on Language, Literature and the Inhuman* (New York: Atheneum, 1982), ix.

17. Chinua Achebe, *Things Fall Apart* (New York: Ballantine, 1959).

18. Lance Olsen, *Circus of the Mind in Motion: Postmodernism and the Comic Vision* (Detroit: Wayne State University Press, 1990), 71–2.

19. Michel Foucault, *The Order of Things: An Archeology of the Human Sciences* (New York: Pantheon, 1970), xviii.

20. Donald Barthelme, *The Dead Father* (New York: Farrar, 1975).

21. Vladimir Nabokov, *Lolita* (New York: McGraw, 1955).

22. Alain Robbe-Grillet, *La Jalousie* (Paris: Minuit, 1957).

23. Alain Robbe-Grillet, *Pour un nouveau roman* (Paris: Minuit, 1963); Jacques Leenhardt, *Lecture politique du roman:* La Jalousie *d'Alain Robbe-Grillet* (Paris: Minuit, 1973).

24. Donald Barthelme, *Snow White* (New York: Atheneum, 1967), 139.

Bibliography

Achebe, Chinua. *Things Fall Apart.* New York: Ballantine, 1959.

Andersen, H. C. "The Emperor's New Clothes," in *The Complete Fairy Tales and Stories.* New York: Doubleday, 1974.

Appel, Alfred, Jr. "An Interview with Vladimir Nabokov," in L. S. Dembo, ed., *Nabokov: The Man and His Works.* Madison: University of Wisconsin Press, 1967, 19–44.

Atherton, John. "The Itinerary of the Postcard. Minimal Strategies in *The Sun Also Rises.*" *ELH* 53 (1986): 199–218.

Axelos, Kostas. *Vers la pensée planétaire.* Paris: Minuit, 1964.

Baker, Carlos. *Ernest Hemingway: A Life Story.* New York: Scribner, 1969.

Barth, John. *Letters.* New York: Putnam, 1979.

Barthelme, Donald. *The Dead Father.* New York: Farrar, 1975.

———. *Snow White.* New York: Atheneum, 1967.

Barthes, Roland. "The Death of the Author," reprinted in *Modern Criticism and Theory,* ed. David Lodge. New York: Longman, 1988, 167–72.

———. "Qu'est-ce que l'écriture," in *Le Degré zéro de l'écriture.* Paris: Seuil, 1953, 17–30.

———. *Michelet.* Paris: Seuil, 1954.

———. *Le Plaisir du texte.* Paris: Seuil, 1973.

———. *Roland Barthes.* Paris: Seuil, 1975.

———. *S/Z.* Paris: Seuil, 1970.

———. *S/Z*, trans. Richard Miller. New York: Hill and Wang, 1974.

Baudelaire, Charles. "Correspondances," in *Les Fleurs du mal*. Paris: Gallimard, 1961, 22.

Beckett, Samuel. *Company*. New York: Grove, 1980.

———. *How It Is*. New York: Grove, 1964.

Benson, Jackson J. *Hemingway: The Writer's Art of Self-Defense*. Minneapolis: University of Minnesota Press, 1969.

Blanchot, Maurice. *Arrêt de mort*. Paris: Gallimard, 1977.

Bonaparte, Marie. *The Life and Works of Edgar Allan Poe: A Psycho-analytic Interpretation*, foreword Sigmund Freud, trans. John Rodker. London: Imago, 1949.

Borges, Jorge Luis. "Pierre Menard, Author of the Quixote," in *Labyrinths: Selected Stories and Other Writings*, eds. Donald A. Yates and James E. Irby. New York: New Directions, 1962, 36–44.

Brenner, Gerry. *Concealments in Hemingway's Works*. Columbus: Ohio State University Press, 1983.

Brooks, Peter. "The Idea of a Psychoanalytic Criticism." *Critical Inquiry* 13 (1987): 334–48.

Camus, Albert. "Caligula," in *Théâtre, récits, nouvelles*, vol. 1. Paris: Gallimard [Pléiade], 1962, 7–108.

———. *Caligula and Three Other Plays*, trans. Stuart Gilbert. New York: Random, 1958.

———. *Carnets I*, May 1935–Feb. 1942. Paris: Gallimard, 1962.

———. "L'Envers et l'endroit," in *Essais*, vol. 2. Paris: Gallimard [Pléiade], 1965, 5–50.

———. "L'Étranger," in *Théâtre, récits, nouvelles*, vol. 1. Paris: Gallimard [Pléiade], 1962, 1121–1210.

———. *L'Étranger*, eds. Germaine Brée and Carlos Lynes, Jr. New York: Appleton, 1955.

———. "L'Été," in *Essais*, vol. 2. Paris: Gallimard [Pléiade], 1965, 805–86.

———. "La Femme adultère," in *Théâtre, récits, nouvelles*, vol. 1. Paris: Gallimard [Pléiade], 1962, 1555–73.

———. "Le Malentendu," in *Théâtre, récits, nouvelles*, vol. 1. Paris: Gallimard [Pléiade], 1962, 109–80.

———. *La Mort heureuse*. Paris: Gallimard, 1971.

———. "Le Mythe de Sisyphe," in *Essais*, vol. 2. Paris: Gallimard [Pléiade], 1965, 99–211.

———. "Noces," in *Essais*, vol. 2. Paris: Gallimard [Pléiade], 1965, 52–98.

———. "Préface à l'édition universitaire américaine," in *Théâtre, récits, nouvelles*, vol. 1. Paris: Gallimard [Pléiade], 1962, 1920–21.

Champigny, Robert J. *A Pagan Hero: An Interpretation of Meursault in Camus'* The Stranger. Philadelphia: University of Pennsylvania Press, 1969.

Con Davis, Robert, ed. *Lacan and Narration: The Psychoanalytic Difference in Narrative Theory*. Baltimore: Johns Hopkins University Press, 1983.

———. "Introduction," in *Lacan and Narration: The Psychoanalytic Difference in Narrative Theory*. Baltimore: The Johns Hopkins University Press, 1983, 848–59.

Coover, Robert. *Spanking the Maid*. New York: Grove, 1982.

Costes, Alain. *Albert Camus ou la parole manquante, étude psychanalytique*. Paris: Payot, 1973.

———. "Le double meurtre de Meursault," in *Albert Camus: Oeuvre fermé, oeuvre ouverte?*, eds. Raymond Gay-Crosier and Jacqueline Lévi-Valensi. Paris: Gallimard, 1985, 55–76.

Cowan, James C. "Allusions and Symbols in D. H. Lawrence's *The Escaped Cock*," in *Critical Essays on D. H. Lawrence*, eds. Dennis Jackson and Fleda Brown Jackson. Boston: G. K. Hall, 1988, 174–88.

Derrida, Jacques. *De la grammatologie*. Paris: Minuit, 1967.

———. *La Dissémination*. Paris: Seuil, 1972.

———. *L'Écriture et la différence*. Paris: Seuil, 1967.

———. "Le Facteur de la vérité," in *The Post Card*, trans. Alan Bass. Chicago: The University of Chicago Press, 1987, 411–96.

———. *Glas*. Paris: Galilée, 1974.

———. "La Pharmacie de Platon," in *La Dissémination*. Paris: Seuil, 1972, 69–198.

———. *The Post Card: From Socrates to Freud and Beyond*, trans. Alan Bass. Chicago: University of Chicago Press, 1987.

———. "To Speculate on 'Freud,'" in *The Post Card*, trans. Alan Bass. Chicago: University of Chicago Press, 1987, 257–409.

———. "La Structure, le signe et le jeu dans le discours des sciences humaines," in *L'Écriture et la différence*. Paris: Seuil, 1967, 409–28.

———. *La Vérité en peinture*. Paris: Flammarion, 1978.

Donaldson, Scott. *By Force of Will: The Life and Art of Ernest Hemingway*. New York: Viking, 1977.

Falk, Eugene. *The Poetics of Roman Ingarden*. Chapel Hill: University of North Carolina Press, 1981.

Federman, Raymond. *Critifiction: Postmodern Essays*. Albany: State University of New York Press, 1993.

Felman, Shoshana. "Beyond Oedipus: The Specimen Story of Psychoanalysis," in Robert Con Davis, ed., *Lacan and Narration: The Psychoanalytic Difference in Narrative Theory*. Baltimore: Johns Hopkins University Press, 1983, 1021–1053.

———. "On Reading Poetry: Reflexions on the Limits and Possibilities of Psychoanalytic Approaches," in *The Purloined Poe: Lacan, Derrida and Psychoanalytic Reading*, eds. John P. Muller and William J. Richardson. Baltimore: The Johns Hopkins University Press, 1988, 147–48.

Fitch, Brian T. *L'Étranger d'Albert Camus. Un texte, ses lecteurs, leurs lectures*. Paris: Larousse, 1972.

Foucault, Michel. *The History of Sexuality*, vol. 1, trans. Robert Hurley. New York: Pantheon, 1978.

———. *The Order of Things: An Archeology of the Human Sciences*. New York: Pantheon, 1970.

Frank, Joseph. "Spatial Form in Modern Literature," in *Criticism: The Foundations of Modern Literary Judgment*, eds. Mark Schorer, J. Miles, and G. McCenzie. Berkeley: University of California Press, 1958, 379–92.

Freije, George F. "Equine Names in 'The Rocking-Horse Winner.'" *CEA Critic* 51 (1989): 75–84.

Freud, Sigmund. *Beyond the Pleasure Principle*, vol. 18 in *The Standard Edition of the Complete Psychological Works*, vols. 1–23, trans. James Strachey. London: Hogarth, 1953.

———. *The Interpretation of Dreams*, vol. 4 in *The Standard Edition of the Complete Psychological Works*, vols. 1–23, trans. James Strachey. London: Hogarth, 1953.

———. *Jokes and Their Relation to the Unconscious*, vol. 8 in *The Standard Edition of the Complete Psychological Works*, vols. 1–23, trans. James Strachey. London: Hogarth, 1971.

Frohock, W. M. "Camus: Image, Influence and Sensibility." *Yale French Studies* 4 (1950): 93–94.

———. "Violence and Discipline," in *Ernest Hemingway: The Man and His Work*, ed. John K. M. McCaffery. Cleveland: World Publishing Company, 1950, 262–91.

Gallop, Jane. *Reading Lacan*. Ithaca: Cornell University Press, 1985.

Gassin, Jean. *L'Univers symbolique d'Albert Camus: Essai d'interprétation psychanalytique*. Paris: Minard, 1981.

Girard, René. "Camus's Stranger Retried." *PMLA* 79 (1964): 519–33.

Harris, Janice Hubbard. *The Short Fiction of D. H. Lawrence*. New Brunswick: Rutgers University Press, 1984, 203–54.

Hemingway, Ernest. *A Farewell to Arms*. New York: Scribner, 1957.

———. *The Garden of Eden*. New York: Scribner, 1986.

———. *Selected Letters, 1917–1961*, ed. Carlos Baker. New York: Scribner, 1981.

———. *The Sun Also Rises*. New York: Scribner, 1954.

Hinkle, James. "What's Funny in *The Sun Also Rises*," in *Ernest Hemingway: Six Decades of Criticism*, ed. Linda W. Wagner. East Lansing, Michigan: Michigan State University Press, 1987, 77–92.

Hoffman, Frederick J. *Freudianism and the Literary Mind*. Baton Rouge: Louisiana State University Press, 1957.

Holland, Norman. "The 'Unconscious' of Literature." *Contemporary Criticism*, eds. Norman Bradbury and David Palmer. New York: St. Martin's, 1970, 131–54.

Hudon, Louis. "*The Stranger* and the Critics." *Yale French Studies* 25 (1960): 59–64.

Hume, Kathryn. "Historical Perspectives on Fantasy and Realism," in *Fantasy and Mimesis: Responses to Reality in Western Literature*. New York: Methuen, 1984.

Ingarden, Roman. *The Literary Work of Art: An Investigation on the Borderlines of Ontology, Logic and Theory of Literature*, trans. with an introduction by George Grabowicz. Evanston: Northwestern University Press, 1973.

Irwin, William Robert. *The Game of the Impossible: A Rhetoric of Fantasy*. Urbana: University of Illinois Press, 1976.

Iser, Wolfgang. *The Implied Reader: Patterns of Communication in Prose Fiction from Bunyon to Beckett*. Baltimore: Johns Hopkins University Press, 1974.

Jackson, Rosemary. *Fantasy: The Literature of Subversion*. New York: Methuen, 1981.

Jameson, Fredric. *The Political Unconscious: Narrative as a Socially Symbolic Act*. Ithaca: Cornell University Press, 1981.

Jewinski, Ed. "The Phallus in D. H. Lawrence and Jacques Lacan." *The D. H. Lawrence Review* 21 (1989): 7–24.

Jones, Ernest. *Hamlet and Oedipus*. New York: Norton, 1976.

Jones, Robert B. "Mimesis and Metafiction in Hemingway's *The Garden of Eden*." *The Hemingway Review* 7 (1987): 2–13.

Kawin, Bruce F. *The Mind of the Novel: Reflexive Fiction and the Ineffable*. Princeton: Princeton University Press, 1982.

Killinger, John. *Hemingway and the Dead Gods: A Study in Existentialism*. Lexington: University of Kentucky Press, 1960.

Krieger, Murray. *Words about Words about Words: Theory, Criticism and the Literary Text*. Baltimore: John Hopkins University Press, 1988.

Lacan, Jacques. "The Agency of the letter in the unconscious or reason Since Freud," in *Écrits: A Selection*, trans. Alan Sheridan. New York: Norton, 1977, 146–78.

———. *Écrits I*. Paris: Seuil, 1966.

———. *Écrits II*. Paris: Seuil, 1971.

———. *Écrits: A Selection*, trans. Alan Sheridan. New York: Norton, 1977.

———. *The Four Fundamental Concepts of Psycho-Analysis*, trans. Alan Sheridan. New York: Norton, 1981.

———. "L'Instance de la lettre dans l'inconscient, ou la raison depuis Freud," in *Écrits I*. Paris: Seuil, 1966, 249–89.

———. *Le Séminaire: Livre II. Le moi dans la théorie de Freud et dans la technique de la psychanalyse,* ed. Jacques-Alain Miller. Paris: Seuil, 1978.

———. "Seminar on 'The Purloined Letter,'" trans. Jeffrey Mehlman, in *The Purloined Poe: Lacan, Derrida, and Psychoanalytic Reading,* eds. John P. Muller and William J. Richardson. Baltimore: The Johns Hopkins University Press, 1988, 28–54.

———. "La Signification du phallus," in *Écrits II.* Paris: Seuil, 1971, 103–19.

Laplanche, Jean. "The Ego and the Vital Order," in *Life and Death in Psychoanalysis,* trans. Jeffrey Mehlman. Baltimore: Johns Hopkins University Press, 1976, 48–65.

Lawrence, D. H. *Apocalypse.* Cambridge: Cambridge University Press, 1980.

———. *The Complete Poems of D. H. Lawrence,* vol. 2, eds. Vivian de Sola Pinto and Warren Roberts. New York: Viking, 1964.

———. *The Escaped Cock,* ed. Gerald M. Lacy. Los Angeles: Black Sparrow, 1973.

———. *Etruscan Places.* New York: Viking, 1963.

———. *Psychoanalysis of the Unconscious and Fantasia of the Unconscious.* New York: Viking, 1960.

———. "The Rocking-Horse Winner," in *Love Among the Haystacks and Other Stories.* New York: Viking Penguin, 1960, 81–96.

———. *St. Mawr* and *The Man Who Died.* New York: Vintage, 1959.

Leenhardt, Jacques. *Lecture politique du roman:* La Jalousie *d'Alain Robbe-Grillet.* Paris: Minuit, 1973.

Leitch, Vincent B. *Deconstructive Criticism: An Advanced Introduction.* New York: Columbia University Press, 1983.

Lemaire, Anika. *Jacques Lacan,* trans. David Macey. London: Routledge and Kegan Paul, 1977.

Lewis, Robert W., Jr. *Hemingway on Love.* Austin: University of Texas Press, 1965.

Luppé, Robert de. *Albert Camus.* Paris: Editions Universitaires, 1952.

MacCannell, Juliet Flower. *Figuring Lacan: Criticism and the Cultural Unconscious.* Lincoln: University of Nebraska Press, 1986.

Maquet, Albert. *Albert Camus ou l'invincible été.* Paris: Debresse, 1956.

McHale, Brian. *Postmodernist Fiction*. New York: Methuen, 1987.

Marks, W. S., III. "The Psychology of the Uncanny in Lawrence's 'The Rocking-Horse Winner.'" *Modern Fiction Studies* 11 (1965–66): 381–92.

Matthews, J. H. "L'Oeil de Meursault," in *Configuration Critique d'Albert Camus*, ed. J. H. Matthews. *La Revue des Lettres Modernes* 8 (1961): 137–50.

Mellard, James M. *Using Lacan, Reading Fiction*. Urbana: University of Illinois Press, 1991.

Michelet, Jules. *La Sorcière*. Paris: Garnier-Flammarion, 1966.

Miller, J. Hillis. "Fiction and Repetition: *Tess of the d'Urbervilles*," in *Forms of Modern British Fiction*, ed. Alan Warren Friedman. Austin: University of Texas Press, 1975, 43–71.

Mistacco, Vicki. "Mama's Boy: Reading Woman in *L'Étranger*," in *Camus's* L'Étranger: *Fifty Years On*, ed. Adele King. London: Macmillan, 1992, 152–69.

———. "Nomadic Meanings: The Woman Effect in 'La femme adultère,'" in *Albert Camus'* L'Exil et le royaume: *The Third Decade*, ed. Anthony Rizzuto. Toronto: Paratexte, 1988, 71–84.

Muller, John P. and William J. Richardson, eds. *The Purloined Poe: Lacan, Derrida, and Psychoanalytic Reading*. Baltimore: Johns Hopkins University Press, 1988.

Nabokov, Vladimir. *Lolita*. New York: McGraw, 1955.

Nancy, Jean-Luc and Philippe Lacoue-Labarthe. *The Title of the Letter: A Reading of Lacan*, trans. François Raffoul and David Pettigrew. Albany: State University of New York Press, 1992.

Nelson, Jane A. "The Familial Isotopy in *The Fox*," in *The Challenge of D. H. Lawrence*, eds. Michael Squires and Keith Cushman. Madison: University of Wisconsin Press, 1990, 129–43.

Oldsey, Bernard. *Hemingway's Hidden Craft: The Writing of* A Farewell to Arms. University Park: The Pennsylvania State University Press, 1979.

Olsen, Lance. *Circus of the Mind in Motion: Postmodernism and the Comic Vision*. Detroit: Wayne State University Press, 1990.

Partridge, Eric. *Origins: A Short Etymological Dictionary of Modern English*. New York: Macmillan, 1958.

Pascal, Blaise. *Les Pensées*. Paris: Éditions du Cerf, 1982.

Pichon-Rivière, Arminda A. de and Willy Baranger. "Répression du deuil et intensification des mécanismes et des angoisses schizo-paranoïdes. Notes sur *L'Étranger* de Camus." *Revue Française de Psychanalyse* 3 (1959): 409–20.

Plimpton, George. "An Interview with Ernest Hemingway," reprinted in *Hemingway and His Critics: An International Anthology*, ed. Carlos Baker. New York: Wang and Hill, 1962, 19–37.

Proust, Marcel. *Du côté de chez Swann*, vol. 1 in *A la recherche du temps perdu*. Paris: Gallimard, 1954.

Pullin, Faith. "Hemingway and the Secret Language of Hate," in *Ernest Hemingway: New Critical Essays*, ed. A. Robert Lee. Totowa, N.J.: Barnes & Noble, 1983, 172–92.

Rabkin, Eric S. *The Fantastic in Literature*. Princeton: Princeton University Press, 1976.

Raffoul, François and David Pettigrew. "Translators' Preface," in *The Title of the Letter: A Reading of Lacan*. Albany: State University of New York Press, 1992, vii–xxx.

Ragland-Sullivan, Ellie. "The Magnetism Between Reader and Text: Prolegomena to a Lacanian Poetics." *Poetics* 13 (1984): 381–406.

Rey, Pierre-Louis. *L'Étranger Camus: Analyse critique*. Paris: Hatier, 1970.

Reynolds, Michael S. *Hemingway's First War: The Making of* A Farewell to Arms. Princeton: Princeton University Press, 1976.

———. The Sun Also Rises: *A Novel of the Twenties*. Boston: G. K. Hall, 1988.

Rice, Donald and Peter Schofer. *Rhetorical Poetics: Theory and Practice of Figural and Symbolic Reading in Modern French Literature*. Madison: University of Wisconsin Press, 1983.

Rieff, Philip. "The Therapeutic as Mythmaker," in *D. H. Lawrence: Modern Critical Views*, ed. Harold Bloom. New York: Chelsea House, 1986, 31–58.

Robbe-Grillet, Alain. *Angélique ou l'enchantement*. Paris: Minuit, 1987.

———. *Les Gommes*. Paris: Minuit, 1953.

———. *La Jalousie*. Paris: Minuit, 1957.

———. "Je n'ai jamais parlé d'autre chose que de moi," interview with Jean-Pierre Salgas. *La Quinzaine littéraire* 432 (16 to 31 Jan. 1985): 6–7.

———. *La Maison de rendez-vous.* Paris: Minuit, 1965.

———. *Le Miroir qui revient.* Paris: Minuit, 1984.

———. "Monde trop plein, conscience vide," in *Albert Camus: Oeuvre fermée, oeuvre ouverte?*, eds. Raymond Gay-Crosier and Jacqueline Lévi-Valensi. Paris: Gallimard, 1985, 215–27.

———. "Nature, humanisme, tragédie," in *Pour un nouveau roman.* Paris: Minuit, 1963, 45–68.

———. "L'Ordre et son double: Érotisme et littérature dans les oeuvres du Marquis de Sade," reprinted as "Order and Its Double: Eroticism and Literature in the Works of the Marquis de Sade." *The Bennington Review* 3 (1969): 3–6.

———. *Pour un nouveau roman.* Paris: Minuit, 1963.

———. "Le Sadisme contre la peur," interview with Guy Dumur. *Le Nouvel observateur* 310 (19 October 1970), 48.

———. *Le Voyeur.* Paris: Minuit, 1955.

Ruderman, Judith. *D. H. Lawrence and the Devouring Mother: The Search for a Patriarchal Ideal of Leadership.* Durham, N.C.: Duke University Press, 1984.

Sartre, Jean-Paul. "An Explication of *The Stranger*," in *Camus: A Collection of Critical Essays*, ed. Germaine Brée. Englewood Cliffs, N.J.: Prentice-Hall, 1962, 108–21.

———. *L'Existentialisme est un humanisme.* Paris: Nagel, 1952.

Saussure, Ferdinand de. *Cours de linguistique générale*, 3rd ed. Paris: Payot, 1967.

Schneider, Daniel J. *D. H. Lawrence: The Artist as Psychologist.* Lawrence: University Press of Kansas, 1984.

Schwartz, Nina. "Discourse in *The Sun Also Rises*: A Cock and Bull Story." *Criticism: A Quarterly for Literature and the Arts* 26 (1984): 49–69.

Snodgrass, W. D. "A Rocking-Horse: The Symbol, the Pattern, the Way to Live," in *D. H. Lawrence: A Collection of Critical Essays*, ed. Mark Spilka. Englewood Cliffs, N.J.: Prentice-Hall, 1963, 117–26.

Solomon, Barbara Probst. "Where's Papa?" *The New Republic* (March 9, 1987): 30–34.

Sontag, Susan. *Against Interpretation*. New York: Doubleday, 1986.

Sophocles. "Oedipus at Colonus," *The Complete Greek Tragedies*, vol. 1, trans. David Grene, eds. David Grene and R. Lattimore. Chicago: University of Chicago Press, 1954.

Stamm, Julian L. "Camus' *Stranger*: His Act of Violence." *American Imago* 26 (1969): 281–90.

Steiner, George. *Language and Silence: Essays on Language, Literature and the Inhuman*. New York: Atheneum, 1982.

Stoltzfus, Ben. *Alain Robbe-Grillet: The Body of the Text*. Rutherford: Fairleigh Dickinson University Press, 1985.

Svoboda, Frederic Joseph. *Hemingway and* The Sun Also Rises: *The Crafting of a Style*. Lawrence: University Press of Kansas, 1983.

Todorov, Tzvetan. *Introduction à la littérature fantastique*. Paris: Seuil, 1970.

Travis, Leigh. "D. H. Lawrence: The Blood-Conscious Artist." *The American Imago* 25 (1968): 163–90.

Vaughn, Elizabeth D. "*In Our Time* As Self-Begetting Fiction." *Modern Fiction Studies* 35 (1989): 707–16.

Viggiani, Carl A. "*L'Etranger* de Camus," in *Configuration Critique d'Albert Camus*, ed. J. H. Matthews. *La Revue des Lettres Modernes* 8 (1961): 103–36.

Wagner, Monique. "Physical Malaise and Subconscious Death-Wish in *L'Étranger*." *Michigan Academician* 11 (1979): 331–41.

Warren, Austin and René Welleck. *Theory of Literature*, 3rd rev. ed. London: Cape, 1966.

Warren, Robert Penn. "Ernest Hemingway," in *Modern Critical Views: Ernest Hemingway*, ed. Harold Bloom. New York: Chelsea, 1985, 35–62.

Wasserstrom, William. "*A Farewell to Arms*: Radiance at the Vanishing Point," in *Ernest Hemingway: New Critical Essays*, ed. A. Robert Lee. Totowa, N.J.: Barnes and Noble, 1983, 64–78.

Waugh, Patricia. *Metafiction: The Theory and Practice of Self-Conscious Fiction*. New York: Methuen, 1984.

Weiss, Daniel A. *Oedipus in Nottingham: D. H. Lawrence*. Seattle: University of Washington Press, 1962.

West, Ray B., Jr. "The Biological Trap," in *Hemingway: A Collection of Critical Essays*, ed. Robert P. Weeks. Englewood Cliffs, N.J.: Prentice-Hall, 1962, 139–51.

Wilson, Edmund. "Hemingway: Gauge of Morale," in *Modern Critical Views: Ernest Hemingway*, ed. Harold Bloom. New York: Chelsea, 1985, 17–34.

Young, Philip. "Adventures of Nick Adams," in *Hemingway: A Collection of Critical Essays*, ed. Robert P. Weeks. Englewood Cliffs, N.J.: Prentice-Hall, 1962, 95–111.

Index

A

B

G

M

R

S

T